A
Queer
Geography

Other books by Frank Browning

The Culture of Desire
The American Way of Crime (coauthor)
The Vanishing Land

A Queer Geography

Journeys Toward a Sexual Self

Frank Browning

Crown Publishers, Inc.

New York

Published by Crown Publishers, Inc., 201 East 50th Street, New York, New York 10022. Member of the Crown Publishing Group.

Random House, Inc. New York, Toronto, London, Sydney, Auckland

CROWN is a trademark of Crown Publishers, Inc.

Manufactured in the United States of America

Design by Leonard Henderson

Library of Congress Cataloging-in-Publication Data available upon request

ISBN 0-517-59857-4

10 9 8 7 6 5 4 3 2 1

First Edition

For Gene

acknowledgments

Many friends, colleagues, companions, and interviewees have given both their time and their imaginations to help me make this book. It is not possible to specify exactly what each person contributed. Often a twenty-minute conversation helped to redirect my imaginative curiosity as much as several months of reading and interviewing. More than any project to date, this book has propelled me into a series of evolving self-inquiries that have led me to reformulate my own understanding of the social meanings of sexuality. By simply watching how succeeding generations of homosexual men and women read the literature and culture of sexuality that has gone before them, I have had firsthand instruction in the malleability of sexual identities. My time spent with new friends in Naples has made it inescapably obvious how history and geography form widely varying sexual meanings and aesthetics that do not easily conform to any particular political program.

While none of the following people bears any responsibility for my expressed ideas and arguments, all have contributed valuable insights and criticisms: Kevin Ayyildiz, Adam Block, Sean Collins, Francesco Durante, Steven Friedman, Peggy Girshman, Fred Hertz, Fenton Johnson, Judith Levine, Jean McGuire, Michael O'Laughlin, Claudio Pellone, Marcello Persico, Raul Ramirez, Scott Sherer, Sharon Silva, Carl Strange, Nina Sutton, John Tambernino, Braden Toan, Frank Viviano, Brenda Wilson, Pat Yellin, Steven Zeeland.

I also owe particular thanks to Jeffrey Escoffier and Gene Kahn, who gave me detailed criticism as the manuscript grew, and to David Groff, who pushed me to undertake the book and who offered always valuable intellectual and editorial advice along the way. Michael Denneny, my editor, is what any writer wants most, a tough-minded ally who never relinquishes the push for clarity.

c o n t e n t s

To ask whether homosexuality is natural is really like asking whether or not it was natural for Socrates to swallow hemlock, whether or not it was natural for Saint Paul to suffer for the Gospel, whether or not it was natural for the Germans to send upwards of 6 million people to an extremely twentieth-century death. It does not seem to me that nature helps us very much when we need illumination in human affairs. I am certainly convinced that it is one of the greatest impulses of mankind to arrive at something higher than a natural state. How to be natural does not seem to me to be a problem—quite the contrary. The great problem is how to be—in the best sense of that kaleidoscopic word—a man.

—James Baldwin
The Male Prison

A
Queer
Geography

introduction

Americans are obsessed with geography, and yet we know so little about it. Since John Winthrop delivered the first great address on the American prospect aboard the *Arbella* in 1630, declaring that he and his fellow Puritans should erect a "citty [*sic*] upon a hill" as an example to all the world, Americans have imagined their destiny in the language of redemptive geography. Believing the land to be a natural gift from God, they—and most of us since—have envisioned the American Dream as somewhere just beyond the next horizon. Leaving the corruptions and failures of "the old world" behind, we have repeatedly convinced ourselves that in some "new world" soon to be discovered we will realize the arcadian promise. Initially the "old world" was Europe or England. Then as the conquest of the frontier rolled forward, the old world became Philadelphia and New York and Boston. Then as the burnished vision of California dazzled us, the old world became the tired-out towns of the Rust Belt.

Today's New World is an interior geography, a geography of the spirit marked by a longing for identity. If as a nation we have left the Cold War for a new era of political isolationism, we have—as has happened frequently before in earlier centuries—turned much of our attention inward, toward a recharting of the essential self. Among conservatives this preoccupation with the self has fueled the Christian right and recalls the preachings of the Great Awakening in the eighteenth century, of the temperance and revivalist movements in the nineteenth century. Among liberals and progressives, the search for personal freedom has led us to plot the contours of identity in the language of psychology and individual autonomy. Yet regardless of ideology, the metaphors of geography, of location, of placement, continue to guide how we imagine our multiple selves. (Perhaps it is not accidental that in our preoccupation with mapping our internal identities we have lost the broader outlines of geography beyond ourselves: our high school students seem to know little beyond their own hometowns, finding themselves unable to locate cities within their states or to distinguish the continental home of Uruguay from that of Madagascar.)

The emergence of "gay people" as a new kind of people in the American demography is high testament to the geographic metaphor. More than any genuine ethnic group, gay people owe their existence *as a separate people* to geography. Original as homosexual desire may be to human beings, the arrival of gay people as a coherent social presence and political force owes everything to the transformations of modern urban geography. Though we are everywhere, our voice, with rare exceptions, is a voice of the urban metropolis. *Gay community, gay ghetto, gay space,* have become common terms in the movement for gay liberation. They speak of the place that gay people have carved out for their survival. But there is another sense of place, of personal geography, that characterizes the queer impulse, and that is the place we afford homoeroticism in the larger shape of our lives. That double sense of place, that double geography, forms the central metaphor of this inquiry: how we as Americans remain obsessed with finding our place in the world, and equally, how we as homo-Americans locate the place of queerness within ourselves.

In *The Culture of Desire,* I asked a single question: Had gay men succeeded in the radical, utopian dream of constructing their own social world based on the exigencies of desire? My intent was not to answer the question straight-out—the question is still unanswerable—but rather to take a visceral journey through some American territories of gender and desire, asking queer people how they felt and thought about the world they were making. Since the beginning of the 1990s, a new kind of question has emerged among queer people both in America and around the world. It is simultaneously a social, a psychological, and a spiritual question. In its simplest form it asks, "Do gay people exist?"

At first, the question may seem ridiculous. After the tormented fussing and fuming about gays in the military, after the enormous gay pride marches and celebrations in Washington and New York, after the gathering of ten thousand queer athletes from all the world's continents, after the appearance of a new generation of slick,

2

upscale gay publications—*10 Percent, Genre, Out, Men's Style, Quotient*—how could gays not exist? Yet it was deep in the midst of the 1994 Stonewall 25 celebrations in New York that I heard startling numbers of lesbians and gay men ask deeply troubling questions about what had become of the original gay liberation movement marked by the Stonewall riots. Had it "matured" into a gay marketing movement? Did its surviving middle-aged leaders have anything in common with young queers in their teens and twenties who looked with contempt at gay ghettos like the Castro and Chelsea? Repeatedly, after the huge Stonewall 25 march, I heard people ask themselves, "Is this all we are? Is this all there is?" For all the gay movement's obvious queer successes during the last three decades, these critical, spiritual, and existential questions have only grown more intense. Moreover, they recapitulate another set of questions: How do we as individuals, as families, as communities, place ourselves in the world? How do we navigate through our requirements for love and fellowship? Where do we locate the need for workmanship in our lives? How do we find language and art to present ourselves? Where do we find common ground when we all feel mutually queer to one another?

Let me be clear about my presumptions. We are all, to use Jeffrey Weeks's term, writing in the "historical present." As an American, as a white man, as a creature of the late twentieth century, as a male who grew up when the *New York Times, Time, Life, Newsweek,* and all of television and radio regarded homosexuality as either criminal or diseased, I am incapable of experiencing my desires with the touch, smell, and sight of a young Neapolitan in Italy or a Sambia tribesman in New Guinea—two places where homosexuality has a rich and ancient history that few make much effort to disguise. The strategies of social and psychological survival I have employed set me apart radically from middle-class Brazilians or Filipinos and even from most of the young men I write about in this book. My history is not their history. They seek jobs at *Time, Newsweek,* and the *New York Times* from recruiters at gay journalism conferences; I would have been blackballed, fired, or frozen out by the *Times'* editor of a decade ago had I spoken of my sexual appetites.

My historical present also differs from theirs in other ways, indeed

3

in the very experience of sex itself. Like most gay men I know of my generation, I spent the better part of my late teens and twenties trying to convince myself to go to bed with women while my eyes knew they were following the hips and shoulders of men. It wasn't that I wasn't interested in women, didn't find women beautiful, didn't get aroused by the kiss or embrace of a woman. My neurophysiological responses functioned just fine with the opposite sex though perhaps a little less quickly. The great fear, my great fear, was that should the woman at hand catch my errant glance at a man, should she divine my lust for a male breast, I would be undone. I would be revealed as a fraud. I would be other than a man. Somehow the exclusionary categories of gay and straight that I had constructed in my mind prevented me—and I believe a vast number of my generation—from enjoying multiple desires in multiple ways. In her dazzling book on bisexuality, *Vice Versa,* Marjorie Garber confronts exactly this conundrum in the development of the modern sexual identity movements. "Why," she asks, "do we resist the idea that erotic life is all part of the same set of pleasures, that there is only one sexuality, of which the 'sexualities' we have so effectively and efficiently defined are equally permissible and gratifying aspects?" Garber asks the question of society at large and answers that such a fluid notion of sexuality is too threatening to established social structure—marriage, family, work, advertising, politics. But the question is just as well applied to ourselves as individuals. Why do we resist the idea that the sexuality we each contain has many forms, the exploration of which can reveal the many faces of our flesh and spirit?

In his *New Yorker* review of Garber's book, Edmund White, the most prominent gay essayist in the English language, makes a startling confession: "[Garber] browbeat me into wondering whether I myself might not have been bisexual had I lived in another era." Despite falling in love with three different women and struggling through years of unsuccessful therapy to straighten himself, White took the Stonewall rebellion of 1969 as a clarion call to personal self-revision, deciding that he "was completely gay and was only making the women in my life miserable. Following a tendency that Garber rightly criticizes, I denied the authenticity of my earlier heterosexual feelings in the light of my later homosexual identity. After reading *Vice Versa,* I find myself willing to reinterpret the narrative of my own personal history."

White, who made his literary name as a professional gay man, is telling us that perhaps he is not gay—at least not gay the way we have all come to understand it. It is a courageous confession, for it calls into question the foundation upon which he has built a psychology of self and it challenges some of the most basic presumptions of the gay movement. If Edmund White isn't exactly gay, then who is? Where can we find the true gay man? What are the boundaries of his life? How do we recognize the topography of his desire? If we cannot trust such a well and publicly examined geography of desire, how can we fully trust our own desires?

A Queer Geography is my own trek into the uncertainties of desire. Chapter 1 begins in bed with my lover and asks if we—and our generation—experience the sliding together of body and spirit in genuinely the same way as today's twenty-somethings and how any of us should understand the universal male fellatio of a tribe in New Guinea. Chapter 2 is a set of journeys to Naples, perhaps the most phallocentric city in Europe, where a gay doctor, two petty gangsters, and transvestite *femminielli* find the American sex system as bizarre as the tribal practices of New Guinea. Chapter 3 returns to Kentucky, my home, to the rebuilding of a room and a fireplace and a contemplation of how the ideology of "coming out" often serves to undermine the aesthetic power of secrecy and erotic mystery. Chapter 4 is an inquiry into the sublime and the ways in which Puritanism and evangelicalism continue to shape the American gay movement. Chapter 5 considers Michel Foucault's proposal that we see homosexuality as a method for leading the creative life and looks at the stories of three men: an African-American political adviser, a jazz pianist from the Midwest, and a radical intellectual turned pornographer. Chapter 6 proposes that our search for a liberated sexuality can and should serve not as the basis for self-protective identity politics but as a model for the renewal of pluralist democracy.

Frequently I have had conversations with friends and activists about the reticence of many Mediterranean, Brazilian, or Filipino

men to embrace North American–style gay identity. Once, a prominent Italian-American writer and activist spoke about visiting his
cousins in Italy, some of whom were in longstanding homosexual
relationships. "All of them, they're all in the closet," he said. "Everybody in the family knows, but they don't dare come out and talk
about it." Of course, I don't know his family, and his perception may
be exactly accurate. But his presumptions certainly wouldn't capture
the nuanced complexity of my Neapolitan friends, among whom
sexual attraction seems to follow passion far more than gender. Nor
would the American approach to "sexual orientation" explain the
Filipino world explored in the 1995 film *Midnight Dancers,* where
handsome young working-class men, married with children, per-
formed as dancers and call boys and gradually developed loving relations with older or richer clients. There, as in much of Central
America, Peru, Colombia, and parts of South Asia, the distinctions
separating love, exploitation, opportunity, and desire make a mock-
ery of the gay-straight divide that has defined so much of the lesbian
and gay movement in the United States.

As George Chauncey demonstrated in his examination of gay
New York before World War II, and as Steven Zeeland has revealed
in his interviews with military men, the successes of the gay movement have sometimes had the unintended effect of *reducing* sexual
contact among men. Often men are drawn to intimate physical contact with other men exactly because it happens sub rosa, away from
the labeling eyes of activists, psychologists, and sociologists. Once
the act is given a name and its practitioners assigned an identity, they
no longer find the sexual contact liberating or powerful. That is not
to diminish the enormous accomplishments of the lesbian and gay
movement in securing rights and freedoms unprecedented in the
modern age. It is to say that the American gay movement is only
that—an American movement that owes its form and direction to
peculiarly American experience and tradition. Now that at last sexuality, including homosexuality, has become a respectable area of
scholarly inquiry, we have come to realize that sexual behavior is not
an unvarying force of history, that the way human beings experience
one another in the flesh is subject to other forces of economy, social
mobility, aesthetic style, spiritual mission, and political generosity. We

cannot tell our sexual story, "gay" or "straight," free of other stories of grief, loss, love, expectation, and dreams. Contrary to our usual national impulses, I believe, we would be well advised to look with generosity and forbearance at other sexual geographies that are organized in other ways, which may in fact change the way we come to see ourselves in future days.

one

Do

Gays

Exist?

Morning in Brooklyn,
March 3, 1994

am lying sidewise in the new bed, awaiting morning. Layers of February quilts weigh down thick and heavy on tucked-up limbs.

Gene has begun to stir. He reaches over to touch his fingers to the always itchy centerline of my back. We turn, in tandem. I plant myself close against him, stretching my head up onto his double stack of pillows. He pulls my left arm around to stroke his tummy skin, then groans and sighs softly.

Another snow and ice storm has hit overnight, the fourth to fall on New York this winter. Dim, cold light seeps through the slats of the wooden blinds. We descend deeper into the covers as a new blast of sleet-laden wind lashes the window. The ice storm kept waking up both of us all night. Even the cats fled from the bed into the quieter center of the house.

A year and a month have passed since I moved in and we began the dance of homo-housekeeping, learning how to sort and tuck each other's socks, accommodating to mutual routines of bath and kitchen and backyard.

I extend an arm from the cotton cocoon and push down the square, plastic button on the clock radio to hear about peace plans and no-fly zones in Bosnia and Iraq and Little Rock . . . no, it's

Whitewater real estate scams and no-talk rules. The mind and the flesh and the ice slide in and out of each other, and then the cats begin whining: they are ready for their first feeding.

Gene disappears into the dressing closet and comes out bundled for sidewalk shoveling. Guilty, I hide deeper in the sheets and listen for the sound of metal on cement. Next blizzard, it's my turn.

I listen and watch the room. Now the sun breaks through the blinds, hard, boisterous, bright. Dust particles turn into floating prisms. Plywood, the yellow cat who spent his formative years sleeping behind a table saw in Gene's carpentry shop, has stretched himself up against the fizzing radiator. ("He's imprinted on it," Gene says; "he thinks it's his mother.")

I try focusing my eyes on the great, beveled, rectangular mirror that hangs on the opposite wall. The mirror is a testament to the invisible hand of New York's invisible, cash-free street markets. Gene found it leaning against a scraggly tree with a pile of other discarded household goods on a lower-Manhattan street. A deft arrangement of hanging clips covers its few chipped blemishes. The mirror is actually six mirrors. A center panel two feet high by four feet wide rests inside a frame of angled four-inch side mirrors, all of which together form a shallow bowl of reflected light. This morning the light shafts strike the center panel at an acute angle and bounce back, across the room, onto a small rug that hangs on the wall just above and to the left of our bed's headboard.

Like Linus, I have carried this rug all over the country as a way of telling myself that I am at home. From Kentucky to Washington (in 1976) to San Francisco (in 1978) to Los Angeles (in 1983) to Ann Arbor (in 1985) back to Washington (in 1986) and back to San Francisco again (in 1990) and now to New York. It is a frayed rug that my aunt Lucie, who lived in Buffalo, gave my parents long ago. Aunt Lucie said she bought it from Seneca Indians when she was young. She was a social worker. She always made it a point to tell us how much she admired the Seneca people, how they and the other "New York Indians" had formed democratic, peaceful governments long before white people had arrived and pushed them out of their homes. The rug is woven of raw, unbleached, beige wool. Four squares composed of red, black, and beige lines anchor each corner.

Two-inch-wide, red-and-black zigzags run horizontally across the rug. A fifth red-and-black box is at the center, itself centered by a beige cross. I wonder if the rug, probably crafted on a reservation overseen by Catholic priests somewhere in the western end of New York State, is at home again.

Slats of mirrored sunlight cut across the rug's bloody boxes and jagged lines, challenging the weaver's design. As many places as I have hung it, I have never seen the rug quite this way. Its colors are already lightly faded, and I've taken care to preserve it from direct sunlight, but this harmless, reflected light has a marvelous, playful effect. I watch the mirror toss the sun onto the rug and the rug repel it back into the mirror's own reflection of the rug. It's like a great childhood game of morning tricks.

Gene has stuffed other visual tricks into the crevices where the flat mirror and its reflective frame meet. There's the postcard reproduction of a Kentucky painter's image of a naked young man and his dog running through fields. There's a skinny French roller skater leaping into the air, knees splayed, skates clicking at the heels, Eiffel Tower in the background. An engraved Christmas card from his late boyfriend's parents. And Paddington Bear mounted on the upper-left corner. Far over, inside the left edge of the mirror, I can see the reflected image of an oil I brought from San Francisco: a small, dark seascape of the Bay and the Richmond tanker tower, painted by the late husband of an old friend.

A half hour has passed and the shovel scraping downstairs has grown more vigorous. I know I shall have to leave this morning reverie very soon, but maybe not just yet. Though I am not a spiritualist, solitary moments like these allow me a meditation on my sense of place. There is an orchestral quality among all these totems to our separate pasts, which in their newfound proximity to one another are helping us to fabricate a new present in this new place.

For Gene this house in the Windsor Terrace neighborhood of Brooklyn, the most soulful of New York's five burroughs, is not new. He has lived here for seven years, knows most of his nearby neighbors, and is a familiar face at the bagel shop, the Italian meat market, and the Korean greengrocer. His method of getting to know people and places is indirect. When, in late 1993, we decided I should leave

San Francisco and move to his house in New York, we didn't address the matter straight on.

"I don't think I can keep renting and subletting the place in SF when I'm really in New York," I said one day.

"Probably not," he said.

"Then I'll have to either store my pictures and furniture or ship them somewhere."

"I wouldn't mind changing what's on the walls."

"There are implications to that."

"Yeah," he said.

So I became a Brooklynite. So I also became half of a couple. A (reluctant) keeper of cats. A novice sailor on Long Island Sound. A subway straphanger who buys his tokens in twenty-dollar lots. I bought the Club, the red steel bar that locks onto your steering wheel and allegedly encourages car choppers to find an easier mark. And I began finding the route to deep sleep in a new bed with a still new, horny man radiating body heat all night long, every night, week after week into the procession of months and probable years. Entering Brooklyn I begin to map a new geography of desire and intimacy.

A peripatetic wanderer, I look at desire as a geographer. I seek its contours, its ragged shorelines, its mud and crystals, the arrangement of its caves and hiding places, the artifacts of its pasts, the sketchpads of its imaginings, the moorings of its departures. As physical geographers know, none of these features are fixed. Shorelines erode. Caves collapse. El Niño stirs up storms that move river valleys. Desire is the enemy of identity, of certainty, of indelible maps. This new geography does not erase past geographies. Early on I learned the value of carting rugs, pictures, and modest *tchotchkes* with me in my movings. They are more than sentimental attachments. They are visual, physical objects that have caught the light and shadow of all the places I have lived, and in the memory of that light and shadow, they are paths across time and space: they recall conversations, embraces, penetrations with the dead and distant. They are locators that make of my body a bridge between the kiss of a young bicyclist twenty years ago in Washington and the slap across the buttocks this morning of a sailor carpenter in Brooklyn—even as this mahogany bed that Gene's dead lover Kevin built brings Kevin's boyish, blond body in touch with mine each night.

■ ■ ■

A while later, toward the end of breakfast, I bring up a conversation from the previous evening, about mating and pederastic sex rites in an obscure New Guinea tribe called the Sambia people. Gene has come to tolerate my periodic, arcane obsessions. This time, however, he is genuinely puzzled over my prolonged curiosity about these more or less Stone Age people and their relation to the topic of this new book, which is about the way Western gay men locate a sense of place in the world. Yet after years of sorting through tracts and tomes on modern sexual identity, I find these premodern people on the other side of the earth endlessly fascinating, for without exception all the Sambia males enjoy at least a decade of exclusive childhood and adolescent homosexuality, after which they embark upon a lifetime of heterosexuality. Sexuality—homosexuality—occupies a radically different place in their lives than it does anywhere in the modern gay rights movement.

Among the ritual burdens of modern, egalitarian mateship is an expectation that each partner will listen to the other's professional obsessions, anxieties, and frustrations—his about suppliers, customers, and taxes, mine about characters, stories, and deadlines. On this topic Gene offers a warning: I had best be careful in writing about such things as young boys being snatched away from their mothers and forced into years of group fellatio. Child abuse, according to the dicta of American gay respectability, is child abuse, whether it takes place in New Guinea or New Rochelle, and it is not a topic the sages and activists of the gay movement care to talk about.

Duly noted. But, I say to Gene—who is finishing his coffee, anxious to get to his shop—it's not just the child sex that seems so upsetting about the Sambian sexual/homosexual system. It's the entire Sambian organization of sex and sexual identification that makes my gay friends fidget. What most distresses them is the extent to which Sambian sexual behavior seems so circumstantial, so lacking in what we call sexual identity. From age seven or eight, according to anthropologist Gilbert Herdt, every Sambian boy is instructed to "eat the penis" and swallow the semen of an older male. Ideally he should ingest semen every day. That is how the Sambians believe they build up their maleness, discover their masculinity. Then, once the child has reached puberty, he undergoes another ritual initiation, is called a "bachelor" and then finds younger boys to fellate him. All this continues until eventually he becomes an adult, marries, and with the birth of his first child turns to conventional heterosexuality.

To the leading authors and strategists of the American gay movement, sexuality—sexual *orientation*—is an identity, something sure, certain, reliable, around which life and literature can be forged, through which rites and rituals are being invented. To the Sambia, whom you have sex with is secondary to the rigid demands of existing tradition, ritual, and collective *Sambian* identity. For a while you are strictly "homosexual." For a brief period you may be "bisexual" in that you can be fellated by either a man or a woman. But by adulthood, you become operationally and happily heterosexual. To a population of middle-class Americans who have argued that sexuality, and particularly homosexuality, is basis enough to build community and cultural identity, the Sambians seem to turn the world on its head.

By now Gene has turned on the dishwasher, wrapped a scarf around his neck, and pulled on his red "Eli Cutter" cap, ready to get on with the practical matters of his workday. He is patient, but he has scant time to spend palavering over the sexual behavior of South Pacific warrior tribes. He interrupts my perambulations about the Sambia to hand me a flyer depicting some decidedly modern if atavistic homosexual rites. Some unknown person slipped the flyer into the mailbox the day before at his shop. (His shop is in an industrial warehouse underneath the Brooklyn Bridge, the sort of neighborhood where wise people carry steel pipes for protection after dark.)

The flyer offers T-shirts, silkscreened with a dozen S&M bondage shots of superpumped muscle toughs in a variety of aroused poses. Bondage not being one of Gene's erotic fantasies, he proposes that it might be more appropriate to my inquiries. He is, however, puzzled that the flyer should have appeared, without an envelope, in his shop mailbox since, so far as he knows, the other occupants in his ware-house are straight. Still, the day before, there it was. But who left it? The two rock musicians who live there and seem to have a steady stream of girlfriends? One of the married guys who works for him? One of the men from the carpentry shop on the ground floor? The UPS man? His landlord? The array of sexual rites and participants in New York is infinite. Anyone, for any number of reasons, might have deposited the flyer in his box. Whoever left it, however, had torn off a corner, including the mailing address for the T-shirt company but leaving the phone order number.

Just as I've begun to ponder the ubiquitous ordinariness of per-verse porn in America, Gene draws me back from bondage boys to New Guinea. "I don't know why anybody should get so upset about them," he tells me. "These people—the Sambians—they aren't ho-mosexual. It doesn't have anything to do with being gay."

"No, not gay," I say. "But they are homosexual, at least for a while. They have sex with other men. They even say they all came to love it. They say swallowing semen was just like their elders told them it was, 'sweet as mother's milk' and just as essential to growing up strong. Like Wonder bread. They even talk about feeling genuine af-fection for their first partners, even romantic attachment."

"Not really, they're not really homosexual," Gene insists. "It's just some sort of rite of passage, and anyway, I gotta get to work."

■ ■ ■

Of course, our experience of homosexuality and the Sambian's is utterly different. However much we and the Sambian men may cel-ebrate and even ritualize the primal experience of cocksucking, however much we may both experience the act as a profound form of male bonding and solidarity, we cannot assume that homosexual-ity has the same meaning for each of us. Indeed, most students of sex and culture argue that ritualized, tribal homosexuality (or for that matter even sexual attitudes at the time of the American Revolu-tion) bear little resemblance to urban sexual life of the last hundred years. With rare exception gay communities, gay families, gay churches, gay psychologists, gay reporters, and gay politicians did not exist before this century. The psychological and social meaning attached to these gay phenomena did not exist: *we,* as individuals whose imaginations and opportunities are shaped by this gay terrain, did not exist.

Nearly anyone with the most rudimentary knowledge of gay history will readily acknowledge as much, but few of us seem ready to acknowledge the corollary: nor is it so likely that *we* will always continue to exist, even if all our adversaries were to disappear and all our objectives to be realized. Even now, midway through the 1990s, there is less and less certainty whom we mean when we say *we* are gay, or a part of the gay rights movement. And that is why I keep returning to the Sambia. For just as we know that the meaning of homosexuality differs radically in our culture and theirs, so we also know that its meaning here in 1955 was radically different from what it has become in 1995. We and they, then and now, may all experience comparable tactile sensations when organs and mucosal surfaces slide together. But the role those physical experiences play in our lives changes continuously. Some fragments of the Sambian explanations make sense to us. Some fragments of Christopher Marlowe's account of the buggering of Edward II make sense to us, and, dismaying as it may be to gay men in their fifties, only some fragments of the cult of Judy Garland make sense to today's queer college kids. Our worlds, our understanding of the relationship of sex to community, is never the same.

Nonetheless, our preoccupation with the place that sexuality holds in community life, any community life, is persistent.

I go back to Paul, a young man I met in that most placeless of American places, Los Angeles. Paul was the advertising manager of the queerest of L.A. publications, *Spunk,* though even *queer* was a term he found too constrictive. Most of the guys who picked up *Spunk,* he told me, found it in skate shops, and they were generally under twenty-five. Since then I've found more and more aggressively queer young men throughout the country who grimace at being called either gay or queer—not because they want to hide their lusts and passions, but because they find more lusts and passions within themselves than the words *gay* or *queer* seem to allow. A year after meeting Paul I had a parallel experience at a suburban "straight" bookstore in Atlanta where I was reading from *Culture.* A torrential storm poured itself all over Georgia that evening, peppering down on the roof so hard that the store's staff put out buckets to catch the dripping water. Even so, a handful of sturdy souls filled the seats. During the discussion period a dialogue developed between David, an athletic twenty-four-year-old, and "Don" a somewhat portly man with thinning hair. Don, a small-town dentist, had driven two hours through the downpour to get there. He explained that he had spent twenty years in a marriage and was the father of three girls.

"I always thought that there was some kind of flaw inside me, and that if I worked hard enough, it would go away. I've spent years in therapy. I got married. . . ."

Don looked at David, who occasionally works as a model. "You never felt that way, did you?"

"No, never," David said.

Both men now say that they are gay, though David leans toward queer. Both crave sexual contact with other men, though Don retains a sense of being somehow flawed. Both find the circumstances of their situations absurd, but the loci of their absurdities are radically different. Don, the dentist, feels his fate at odds with his heritage. His sexual "flaws," over which he now acknowledges he has no control, have made him feel absurd, "out of place" in the traditions that have shaped the bigger part of his life. David feels his homosexual desires are thoroughly natural and it is society's response that is absurd. He regards being gay as simply "a piece of the mosaic of my life." If the queer stone in that mosaic doesn't occupy as much psychic space for him and his friends as it does for slightly older gay activists, it doesn't, he assures me, mean that they are any less ready to struggle "against our society's homophobia and bigotry. It just means that we see the whole issue of being gay as being that much more absurd."

Unlike Don the dentist, and unlike most middle-aged American gay activists, David's realization of his sexual desires was not accompanied by prolonged torment and crisis. "When I was thirteen," he said, "I went to the public library and buried myself in a corner with books on homosexuality, praying that no one saw what I was reading. I was desperately trying to find a clue on what was going on and how I could meet other queers. The only thing I learned was how to pick up guys." By the time he was in college, it could happen that his straight fraternity brothers joined him at a gay bar to meet his then boyfriend.

I recount these stories not because they are universal—prospectively homosexual teenagers still commit suicide at alarmingly high rates—but because they reveal an extraordinary rift in how two queer generations have come to understand their place in the fabric of American life. When I relate these stories to gay activists and writers of my own generation, I often hear two reactions: first, these young queers are naive and haven't realized how hard we fought to win the gay freedoms they enjoy; or, second, the young queers are denying how deep the closet really reaches into their lives and how long it takes to come out of it. There may be some truth to each of these self-defensive critiques. But on balance I think we must trust people to tell us what they are feeling—and what these young queers are saying is that they experience their sexual selves in different ways than their immediate elders do. I see that difference as an expression of place. Don places his sense of sexual absurdity at the center of his being and sees himself removed to the periphery of his heritage: a man whom fate has tossed to the margins. David gives his homosexuality a vital but secondary place in his personal identity: he uses it as a tool in the formation of his career and family in the mainstream of middle-class American life.

Sexuality occupies a different place in daily life for David, in Atlanta, or Paul, in Los Angeles, than it has in my life or the lives of most other middle-aged men I know. For David it is an asset, an area of experience he can draw upon in his professional life, working for gay political causes, publicizing gay events. For Paul, it is a route into the edginess of bohemian Los Angeles. For all of us it is at the threshold of ecstasy, intimacy, and love. Each of these young gay men—shall I call them gay?—uses sexual identity as an instrument, but only one instrument, to locate various dimensions of their lives.

By contrast I look at Gene's experience and my own. We both began our postcollegiate lives in 1970 as professional journalists, he in New York, I in San Francisco. Within two years, he left journalism. There were many reasons for his decision, but prime among them was "coming to terms with being gay." He felt that the overwhelmingly heterosexual ambience of the small daily newspapers where he was working blocked him from his development as a gay man. Instead he became a cabinetmaker, where he could control his workplace and make no explanations to anyone about how he conducted his social and erotic life. He moved to lower Manhattan, near the clubs and the baths and the piers—the preeminent gathering spots for post-Stonewall gay men. He tasted of all the delights available there, found several boyfriends, and eventually took up housekeeping with Kevin. He and Kevin lived together for thirteen years.

At about the same time, I was busy sorting out my life as a political magazine writer, producing investigative reports and essays on drugs, crime, and issues of social justice. I, too, chose self-employment, where my romantic life would not be subject to the same sort of scrutiny it would have been at the watercooler in the city room of a daily paper. More to the point, I made a clean distinction between what then seemed to me to be "serious issues" and my private, erotic interests. As an educated white man who was raised to believe that social problems belonged to other kinds of people, I was hardly unusual. In my twenties and thirties, gay men who wanted to work on frontline issues of the day almost never rummaged about the attics of their own sexual anxieties. Those who did elect to write about being gay risked being taken as activists or being remembered—and rehired—only for gay topics. As a result we came to accept the division between our lives and our work as normal.

No matter which choice we made—to reframe our work life in order to concentrate on being gay, or to containerize being gay in order to preserve our professional options—our queerness held the primary place in the organization of our lives. For more and more young queers now, however, sexuality is, as David said, only "a piece of the mosaic." As sexuality occupies a different place in the psychic makeup of our lives now than it did then, we experience the queer world around us in very different ways.

To take a quintessentially queer case, we cannot feel and interpret drag costume the same way in the 1990s—when, as one salesclerk assured me, a business executive in an Armani suit recently walked out of Lord and Taylor onto Fifth Avenue on spiked pumps—as we did when any cross-dresser caught on Fifth Avenue was subject to arrest for "unnatural" solicitation. The very same drag queen who dared sashay down the avenue in 1956 will have a profoundly different experience when she tosses her locks in 1996. S/he will experience it differently performing before us (whoever we are, with *our* earrings and studded leather belts and ceramic red ribbons set in place), and we will react in radically different ways than we would have felt free to react at the height of the McCarthy era. At the very least, we will be neither as bohemian nor as fearful now as we would have been four decades ago.

More to the point, we are all moving through our identities on roller skates—backwards, forwards, and sideways. We know as good postmodernists that we are all performers and viewers, foreground and background, subjects and objects. Today, the Brooks Brothers man is also a drag queen, a performer whom others describe as "a suit." Once the epitome of unself-conscious normalcy, he is now a figure in a costume (albeit a powerful figure). He can no longer be assured that he represents the standard, that his dress and manners and traditions and worldview constitute the normal, common ground against which everyone else seems aberrant and a little queer. For there is no longer a common ground of American normalcy. A twenty-four-year-old, openly queer public relations agent driving his new Isuzu Trooper can feel just as normal as the dowdy bank officer who approved the loan on the vehicle.

The notion of common ground among Americans, gay or straight, has always been at best provisional. At least since the great Irish immigrations of the 1820s and 1840s, Americans have battled over who owns the idea of the nation's common heritage. If middle-aged gays and young queers see themselves as elementally different, even when they are both white, middle class, and university educated, then the broader upheavals in our national story often leave many of us feeling as though we come from entirely separate universes. The totems of our disparate myths of origin—Mother Africa, Atzlan, Magna Carta (each with its own version of the perverse and the normal)—locate us and our fables in moral and aesthetic landscapes that seem to share nothing, that indeed seem only to reflect the legacy of Western conquest and opportunity played out over the last five hundred years and reenacted for video cams in the streets of South Central, Los Angeles, or Crown Heights, Brooklyn.

These all-too-real and all-too-bloody pageants are in fact struggles over ground, over social space, over the idea of place: at once racial and theological, economic and physical. They are about order and who has the authority to maintain it: theocratic Jews awaiting the Messiah or the great-grandchildren of African slaves hustling for a slice of the service economy, sons and daughters of Oaxacan shepherds who pray to the Virgin and sew the gowns of Beverly Hills bon vivants or Korean shopkeepers whose sons and daughters and aunts and uncles provide the labor to accumulate the money to buy up the stores that used to belong to the grandchildren of the African slaves. Or does authority remain with the Episcopalian WASPs who run law firms, convene civic commissions of inquiry, and undertake "public service" at the State or Justice Departments when their party wins the White House? These are the dreamtrails of American life in the nineties, exuberant and crazy with expectation for those who see their space expanding—terrifying and apocalyptic for those whose world seems to be collapsing. It is into that maelstrom of rising and collapsing social space that the call for queer space has emerged and continues to evolve.

■   ■   ■

To get a grasp on our conflicting dreams and myths, to see where I, too, stand in that conflict, I take myself back into the stories of my childhood, magical stories that have drifted down through the generations. The best two concern a certain Parson James Keith and his family. Keith was my grandmother Browning's maiden name. Parson James, having been educated at Edinburgh in Scotland in the early seventeenth century, found his way to Virginia and led a prosperous, though lusty and roustabout, life. The story has it that one day a rather peculiar fellow appeared at Parson James's door asking about him. The parson was out; the housekeeper answered. With considerable gravity the visitor told her that he had gone to university with the parson, and upon graduation the two had made a pact. Despite their training in theology, both men were doubtful about the existence of heaven and hell, even of an afterlife. Their pact required that if there were an afterlife, whoever died first would return to tell the other about it. Since their graduation, the two men had not seen one another, Parson James having shipped off to America, the visitor having spent his life in India.

"There is indeed a heaven and a hell," the visitor advised the housekeeper, adding that the parson himself had but a few months to live and, further, that if he wished to inherit the happier venue, he would need to change his ways immediately.

A sensible woman, the housekeeper shooed the peculiar visitor off and declined to mention his appearance to Parson James. The next day the visitor appeared again, sharply upset.

"You did not give the parson my message!" he scolded her. "I cannot return again. You must tell him that he has little time left and will have to reform his ways if he is to find a place in heaven!"

This time the housekeeper was shaken to the core. She passed on her message to the parson the same night. Parson James learned that his old university friend had indeed died a year or so earlier, so he took the visitor's admonitions to heart, repented of his ways, and shuffled off to his own grave within the year.

For emphasis, we were told that not only had the story of Parson James's visitation been passed down the Keith family line, but the descendants of the housekeeper's family were also told the same story at least up through the 1950s.

The second of the Keith family stories concerned Parson James's wife, Mary Isham Randolph. Mary was born to the famous and notorious Virginia Randolphs, and it seems she was an independent lass—so independent that in late adolescence she eloped one day with the bailiff of the family estates. The Randolphs were variously gamblers and wastrels, but they were also among the largest landowners in Virginia, holding thousands of acres of Piedmont and Tidewater land. Their children did not marry servants.

Mary's brothers did what any such brothers would have. They committed themselves to finding the errant couple and annulling their "marriage." More than a year had passed when one night the brothers found the lovers' retreat on Ilk Island in the James River. Without warning they burst through the door, snatched Mary, and bound her to a horse while taking an ax to her infant child and husband. She was returned home and eventually married to the apparently socially acceptable Parson James.

Once again fate intervened, this time on the parson's widow. One day Mrs. Keith received a letter purportedly from her long-lost love, who had somehow survived. He would not afflict her further, he wrote, advising her to forget him as he had more than died for her love. The parson's poor widow became unhinged; at first she searched for him, then slipped between moods of melancholy and "folly," ending life a veritable "lunatic."

My own aunt Lucie Keith Browning and her brother, my uncle Keith Browning, relished such stories, and they told them well, with a modern sense of humor and irony. But these were also instructive stories. None of the characters was free of blemish. Surely the murderous Randolph boys were not, nor was their rambunctious sister, who by failing to observe the rules of station and social obligation had brought stain upon the family, suffering to the stableman, and death to her own child. And the parson, energetic, attractively worldly, and intelligent, came to understand that even on the frontier, faith in God and heritage was the only protection against perdition.

Beyond the obvious moral lessons, however, there was a more rigorous message in these tales of Scottish ministers and yeomen, and later Virginia farmers and speculators and then Kentucky factory owners and even a famous poet and "distant cousin" of my own last name. I was given to understand that these were the people—we were the people—who had woven the civil fabric of the globe's most envied land. There were those who retained a history and those who did not. There were those who established the land— however speckled their use of it—and those who worked it. There were those who carried the imprimatur of Edinburgh—and in the seventeenth century Edinburgh was the center of British enlightenment—who fabricated the vision articulated finally in the documents of the founding fathers, fulfilling the destiny of the New World. And there were those later huddling masses who would become the beneficiaries of that vision. The preservation of the Keith name through two centuries to the very storytellers, my aunt and my uncle, left no doubt where my presumed place was.

These are the sorts of stories that give people their sense of place, their confidence that, as a matter of family right, they *have* a place in the world. In parallel ways, immigrant stories of relocation and arrival often impart values of energy, ambition, and anxiety over survival. These stories leave us with the sort of knowing that comes before knowledge. They lay down inside us a cultural and psychological template that we use to manage the "factual knowledge" we later learn. These are the stories that tell us what is "normal" before we could even guess what it is to be abnormal—for most Americans and Europeans to know what it is to be white before they have ever met a person who is not, to presume what it is to be "straight" before they have ever imagined what it is to be "queer." Stories like these teach us that our story is the ground, the foundation, the context against which other newer, more outsiderly human stories are played out. Even though there may be aberrations and adventures in our pasts, we learn before knowing that we have learned it that we have a coherent past and a reliable future. Ours was a seamless dream: our bodies, our spirits, our names, our place, were one, and there was nothing queer within us.

Or so it seemed until we were smacked by the great inversion of the modern era.

I say *inversion* with a double meaning. First is the psychological sense of my father's generation—as a homosexual I am an "invert." But I also mean a broader cultural inversion that has left the Americans of my father's generation (and of Don, the dentist's) feeling that their entire world has been turned upside down, inverted, that the cultural heritage that assured them of their place in the world has been disrupted. It is this double inversion—through which I invert my head and my penis, my penis and my anus, and upon which I exchange my inherited privilege of dominion for a marginal position of disruption—that has made homosexuality more than a matter of private behavior for Americans. We have not only inverted our organs and our orifices, as humans were doing long before my ancestors arrived on these shores. We have called upon our national myths—of heroism, the frontier, the promised land, the faith in rebirth—to insert ourselves into the national story. We have inverted the cultural codes that made us moral outcasts and used those codes to claim "our" place in society.

The contest for place in America, for a piece of the American idea, is not only about where we have come from; it is equally tied to our sense of present identity and future possibility. The Yoruba hunters sold into Virginia slavery, the New Rochelle whores shipped into Louisiana servitude, the English Puritans shuttled to Holland and on to Massachusetts, the Irish debtors hired to open the new lands of Georgia and Alabama—all these people who invented America arrived here as displaced persons. As did the merchants and planters who controlled their lives.

At its core the central faith of America has always been Protestant rebirth, the new beginning, through which we will be delivered into the new land. From the westward lurch of the Conestoga wagon trains to the spiritual promise of the criminal's redemption in a penitent-iary to the lure of "virtual intimacy" in the unbounded cybernetic community, we, as Americans, are suffused with the religion of realizing new identity through the location of new vistas. It was true when developers sold middle-class Brooklynites on moving to the green lawns of Levittown for a wholesome family life. It was true when Mao's former Red Guard revolutionaries swam to Hong Kong and finally transformed themselves into San Francisco stockbrokers. It remains true as unhappy drug users, drinkers, and overeaters sign themselves over to twelve-step temples for rebirth as clean and temperate children of the higher power. The promise of American redemption, both at home and in the world, relies, insists, upon the transformation of physical place as the guarantor of psychic, spiritual renewal. If we would be reborn, remade, or recovered, we must enter upon a personal journey, we must "walk that lonesome valley," as the gospel song put it, so that we might pass into "Beulah land."

That search for place is at the heart of the gay faith of coming out and being reborn into our own queer culture.

And there, of course, lies the rub. To be reborn, to be remade, to come out of the closet of our denials, we must go away, leave the old repressive world and build a New World, fabricate, in our case, a

Queer World. Gay liberation was, in this sense, no different from all the other subordinated-identity movements that have populated American history. Not only did we migrate to the great urban enclaves of the East and West Coasts as our immigrant forebears did. We even interpolated the metaphors of place and movement into a psychological praxis of gay identity. By "coming out" of our psychological closets we asserted a neat geography of identity. We visualized our psychic torment in clear, spacial terms. Our proposition—to ourselves and to the "straight" world—has been that there actually is an "inside" and an "outside" of sexual identity, replicating the Christian promise of the old and new testaments through which the sinner could achieve redemption by moving from the territory of the old faith to the territory of the new. Having "accepted" our new identities by "coming out," we have saved ourselves from the damnation of failing to believe in the goodness of our sexuality.

But there is a price to be paid for this deeply American ritual. We continually replicate the ordeal of displacement, inventing and reinventing the frontiers of our psychic identities just as our ancestors reinvented their New World dreams by slashing and burning new trails across the continent. In each new location we invest our expectant dreams in the language of community and renovated tradition: as Oneida and New Harmony and Arcadia, as the republics of Texas and Utah and California, sure that we have arrived at last in the community of our deliverance. Yet what we have left behind in each case is the tactile memory of our multiple pasts, the ordeals of earlier communities and earlier deliverances, the physical artifacts of our ancestors (not only their headstones, but also their rocking chairs and snuffboxes), which might somehow have reminded us of how many selves still reside within our new-made identities.

What we "gay people" are learning now, two decades into AIDS, three decades into the modern gay movement, is that the politics of self-redemption is no more reliable for queers than for any other Americans. Well before the first modern generation of "gay people" has approached retirement, before its own pantheon of ancestors could be carved into stone, the viability of gay identity itself is in question.

"Nobody is happy with 'gay' anymore," my activist friend Eric
Rofes told me one morning over breakfast in San Francisco. Eric
has been one of the architects of gay activism since the 1970s, an editor and writer at Boston's *Gay Community News*, executive director
of Los Angeles's Lesbian and Gay Community Center and later of
the San Francisco Shanti project, and a board member of the National Gay and Lesbian Task Force.

Eric had been the first prominent gay leader I heard use the word
queer to describe himself. He was speaking at a Task Force conference in 1988. "I realize I've always felt queer," he said. "It used to be
because I was a gay man in a straight world. Then I realized I still felt
queer even when I was surrounded by gay people." Six years later, in
1994, twenty-five years after the Stonewall riots, after Queer Nation
had come and gone, after gay clone mustaches had been replaced by
queer clone goatees and then been replaced themselves, the dazzling, expansive, inclusive promise of queer identity had imploded
upon itself. What had begun in the streets as an exuberant expression
of rage and flamboyant gestures—guerrillas invading department
stores, chanting, "We're here, we're queer, get used to it!"—became
subsumed under an academic discipline called queer theory where
serious students of aesthetics and epistemology examined the linkage between identity and social action in the postmodern universe.
Brilliant theorists like Eve Kosovsky Sedgwick and Judith Butler
were developing literary and philosophical works that demonstrated
how buried issues of gender and sexuality and "the closet" were
never far from the story lines of most Western literature. Yet in
everyday life—going to work, going to the polls, going to parties,
going to bed—both the old language of "gay" and the newer language of "queer" seemed inadequate.

Queer remains a signature of generational difference, a marker of
a more freewheeling, combative social style. But replacing the word
gay with *queer* hasn't resolved the trouble that brought about the
change in terminology. Younger men like David and Paul still find
themselves pinched within the boundaries of both words. As do I.
And Eric. And a great many of the people I write about in this
book. The trouble we feel with *gay* is deeper and more difficult than

language. The semantical shift to a more expansive and edgier term like *queer* reflects a psychic and philosophical problem at the foundation of an identity politics built around sex and gender. For me that problem becomes clearer the more I read and listen to the stories of gay African-Americans.

Audre Lorde, the late African-American poet, wrote at length about the power of difference in American life. Lorde was lesbian; she loved and made love to other women. But she was not exactly "a lesbian." "I have always known that I learn my most lasting lessons about difference," she wrote in one of her last essays, "by closely attending to the ways in which the differences inside me lie down together." Lorde understood how closely empowerment lies to imprisonment in group identity. Categorized as a "woman poet" rather than a poet, she experienced both the exclusion implicit in the phrase (one never hears Whitman or Auden described as a "man poet") and the solidarity of being anointed a feminist voice. Born black, she knew, too, about racial responsibility and the patronizing manner of white critics who could only hear her as a voice of *her* people (and therefore not as a writer of universal power). It is not enough to say that as Americans we are a pluralist society and that as queer Americans we carry our plural identities to their furthest extreme. For Lorde or James Baldwin before her, the pluralities are inside ourselves just as much as they are among ourselves. We are creatures possessed by multiple demons (and daemons).

"A culture," Baldwin writes in *The Price of the Ticket,* is not "something given to a people, but, on the contrary and by definition something that they make themselves." Baldwin was writing about the longing of black Americans for an authentic heritage in Mother Africa that would offset the almost uniformly white story presented in the history texts. Important as Africa was to the culture of the diaspora in the New World, he rejected it as a singular heritage, arguing that both in Africa and in America, culture emerges through the interaction of diverse individuals joined in common purpose.

Baldwin pressed his point further, however. Even contemporary Africans cannot look only to Africa to find their identities. "They were all now, whether they liked it or not, related to Europe," he argued, "stained by European visions and standards, and their relationship to themselves, and to each other, and to their past had changed." Africa, he insisted, must not be seen as a museum where the African-American diaspora could find its roots. After two centuries of European colonial rule and two generations of postcolonial warfare and disease, the continuities of African classical heritage have become as fluidly postmodern as gender-fuck drag life in Gotham—a point that RuPaul and his enthusiasts understand intuitively. Culture does not exist in a museum, and an identity does not derive from the artifacts contained in its display cases. But the way we visit the museum, how we see and use the artifacts in it, shapes and illuminates the cultural life we are constructing—whether the museum show is about the tropes of post-Stonewall gay visibility or the healing power of Senegalese carvings.

Identity, finally, represented a failure of faith for Baldwin. He saw it ultimately as an oppressive approach. As he told *The Advocate* in a 1983 interview, "It's not important to be gay . . . or important to be white . . . or important to be black. What's important is to be *you.*" Instead of identity, Baldwin proposed an altogether different solution. A unified, coherent culture of the sort African-Americans imagined in the mother country, Baldwin argued, permits "a much lower level of tolerance for the maverick, the dissenter, the man who steals the fire." That image of a black Prometheus, the man who steals the fire, is what Baldwin relied upon as both a method and an image for liberation. For Prometheus represents the human soul in perpetual rebellion to all the gods and demons that would contain it. As the poet and critic David Bergman noted in *Gaiety Transfigured,* Prometheus is a figure that speaks on multiple levels. Both European and pre-Christian, Prometheus comes from a polytheistic world where humans are acknowledged to be possessed by multiple daemons and multiple sexualities, a worldview that is remarkably similar to the Yoruba spirits that accompanied Baldwin's forebears in their slave ships to the New World. Still more intriguing as an idea, the Promethean spirit brings us to interrogate ourselves about who "we" are (who "I" am) and how the many selves inside us can relate to each other.

While he uses very different language, Baldwin's Promethean approach to identity feels very close to the philosopher Michel Foucault's playful admonitions about "gayness." As much as he loved the exploratory sexuality of the baths and the bushes, Foucault was suspicious of the organized institutions of the gay movement. He was particularly doubtful about "the tendency to reduce being gay to the questions: 'Who am I?' and 'What is the secret of my desire?' " Initially, I supposed Foucault and Baldwin to be intellectual antagonists. When Baldwin said that the important thing "is to be *you*," would he not have you ask first, "Who *are* you?" How can I *be* myself if I do not *know* who I am? Yet I think these two queer writers, Baldwin, the grandson of slaves reared in Christian Pentecostalism, and Foucault, the atheist, intellectual descendant of Nietzsche *and* Descartes, were getting at the same thing. Neither of them believed that the self could be easily located on anyone's sociological map, even a map that offered itself as the route to liberation. Both approached personal integrity through relentless self-interrogation, asking not "Who am I?" but "What must I do, where must I go?"

The question "Who am I?"—gay, straight, black, white, French, American—is a question every adolescent asks in hope of finding a clear, singular answer. To *be* myself, on the other hand, I do not have to answer categorizing questions about myself. Men were falling in love with each other long before they began calling themselves gay. By declining to ask or answer the question of who I am, I can, with courage, allow myself many selves and multiple possibilities.

The distinction is subtle but important. If I tell you, "I'm a gay man," I am making an exclusionary statement. More than anything else, I am telling you *what* I am not: I am not a man who has sex with women. But I'm revealing very little of who—a Southerner, a political writer who shuttles back and forth between the power obsessions of Washington and the pixilated marginality of San Francisco, a would-be actor who grows apples in Kentucky and is learning to make champagne cider—I am, and I am telling you nothing about how the force and form of my sexuality plays with all those other personae I inhabit, how my sexuality has surfaced as a door of introduction to the world of cider-making, or how its sublimated effects emerge when I climb onto the tractor to rip open the soil with a set of shiny steel plows.

And yet, the simple declaration of my "gay" identity releases the power of solidarity and provocation; therefore I don't want to relinquish it. I go to Oscar parties on Academy Awards night and share in camp jokes about famous producers who thank their wives but not their boyfriends. I stop in at the adult bookstore in Lexington where I know I can meet other farmers, students, and assorted randy men who don't like bars. I join a gay journalists' association and draw sustenance from the realization that I am not alone in proposing "unconventional" stories about "family life." I watch gymnastic Olympic events and relish the particular pleasures my friends— dykes and homo boys—derive from watching beautiful men and women glide over the exercise horse. I am enlivened at "community meetings" when "my people" come together to wage war against bigoted political initiatives or to develop strategies against the scourge of AIDS. Gay identity links me to other people through whom I find direct, collective social, sexual, and political voice. It tells me I am not alone.

But just as powerfully, gay identity polices the profusion of my possible selves and the possible, profuse contacts I may have with you. It focuses and limits the erotic possibilities we might share. By *erotic* I mean all the powerful attractions we might have: for mentoring and being mentored, for unrealizable flirtation, for intellectual tripping, for sweaty mateship at play or at work, for spiritual ecstasy, for being held in silent grief, for explosive mutual rage at a common enemy, for the sublime love of friendship. All or none of these ways of loving might be connected to the fact that I usually have sex with men because all of these loves can and do happen with both men and women in my life. Any one of these loves—rage, ecstasy, mateship—can drift into each other, further complicating and entangling our lives, leaving us to realize on parting that the one with whom we feel the most powerful love may be neither the one we most respect nor the one for whom we feel the greatest lust. If I tell you first that I am gay, our love will move in one direction. If first I tell you that I love you—as a mate, as a comrade, as a spiritual voyager—you will know my queerness in quite another way.

"Might it not be better," Michel Foucault proposed, "if we asked ourselves what sort of relationships we can set up, invent, multiply, or modify through our homosexuality? The problem is not trying to find out the truth of one's sexuality within oneself, but rather, nowadays, trying to use our sexuality to achieve a variety of different types of relationships. And this is why homosexuality is probably not a form of desire, but something to be desired. We must therefore insist on *becoming* gay, rather than persist in defining ourselves as such."

Reversing the fierce, maudlin lyrics of the stoic homosexual in *La Cage aux Folles* ("I am what I am"), Foucault—and the emerging generation of antigay queers—would rephrase the song, "I am what I can become." The identity of becoming is a dynamic identity. It acknowledges that "coming out" is a fluid, continuous experience, more akin to Heraclitus' river, which can never be touched, because during the time it takes to dip your hand into it and pull it out, it has moved somewhere else. Both eros and love are not knowable, not capable of being fixed, any more than the force of the river, even the Mississippi River with all its engineered locks and dams, can be contained. The paradox of the Heraclitean river, of course, is that even though it cannot be touched, it forms the very definition of place. By its course it orders the land it divides, and more, it provokes those who live on that land to Promethean daring. It challenges them to snare its power for transportation, snatch its fish for sustenance, drain its water for irrigation—all the while risking death by drowning.

I linger on the metaphor of river as identity because it seems to speak to the dilemma we face now, at the end of the millennium, in our yearning for community and liberation. Like the river, we cannot retreat. That is the route of sentimentality, along which we would wistfully and hopelessly search, like the pope's speechwriters, for the nostalgic, small-town communities of our grandparents. The answer to the barrenness of the consumerized, zip-code-organized gay communities identified by bars, buns, and boutiques is not a homo shtetl marked by its own codes of fearful self-preservation.

If, on the other hand, we dare to see "coming out" as a simultaneous "going in" to the uncharted potential relationships we contain, then we may find in our sexualities a new method for finding community. Then "queerness" becomes a tool of navigation, an interrogatory technique for revealing the queerness in others, establishing spiritual and communitarian bonds with and among others too mysterious for the reductionist moguls of marketing to comprehend. Our charge, engineered at once through confrontation and seduction, is genuinely shamanic: it is not to protect ourselves, but to subvert certainty and to destabilize power; it is not to build new families, but to open up and nurture the queer spaces already inside them; it is not to retreat into our own safe space, but to discover, protect, and electrify the queer zones in calcified, dispirited communities everywhere. Our mission is, in the very best sense, spiritual: it is to provoke passion where planners, preachers, and commodity marketers have done their best to deaden it.

Midnight, July 28, 1994, Park Slope

Nearly half a year has passed since the morning of the ice storm when Gene and I cocooned ourselves beneath the covers, and I kept talking about the Sambia tribesmen. As bitter cold as the winter was, this summer is meltdown hot. In another week he is going to sail out Long Island Sound up to Buzzards Bay through the Cape Cod Canal to Provincetown. It is a hard sail just leaving the Sound. The tides through The Race at the end of Long Island are pernicious. Timing must be exact to pass through them.

Gene is facing his perpetual dilemma. He needs a crew of at least three experienced sailors to get through the first twenty-four-hour run to Block Island, and he'd like them to be gay guys. He goes into his usual lament: "Gay guys don't sail."

"That's nuts," I say. "You just haven't found them."

"Yeah? It's twenty years now I've been sailing around New York. They all say they want to, but when it gets down to particulars, they'd all rather go to Fire Island or the Hamptons or Vermont or the discos."

(I am not an experienced sailor, especially for the night-sailing section near the ocean. I'll take public trains and ferries to meet him on Block Island.)

Just this month, July, Gene heard about a new group of gay sailors that's forming. I find it hard to believe that, with the plethora of gay sports events, such a sailing group hadn't been formed years ago. But in all the guides to New York homo life, nothing has shown up until now. Certainly, the reason isn't money, given the thousands of dollars gay men spend every summer on shares in Fire Island houses.

Last night Gene got home just after midnight. He'd gone to the gay sailors' first meeting—on board a thirty-eight-footer moored in a harbor in Jersey City. Gene hasn't been this effervescent in months. Thirteen men showed up. Two-thirds of the guys own their own boats. The others were experienced at handling lines and reading charts. The owner of the boat where they met was in his late forties. Most of the rest were in their twenties or early thirties. Gene brought a deli sandwich, but many of the others arrived with more elegant fare: marinated fresh asparagus, homemade pesto, bourbon-infused walnut brownies. The meeting had turned into a six-hour sail across New York harbor and out beneath the Verrazano Narrows Bridge. Finished and back on the dock, one of the young men, who until then had held a rather serious, rangerlike demeanor, let go.

"He just started prancing around, being very gay, and said, 'Now I can do what I want!' Then he came up to each one of us and gave us a big kiss."

Gene, for whom sailing is very serious play, turned to me and smiled. "It was wonderful."

I listened, asked a few questions (none of the guys are likely to be free for the Provincetown sail), and said, "I think I've figured out why the Sambia people are so interesting."

"The who?" he asked, wrinkling his nose in a grimace.

"The Sambia tribesmen, remember? In New Guinea. Where all the boys suck cock until puberty, and then after marriage become exclusively heterosexual."

Silence.

"All right. It's too late to go into now," I said. "But thinking about the Sambia sex system even makes it a little clearer to me why you've had so much trouble finding gay men to go sailing with."

■　　■　　■

First, the gay sailors problem.

Like stonemasons, sailors develop their own tribal knowledge and sensibility. The wind and the sea are global. Everywhere sailors face the same kind of challenges in coping with the elements. Even when they don't speak the same language, sailors find a method of common communication, united in an almost spiritual fear of and respect for the sea. The experience of working the water forms its own brotherhood. Those who are guests and fair-weather passengers, as I am, stand outside it.

I have brought others, gay and straight, aboard Gene's boat, and he has taught them the rudiments of sailing. He has turned over the wheel to them. Usually, they say they have had a splendid time. Still, those who are not sailors know that they are not quite in the same world as is Gene, who, if possible, will be on the water every weekend it is warm enough to sail. There is a camaraderie that appears between him and other seasoned sailors that is altogether different from what happens when the nonsailors join us. Even when the newcomers are skinny guys in cutoffs.

Sometimes the gap between sailors and nonsailors seems as great and as profound as the gap between gay and straight, the insider-outsider dynamics even more invested in history and practice and spirituality. Thinking about these differences has given me another glimpse of what Audre Lorde means when she writes that she "learns the most lasting lessons about difference by closely attending to the ways in which the differences inside me lie down together." This summer, for example, Gene began flying the rainbow flag he picked up several years ago at a marine store in Newport, Rhode Island.

"It's the friendship flag," he told me. "That's the way they were using it in Newport. The shop that was selling it certainly didn't think of it as a gay flag." Then, several months ago, when he came to help me pack up my house in San Francisco, he was stunned at the ubiquity of the rainbow flag as a marker for gay turf. Gene had not been in San Francisco in more than twenty years; in New York the rainbow flag has not held the importance it has in the Castro district.

Gene is thoroughly comfortable being gay, but he told me once that he never fully trusted the community identity of gayness, never wanted to be identified by its iconography. He is Jewish (but not religiously so). He is a cabinetmaker. He is a Brooklynite. He is a sailor. He "likes guys." But he does not wear the insignia of gay community identity. His decision to fly the rainbow flag this summer came in part from his excitement at seeing how relaxed and convivial gay men seemed to be in gay San Francisco, where, unlike New York, they operate large parts of city services and administration. After that the "friendship flag" from Newport became much more important to him. Even so, he fits his use of the flag as a gay icon inside the context of sailing. He does not hang it from our window at home, nor does he paste it on his bumper. It flies from the mast along with his personal flag (a penguin named Burgess) and along with the standard American flag attached to the guyline at the back of the boat. I think of the way he uses the flag not so much as an identity, but as a part of the guidance system of the boat.

Flying from the mast, it does not guide the boat, but it may provide us some internal sense of guidance. To other sailors on the Sound, it is far from the first thing they see. Their first knowledge when they see us is the type of ship, the direction and force of wind, and how astutely we are sailing. All of this information also tells them something about themselves. Most important they will determine whether one of us must alter course to avoid collision. Further, if we are upwind, they get an idea what to expect when they reach our location. If they are leeward of us, we will steal their wind; if we are leeward, they will steal ours. By watching the shape of our sails they can evaluate whether they should retrim their sails. They may even learn something about the comparative dynamics of our two craft as they move through the water and, should our boats be comparable, whether their slower speed indicates that their bottom and keel have become encrusted with barnacles and shrimp.

All this information likely arrives before they can see the rainbow flag clearly. Even among the homophobes, they are more likely to say "That sailor's a queer" than "There's a queer with a sailboat." The commonality of sailing precedes the difference of sexuality. The meaning, I think, is radically different from the iconography and cultural meaning of summer weekend life on the Fire Island Pines.

At the Pines, identity seems simple and singular: young, hunky, mostly white gay men whose navigations are more directed by hot breath than fickle southwesterlies. Being there is more about status than movement. The rules and customs of behavior are local. They are provisional, confected from within the group that happens to be there, and like the sandbar that is Fire Island, they don't pretend to permanence. The tingling excitement at tea dance is suffused with flighty giddiness: it is not about moving through the world so much as relief from the world. It is, in short, the inverse of the sailor's world. While no boat ever moves through the same water twice, the customs, manners, and methods of living aboard the boat, of living atop the unstable sea, are almost primordial. The physics of how solid objects move in water and stay afloat do not change. They were as predictable in the Pleistocene as they are in the age of heavy metal, as regular in the Gulf of Tonkin as in Buzzards Bay. To enter into that world is to enter into a time-transcending system of codes and rituals, altogether the opposite of a weekend at the Pines. The expectations of permanence and impermanence on land and sea are turned upon their heads.

I think of the world the Sambia live in as parallel to the world sailors inhabit. Despite the advent of satellite guidance telemetry and fiberglass-hull fabrication, sailing is premodern. To enter into the world of sailors is to enter into a world of customs and physical laws most of which antedate the discovery of gunpowder and steel. Much of the appeal of sailing is the harmonious contest—a tango if you will—between individual will and transcendent order. The wind cannot *be made* to blow backward nor can the current be forced to run upstream by the will of the sailor. At the same time, the rush of wind in the face, the slice of the bow through the rhythmic swells, carries its own proto-erotic sensations. It is a seduction that goes on continuously between sailor and sea in which the archetypal male wanderer relentlessly contrives to outwit the ultimately unknowable and uncontainable (and female) force of the sea. It is a sublime confrontation in which the sailor's only hope of success (and often survival) depends upon his knowledge and manipulation of nature's ordered rules.

The territory of the Sambia is just such a world, where survival demands that they navigate personal volition through a fast system of code and ritual. Passion and eros are central to their collective myth; at the same time, the codes and rituals of war, maturation, and mateship organize and intensify the power of passion and eros. As it happens, homosexual experience is central to those codes and rituals. Yet it never stands alone as a distinct individual "identity" that would distinguish one man from another. Instead, homosexual acts—fellatio—and bonding are deeply embedded in psychological and spiritual belief systems they rely on to "navigate" through a dangerous world. As much could be said of a number of other premodern or "classical" societies where love, affection, and sex were shaped by strict ritual.

Clearly, the Sambia are not homosexual in the way that we mostly European-descended people understand that word. Yet as I read Gilbert Herdt's intimate and expansive descriptions of their sex acts, much of what they do could be written down in S&M handbooks, complete with blood rites, bondage, and flailing techniques. Nor does the fact that their couplings are ritually governed mean they lack affectionate interest in each other. Ritualized sex is not without passion, as any participant in Faerie gatherings or Chicago (S/M) Hellfire knows well.

Sambian men understand "eating each other's penis" as a nurturing rite of passage. They believe that boys cannot become men unless they suck out male essence—semen—and fill up their "semen organ" through which they become *jerungdu,* or strong. Their understanding of biology is that males cannot generate their own semen but must get it from other men, from outside themselves, and then, once having it, they pass it on.

"We men [ejaculate into the mouths of] women and their children. We copulate with a woman and she produces breast milk; then she feeds the infant," Tali, one of the Sambia men, explains to Herdt. "We men complain: we give semen to a boy, we *moo-nungendei* him. And he turns around and copulates with a younger boy. We big men copulated with him and we said, 'We completed his *moo-nungendei,* but he has gone and given his share to other boys.' " Among the Sambia men, semen is a genuinely masculine elixir. Tali confesses to Herdt, "I still never stop thinking semen or eating it," adding with a smile, "A married man who didn't play around enough will die quickly, like an airplane without gasoline!" Fellatio is what enables the men to breed and make babies in the bodies of women, and it is what binds the men together across generations.

To us the Sambia may not be an appealing culture. They are deeply misogynist; they fear and sometimes hate women, and therefore subordinate women mercilessly. Moreover, they guard their homosexual exchanges with great secrecy, possessed by all sorts of fears about how women would, if they found out about male homosexuality, use evil powers to destroy the men. For it is, in their view, only fellatio, cocksucking, that they can share with one another and thereby become bonded in a dangerous and threatening world.

Over the more than two decades that Gilbert Herdt has studied and made friends with the Sambia, they have told him of the genuine eroticism, of the deep affection, that their years of cocksucking brought them. A gay American himself, Herdt came away from his research convinced that genuine emotional and psychological bonds developed among the Sambia—though never apparently on the paired-off model we find in the Judeo-Christian West. Still, to our American gay minds, the fact that Sambian cultural rules specify and regulate their homosexual events—the young may suck, adults *are* sucked, and after an adult man's first child has been born he may *not* give his penis to boys at all—demonstrates that they are not *in essence* homosexual. Their homosexuality is provisional, undertaken only to fulfill the greater purposes of Sambian society—namely to forge a powerful, secret bond among the males through which they underwrite their power and dominance. It is not freely given, individual, erotic love, but eros chained to the dictates of community preservation.

In America, and to a growing degree in the Americanized sectors of the globe, we go about our affairs in just the reverse of the Sambia people. Having sacrificed the sure rituals of local community life for the lures, opportunities, and mobility of the modern city, we find ourselves in a social geography where we label and map our internal identities and then go about the self-conscious enterprise of constructing temporary public communities based on those accumulated personal identities, to wit, the organized gay worlds of the Castro, Chelsea, Newtown, Midtown, South Beach, the Marais, Earl's Court, Nollendorfplatz. These homo-communities are the peculiar gift of America, the earth's largest collection of individually displaced people.

Through a hundred years of psychological adventure and social activism, we have fabricated something called a gay identity. That identity, like all the other racial, ethnic, and nationalistic identities that bubble to the surface in an immigrant consumer society, longs for the security, the community, of the ritual-heavy home that was left behind. But save for the forests of New Guinea, such communities of unquestioning ritual scarcely exist any longer. (And even there, as Herdt notes, questioning and change are altering tribal life.) To replace them, we look to the only place we can, to our accumulated self-identities, hoping that by force of will we can invent the strength and reassurance of community that the modern world has eliminated.

What we do is, as Gene says, the opposite of what the Sambia do: they locate their sense of self and the trajectory of their lives through the application of abiding community ritual; we would locate our dream of community through reenacting internal psychodramas of the reborn, fabricated self. Straight and gay alike, we turn to the marketplace of myths and images, hopeful that we will find, invent, or renew ourselves, anxious to discover collective meaning somewhere on the social internet. As urban postmoderns, we are driven to the metaphors of navigation and geography. The ground beneath our feet is always moving. Literally. Since World War II, nearly a fifth of all Americans have moved to a new house or apartment every year, while fewer than 10 percent of French, British, Japanese, or Swedish citizens move each year. The statistics of family life are equally voluble. Only half of those who marry spend their lives with the same partner, and hardly anyone, except for large Hispanic and Asian extended families, see their adult siblings or grandparents on a regular weekly basis. We don't even stick to our own trade. A 1991 federal survey found that fewer than half of professional and managerial employees were in the same occupation they had six years earlier and that among American factory workers, fewer than half had been in the same trade for more than four years. Why should we expect our experience of sex and sexuality to be any more stable than the other prime forces in our lives?

A hundred years ago, at the prime of my grandparents' lives, bourgeois understanding of sexuality was little different from what it had been in the Christian Renaissance: sex acts were evaluated as matters of moral behavior (most of the possibilities regarded by Christians and Jews as immoral), a few celebrated through the romance system for cementing family life and perpetuating the community. Since the triumph of Victorian scientism, when medicine set about carving up the black box of the mind based on human beings' external, observable behavior, and the mass organization of work and consumer spending, transforming us into "virtual households" on a digital mailing list, sex and the uses of the body have been reinvented. What we do (and how we spend) determines who we are. We know ourselves by the categories of mind revealed in our actions. If I willfully take a penis into my throat or my rectum, I *am* a homosexual. (Establishment of those facts is the one sure defense against libel if I describe another man as gay.) I can then be identified and zip-coded into a class of people for whom Absolut vodka or Levi Strauss will supply target-designed advertisements, reassuring me who I am each time I sign my credit-card slip. As the drag queen says to the swaggering, butch boy, "Don't jive me, girl, I know where you shop!"

If you're a boy and you screw boys or get screwed by boys, then, boy, you are gay. If you tie down your dick, then cinch up your gown and straighten your wig, well, girlfriend, you *are* a drag queen. In the gay cultural system that has swept the world from Berlin to Sydney during the last quarter century, these verities have come to be accepted as Truth: we are what our genitals tell us we are, and the kind of communities we build sustain us in that belief. If ethnographies on the sex lives of New Guinea forest people suggest a more complicated erotic landscape, it is easy to categorize (and dismiss) them as a people of prehistory, a people so enslaved by ritual as to bear no relevance to us postindustrial, poststructural moderns.

Even so, there are cracks in the walls of sexual truth.

David Mills, a twenty-five-year-old queer man I met in San Francisco (who grew up in northeast Pennsylvania and was educated in San Diego), articulated his view of the world starkly. He arrived in the city with great expectations that this global gay mecca would give him a home. "When you come out, there is this promise that, because we haven't felt part of so much for so long, [because] as a kid you're not part of what the straight kids are doing—the romance and dating, the dances in high school—[you are] going to feel a part of something else . . . part of the great community.

"Then I come to this city, and it's all this bunch of older guys with houses and dogs and dinner parties, and it has nothing to do with me. They're not interested in my ideas, and I don't know anything about the seventies, and I don't know anything about living with HIV, and I don't know anything about leather daddies, and I don't know anything about Broadway musicals, and all these things are tickets to the gay world."

By the time he ran down the long list of "gay tickets" he didn't hold, I asked David if he really wanted into that world. Without hesitation he answered, "I want into a gay world, but not that one!"

A war is going on inside David. He is a highly sexed, attractive, magnetic young man. He talks about sex in almost sacred terms, and he knows something of the literature that would link sexuality with fundamental notions of liberation. He would like to find a "community" that would protect and celebrate that journey of liberation, but to his dismay he has found instead a gay community of shopkeepers, lawyers, and real estate men. When he says he is searching for *"a* gay world but not that one," he is revealing a genuine crisis in the whole American enterprise of forging self-conscious "identity communities." For in fact there is no necessary linkage between the hot young men of the seventies who have either died or become homeowners and the hot, young men of the nineties looking for a homosexual place in the world.

The maps that David Mills carries around inside him of sex and work and art and family may or may not guide him into the gay and lesbian communality currently available in San Francisco. The fact is, he tells me, he has no "map" to lead him through his life.

"There is some sort of track for straight twenty-five-year-olds," he says. "They know what's coming. They know there's going to be a wife, or a husband, and kids, and a house and a career and promotions. I feel like I have to create my own track, my own future. Whatever happens is because of me, not because of some sort of track I'll get on. I'm going to be essentially on my own the rest of my life." Never mind that throughout America the level of anxiety over all these life stations is steadily rising, that neither six-figure-salaried executives nor factory line workers can count on job security or pension or health care. Or long-term marriage. Insecure as those promises are, they are still held out as the ideal in presidential speeches and high school family-life classes. Queer adolescents realize that even the promise is gone, that it isn't only their sex acts that are queer, but that the map that would guide them along their social lives will be equally queer. Queer because it has so few vistas of what daily life will look like past the age of tumescent sex parties, club life, and street demonstrations.

Then there is Daniel, who grew up in California and took his life east across the continent. I met Daniel one winter day in 1994, not long after the ice storm that kept me bundled under the covers in Brooklyn. Daniel is Jewish. Daniel is an architect. Daniel works for a public housing agency in a large East Coast city. Daniel grew up in Beverly Hills. When I met him, Daniel was visiting New York with his boyfriend, Michael, whom I had known for several years.

We sat at the kitchen table of a borrowed Upper West Side apartment. Two strangers, drinking tea, one forty-seven, the other twenty-seven, talking queer.

"I slept with girls in high school," Daniel said, "but it wasn't until I finally started having sex with men my freshman year in college that I really enjoyed having sex with women."

"And now?" I asked.

"I like having sex with women a lot."

"Yeah, but . . ." I tossed my head toward the bedroom where Michael was napping.

"I usually sleep with men. But I don't know if that will always be true."

"Does that leave you feeling like an outsider both ways? To men and to women?"

"I always felt like an outsider. Being a Jew in a WASP high school."

Daniel and I stayed in touch. A year or so later we met and drove up to the Green Mountains of Vermont for a weekend of cross-country skiing. He and Michael had parted, as friends, shortly after I met him. We talked a lot about design and space, about the family house I was gradually reworking in Kentucky, about the city-owned houses he was restoring for low-income people, about how certain types of interior design encourage or inhibit playfulness and eroticism.

The sun that weekend was blindingly bright, the snow thin and more like granulated ice than fluffy powder. Neither of us had logged much time at cross-country, so we both fell down a lot (I more than he). Wet with the sweat of exertion, shivering with ice in our socks and pockets, we zipped back to the Grafton Inn, jumped under the covers of our rather fussy, canopied four-poster bed, and held each other into a dreamy sleep as the winter sun went down.

On the rainy drive back to his house Sunday night, Daniel told me about the woman he had been seeing for several months and about a man he was seeing. The relationship with the man was ending and, he thought, would likely become a friendship. The relationship with the woman was growing.

"I think we could become life partners," he said.

"Does that mean you're thinking of marrying?"

"Yes. But much more."

He seemed concerned that I would feel hurt at this revelation. "I liked being with you a lot this weekend. I've been looking forward to it since last fall when you first mentioned it."

I told him that I, too, had enjoyed our time together and understood it as a special weekend affair. I added that it was neither a secret from nor, I believed, a problem for the man I live with, Gene. But I had a question.

"How does. . . ?"

"She knows that there are men in my life."

"Generally you've been monogamous in your serious relationships, you said."

"Yes. I've fallen in love three times. In love I want monogamy."

"You don't perceive a problem wanting men outside your life partnership with a woman?"

"I don't think so. I can't predict the future, but for me a partnership is more powerful than sex."

"Do you feel comfortable with calling yourself bisexual?"

"*Queer's* the closest word to how I feel. I like *queer.*"

Bisexual felt to him too much like another add-on category in an already crowded shelf of sexual categories. The wonderful thing about *queer* was the way it had opened up space for him. Space inside himself that was no longer worrisome, erotic space he felt free to celebrate, and space in the world for an erotics of exploration. To be bisexual was more constraining. It suggested that he must continually be looking for both men and women at the same time, where in fact he was looking for another human soul who might be a man or might be a woman. He thought, as we parted, that it would likely be this woman, the sort of woman he supposed he might never have been able to find had he not opened the queerness within himself.

■ ■ ■

As I listen to Daniel and to David in Atlanta and Paul in Los Angeles, as I read and reread Baldwin and Lorde, as I notice the spreading discontent with Stonewall 25 and the almost universal enthusiasm for the highly structured Gay Games IV, the emergence in the summer of 1994 of New York's first gay sailors organization doesn't seem so accidental. Everywhere there is a sort of double sense about the "gay culture" that has come about in the twenty-five years since Stonewall. On the one hand it is a haven, a defensive zone of experimentation and growth in a culture that has long been marked by panic around sexual matters. At the same time gay people—queer people—homos—seem to be expressing an unmistakable dissatisfaction with the flat, horizontal, stylized uniformity of commercial, consumerized "gay life."

Everywhere people seem to be looking for a landscape of desiring identities that are more complicated than "gay identity" permits. Everywhere, it seems, more and more queer people are saying that they are ready to go sailing, to move away from the sandbar, to navigate unknown waters and to press ahead, into the winds of mystery.

t w o

Genius

Loci

A man and a woman sit beside each other in a passenger-train compartment. Across from them on the opposite bench are two men. The train shoots south, through whistling tunnels, across bare bridges along the Italian Riviera toward Rome and Naples and Palermo.

An American enters. She is wearing a straw pith helmut, carries a valise, and has a small daypack strapped over her shoulders. One of the men, about sixty, wears a brown tie and a beige linen jacket. He rises to help her stow her luggage.

"Every train ride is different," he says with a bemused sigh. "It's an adventure. Sometimes fantastic. Sometimes terrible—if you get a jerk!

"Where are you from?" he asks the American woman.

They speak, hesitantly, in the manner of railroad acquaintances.

Diego, who sits opposite the American, introduces himself. He is a "professor," in a high school, in Rome. He wears a red silk tie, a dressy blue shirt, and a checked jacket. He asks the American if she is going to Rome.

No.

And if she is married.

No.

"Not ever?"

"No, never," she answers flatly. "A husband is not necessary."

The professor extends his hand. "I wish the women here were like you."

The American sorts through her papers, the *Herald Tribune, La Repubblica,* and an Italian paperback book whose cover displays a painting of a Roman-looking man with deep, inky eyes and a red rose behind his right ear. The author, Giuseppe Patroni Griffi, is a well-known playwright and novelist who is homosexual.

"Giuseppe Griffi!" the young professor says. "He is from Toledo. That's where I come from. What a wonderful writer. He has written many great books. But I think he is not so known outside Italy. Do you read him in America?"

The American explains that she is reading Griffi's novel because she is joining an American writer, as an interpreter, and he is interested in homosexual life in the south, in Naples.

"Naples! Yes, Naples. That's the place to go!" Diego exclaims. "Homosexuality has always been more acceptable there than anywhere else in Italy." A subtle electricity seems to enlighten the compartment, brighten the eyes, lift up the shoulders of the other passengers.

"There's a tradition there," the professor continues, "especially since the turn of the century."

"It's the Greeks who brought it in," advises the older gentleman, who has been quietly following the conversation. "Naples was founded by the Greeks."

"Oh, and there's the *femminielli,*" the Italian woman, silent until now, interjects.

"Where, how do you find the *femminielli?*" the American asks.

"You can find them in the Spanish Quarter."

There are many male prostitutes in Rome, the professor says. Some are butch men. Some are *femminielli,* who dress as women. "You can find them every Saturday night. They take the train to Rome. For work. Then they go back to Naples when they are done."

Why to Rome? the American asks.

"The money. In Naples a customer pays twenty-five thousand lire [less than $20]. In Rome the hustler can get a lot more."

The whole compartment breaks into laughter.

"Come on!" says the Italian woman's husband. "Twenty-five thousand is nothing. That's a long time ago. You haven't asked them lately."

"Inflation," the American says, smiling.

"Right!" they agree with more laughter. Everyone in the compartment is drawn into an animated conversation about prostitutes, male and female. Which cities are busiest, which are most expensive, the nature of local tastes.

"I'll tell you about the transvestites, the *femminielli*," the chivalrous older gentleman declares. "They all have beautiful legs!" The others heartily agree.

Then the American tells a story.

"I took a train late one night from Milano, the central station. Maybe three in the morning. The waiting room was full of pimps and prostitutes and pushers. Some men. Some women. Many transvestites. They were, well, older people. They weren't attractive."

She looks to the professor and to the older gentleman on the opposite bench. "How do they get any business?"

"It's loyalty," the older man says. "They keep some customers for thirty years or more. Since they were all kids together."

■ ■ ■

I have come here to Naples to sort through a kaleidoscope of myths—some my own, some the American gay movement's, some about the roots of masculinity in the West. The first image that washes through my head when I hear the word *Naples* is a color. Naples Yellow, rich, thick, like sunflowers in August. It was an oil paint manufactured for artists by the Permanent Pigments company of Cincinnati. In my teenage years, when I began to paint, I both cherished and feared Naples Yellow. My painting books, warning of its intensity, advised that Naples Yellow be applied sparingly, lest my compositions be overwhelmed by it. When I would look down at the squat lead tubes of Naples Yellow, I wouldn't see paint; I would see a blinding sun that could burn through the mist of my sullen moods. What a magic, magisterial place Naples must be!

Naples had taken up lodging in my imagination even earlier though. The first real book—that is, a book like my father's books,

books made all of words instead of pictures—I remember reading and having read to me was about three men who sailed from Naples to Capri, where they met a boy named Michele. Michele spotted the men far out in the Bay of Naples because their boat was so strange: their sails were deep red. And so the book's title: *Red Sails to Capri*. Michele was a kind of wild colt, always troubling to his parents, who let out rooms to the strangers. He became their guide to the charms of Capri—and they became his telescope onto the great cities like Naples, so far beyond the quaint fishing villages of Capri.

Red Sails to Capri, a Newbery Prize winner, is still in print. It still charms me, although now in a different way. The three men on the sailboat, a writer, a painter, and a gentleman of affairs, might easily have been—perhaps were modeled upon—the famously homosexual artists and poets who fled England, France, and Germany in the nineteenth century and turned Capri into one of modern Europe's first homosexual retreats, rendering pretty, smoky-eyed boys like Michele as mythical phantasms from antiquity. *Red Sails* still captivates me because, whether by design or not, it is essentially homosexual: it is a dream world of boys and men who are in love with the magic they present to each other, a magic that plumbs the mystery of origins and the majesty of undiscovered possibility. The red sails are wings of deliverance as free as the winds of imagination.

Naples and her people, of course, are not phantasms for the delectation of cosmopolitan aesthetes. But there is in Naples, despite the notorious desperation of the city, a persistent magic of place. More than anywhere else I have been, it opens windows on the meaning of the homosexual journey.

It is May 1994, my second time in Naples, and Pat, my American interpreter, has introduced me to a number of gay Italian men there who are her friends. Two of them, both named Marcello, grew up in Naples. I'll call them Marcello L. and Marcello D. Marcello L. is a doctor, a liver specialist. Marcello D. is a designer of wondrously playful glass and ceramics.

We have met at Marcello L.'s place, a newly remodeled apartment in one of those old ocher buildings with a central wrought-iron cage elevator, the kind that requires a fifty-lire coin to operate. It is a bright, white-walled one-bedroom that his parents bought him. A cleaning lady, whom Marcello has hired with his mother's advice, comes three times a week to shop, clean, and do the laundry for him and his boyfriend, who is a homeopathic doctor. Tall French doors give onto window balconies, two in his living room, one in his bedroom, overlooking Mergellina harbor, the American consulate, and the Villa Communale, the seaside park where from 4 P.M. to 4 A.M. men pluck other men from quiet benches. Capri floats on the distant horizon.

Day or night, the phone rings incessantly. Marcello L. often finds fifteen or twenty messages on his answering machine when he returns home. Most seem to be from close women friends, or from family or from patients or from mothers, brothers, sisters, sons, of patients. To know a young, accomplished doctor who has studied in the United States (University of California, San Francisco) and has a good position at a good hospital can be vitally important—no matter that the doctor is a liver specialist and your uncle has arthritis. In Naples, quality is personal. Care comes to those who know a caregiver. *Clientelismo,* the critics call it. A caregiver, among other things, is a person who can make the hospital respond to his patient, even if he is not the assigned specialist. On my first visit, Marcello L. was attending to a family friend who had just had a severe heart attack.

"The telephone is the plague of my life," Marcello tells me one evening in his *molto rapido* lilting English. When I propose that he relax awhile—he had already taken four calls in the half hour he'd been home—he looks at me with puzzlement in his black eyes. "I could never do that. It is my lifeline."

"But I thought it was your plague," I say.

"Yes, it is that, too. It is both. It is my plague and it is my lifeline."

It is a little like the way he thinks about sex. And men. And women. And passion.

"With me, everything is two," he once told me, a sly smile in his manner. "I am truly Neapolitan. Each part of myself is always two. I have two eyes, two ears, two lips, two legs, two arms, two feet, two balls—"

"But one dick," I interject.

"No, two," he goes on with another sly laugh. "Everything is two."

To be two is an exasperating conundrum for most Americans.

Descendants of Calvin, Condorcet, and Descartes, fabricators of the New World, we like to believe definitively in the labels we give ourselves and the claims we make for ourselves. We are Christians or we are pagans. We are "law-abiding citizens" or we are "criminals." (Never mind the tax laws we break.) We are men or we are women. We are straight or we are gay. In the theology of ordinary living, this is the litany most Americans embrace. It is at the foundation of our system of laws, at the core of our faith in scientific progress, at the font of our positivist, binary, cyberspacial dream. But it does not describe the cosmology of mind, body, and sex that Marcello and his fellow Neapolitans inhabit. For them, to be two things at once, to advance two contradictory beliefs at once, is as natural as the annual menstruations of San Gennaro, the (male) patron saint of Naples.

Of all Marcello's twos, it is his "two dicks" that seem most Neapolitan, most redolent of the sexual complexities that the American gay movement neatly sidesteps. "All parts of myself are basically two. I am always double," he explains. "When I'm speaking, I'm thinking differently. Always I'm saying something, but inside I'm criticizing the something I'm saying."

For example, the matter of family.

Families are never far from the topic of talk in Italy—from Lina Wertmuller's films to papal encyclicals, from the relentless crises of political corruption to the red harvest of Mafia massacres. Family, its strength and its crisis, pervades all. Much of Marcello's reason for living in Naples is his family's presence there, especially his mother. Marcello speaks to his mother two or three times a week. "If I'm out of town and I need her for the house, to let someone in to clean or fix something, [she takes care of it]. I find everything done better than I can do. If she sees something missing, like a carpet or kitchen appliance, she buys it. I feel protected. I feel like if anything happens, if I need money, if I need a shoulder to cry on, she'll be present." That's one side. But in opening his description of their relationship, he tells me how "possessive," how "obsessive" she is, how she is always asking medical favors of him to see family members whenever anyone has a fever. "It's a way to keep me tied to her," he sighs, continuing, "In another way she seems the best woman I've ever seen in my life."

Nor is Marcello's description of his relationship to his mother unusual among his gay friends. On my second night in town, we go to dinner at one gay couple's apartment. We are served an exquisite five-course meal that includes, after dessert, home photos, digitally transferred to a twenty-four-inch TV screen, of hauntingly beautiful men at play on a beach. Several of the men are our dinner mates. Altogether, it wouldn't be an atypical evening in certain homes in the Hamptons or Fire Island. Nonetheless we are in Naples. During the banter I tell our host that his gnocchi in pesto is unquestionably the lightest, creamiest, most nearly angelic gnocchi I've ever bitten into. "Oh, they're one of my mother's specialties," he says.

Later, Marcello explains that the host's mother lives next door and prepares almost all the meals for her son and his lover. If mother-son anecdotes like these stretch the limits of cliché, the story he tells of his mother's mother seems more like an outtake from Fellini's *Amarcord*.

When Marcello's grandmother was forty-five, her youngest son died. The boy was his grandmother's last child. "Each year, until my grandmother was seventy, she hired two men to go to the cemetery and open the tomb of this little child who had died of cancer of the liver. Each year, she opened the tomb, and she held in her arms the little body. Each time she had a new sheet, a kind of big white towel, that she put the boy in. Each time she would clean up the body with the towel. She went by herself with the two men.

"I remember when my grandfather died. He was young, only sixty-two. Her children wouldn't help her open up her husband's grave, but she was in the mood to do it." At the time of his grandfather's death Marcello was fourteen and went to stay with his grandmother to keep her company. "One night after I was in bed, I looked at the wardrobe and I saw my grandfather standing there. I opened and closed my eyes, wondering if it was a dream. It turned out she had put my grandfather's picture on a hanger with a jacket in the wardrobe, so it looked like my grandfather was just standing there. It scared me so much I thought it was the devil or something. She told me later, 'Oh, each time I open the door now I see my husband.' "

These are the ordinary stories of an upper-middle-class Neapolitan family, not the mysterious tales of death spirits and shrines that hang like dust in the air of the impoverished Spanish Quarter. As much as modernism, the marketplace, and global migration have rent apart the traditional southern-Italian family, these extrarational, premodern shadows of family linger on in the tales and rituals of daily life. These layered memories of family loves and labor, of mamma's gnocchi and dead babies and ghostly grandfathers, paper the inside of the mind. They shape the irrepressible flashbacks let loose whenever anyone mentions *la famiglia,* proposing, with peculiarly American naïveté, the notion of fabricating a "gay family."

"A gay couple is something different from a family," Marcello tells me. The sun has fallen down into the ultramarine Mediterranean, and he has snuggled himself like a puppy into the pillows of his couch. Nicolo, his tall boyfriend with the bedroom eyes, hasn't come home yet.

Pat and I have been talking with Marcello about what it is that makes a family, whether there can be a family without someone like his mother, or his mother's mother. Through the French windows we look out on the lights of the ferryboats returning from Capri, notorious for the sirens who lured ancient mariners onto her rocks and the nineteenth-century aesthetes who seduced curly-haired peasant boys into their bedrooms. We drift into the matter of children.

"I do not agree with gay adoption," Marcello declares. "Not at all. I am completely against that. A child needs a mother. He cannot miss it. He needs boobs, he needs breasts."

"You mean symbolically," I say.

"Well, not only. He needs to suck."

"Lots of gay men make arrangements with lesbians or straight, single women. What's wrong with that?"

"I don't know how the kid will grow up missing the mother side of himself," he answers, doubtful.

"How about the reverse, with lesbians?" Pat asks.

Marcello sits up, clearer in his thinking. "Not at all. Because you need a father, your male part. The only way to do it is just to live with it. There is no other way when you are very young. You recognize that the one is your father because you have to recognize where is the power. If you miss all that, it will be a mess for you."

He stops, wrinkles up his chin, laughs, and lets the other side of his mind out: "It probably is [a mess] anyway because we confuse everything about power, mother and father, but at least with a father and a mother we know where is the female and where is the male sex."

This is the third time Marcello and I have wandered off into a conversation about maleness and femaleness and families and children and being gay. I am wrestling with something that feels profoundly different here about the texture, maybe the foundation, of gayness among Marcello and his Neapolitan friends. Marcello's objection to gay childrearing is altogether different from American fundamentalists' warnings about the corruption of impressionable youth. He is concerned with protecting the mysterious dimensions of masculinity and femininity that inhabit us all as human beings. He believes that it is in the infant's direct physical contact, body to body, suckling and clutching, that the profound knowledge of maleness and femaleness emerges, that we know more than we can ever say about the contours of masculine and feminine power, and that if we separate our young from that precognitive knowledge, we are impoverishing them as human beings. The polarities that seem most important to Marcello are not between gay and straight, but between masculine and feminine.

"Growing up I understood that there were some differences between masculinity and femininity," he tells me, wriggling back into his pillows, "but it's not strongness or weakness or power. It's something untouchable, not predictable, not possible to say by words. It's really something deeper, probably . . . tenderness that is more typically feminine." As soon as he finishes that line, of course, he acknowledges that tenderness is also what he looks for in a man.

Like most of the gay Neapolitans I've met, Marcello is dazzled by women, and he does sleep with women periodically. Women have "color," he says. "Women have different colors, different taste, different smell, different sounds. Without women around there is sadness. It's a little like being handicapped. I feel like something's missing in my life if I go more than three or four days where it is all males there. It's horrible. It smells bad. It smells wrong, rotten, in a way that what's going on is not true."

"But why do you sleep with a man every night?" I ask.

"Because I like it. Just . . . I like it. And I love it. It doesn't mean that afterward I have to see only men in my life, or avoid friendship with females or avoid the color of feminineness."

I am intrigued by this word *color* and ask Marcello to tell me what he means by it.

"Color? I mean joy."

■ ■ ■

This conversation in a young doctor's living room overlooking a three-thousand-year-old city built by the Greeks, colonized by the Romans, conquered by the Spanish, ruled by the French Bourbons, and left exquisitely destitute after the unification of the Italian state was not a conversation I could have had with a gay American in the United States, even if he was of Italian ancestry. On my first arrival there, in 1993, I looked up a gay Italian-American doctor, raised in suburban New York and serving at the American military base outside Naples.

Dr. Bill, as his friends called him, found Naples baffling. Naples had no "gay life," he said, save for the expatriate world of diplomats and military men posted to the NATO complex. "There are two bars, and only one is busy," he said. "There are pickups in the parks and movie houses, but if the guys are middle class, they're still living with their families and they never talk about it." And yet, like the fellow travelers in Pat's train compartment, all the Italians Bill met told him Naples was the gayest city in Italy. Even a visiting American friend waxed rhapsodic about how easy it was to encounter available men on any street corner.

American gay activists tend to reduce this perplexing situation to "the oppression of the closet." Because of the power of the family and the influence of the Vatican, they say, gay Italians live lives of transparent secrecy—as in Marcello's family, where "everyone knows, but no one says." Decorum forbids discussion of a "perversion" that all society acknowledges exists and that has never been outlawed in the Italian criminal statutes. Indeed, parliamentary lawmakers in 1889 concluded that silence was likely to be a far more effective method of containing the homosexual impulse than prohibition; in the words of then prime minister Zanardelli, "In this field a general ignorance about this action is much more useful than knowledge of punishments against it." Nearly a hundred years later, when the U.S. Supreme Court affirmed Georgia's sodomy statutes in the notorious Hardwick case, conservative Italian newspaper columnists condemned the American ruling as an invasion of the private citizen's rights—and worse, one wrote, it had the effect of aiding the homosexual cause by forcing discussion of their "disgusting" habits onto decent citizens.

But the American notion of "the closet" doesn't quite capture the paradox that so puzzled Bill. Nor is it quite enough to look to the condemnations of homosexuality by the Catholic Church as adequate explanation for the absence of an American-style gay milieu. As countless travelers to Naples have discovered for themselves, the easy sex available on the streets and in the parks is not particularly furtive; if anything, it is just another face to the famously robust and guileful sensuality that has distinguished Naples since the Greeks and Romans built their summer resorts there.

Before applying the categories of my own North American experience, I have tried to follow the advice of other travelers through the Mezzogiorno: first look, then listen and smell. Watch how people move through the streets. Notice how they look at one another, how their eyes rise and fall, how the men idly tug at their crotches. Note the family intimacies tucked inside the ubiquitous "Catholic" shrines carved into old walls. Linger on the voluptuous and tortured limbs of the saints, the Madonnas, the cigarette hawkers, the pickpockets—and the peripheral vision of the shopkeepers, who are watching all of them. Observe the silent gestures of flirtation and rejection that pass continuously among all these actors jumbled together in the streets. Follow the layers and levels of "cruising"—for money, for hope, for guile, for lust, for forgiveness—that form the visceral texture of daily life.

We—writers, activists, professional "investigators"—live in an avalanche of postcard reductions and abstractions. They are the tools, essential tools, we use to render the world. Without them we bury ourselves in a cycle of endless, formless tales. But just as often the abstractions are no more than the projective lenses through which we protect ourselves from hearing and seeing the bizarre frailties of our own picaresque tale-telling. For the activists and the reformers, Naples is the reactionary closet of denial and personal repression. For the historians, she is a premodern cacophony of the corrupt and the dispossessed. For the economists, she is a backwater of feudal resistance to industrial efficiency. For the sociologists, she is a harbor of superstitious codes and family obligation that stymie the young, block education, and prevent new generations from imagining a future that works. And of course, for the efficient, democratic Northerners she is the symbol of the lazy, corrupt South that sucks at the national destiny—the flip side of which surfaced among the American's railroad companions, who saw in Naples an atavistic, high-libido Disneyland for the prurient.

"It's the Greeks who brought it in," the elderly gentleman on the train had said. He was only repeating the truism that Northerners have been ascribing to southern Italy since Boccaccio's *Decameron* appeared in the fourteenth century. Naples, whose people are still regarded as the most lingeringly Greek of all the Italians, continues to be credited with having carried the blessed stain of Greek sexual predilections into modernity. Lord Byron, Johann Winckelmann, Wilhelm Von Gloeden, Walter Pater, E. M. Forster, Norman Douglas: they and many other men of arts and letters found in the Mezzogiorno the mythic affirmation of their deepest desires. There, among the "Praxitelean youth" and the "olive-eyed, bare-armed boys," they searched for the descendants of that golden, ancient era of homosexual expression that would demonstrate the power and beauty of their deepest same-sex desires. To judge by their diaries, their poetry, their paintings and photographs, they seemed to find the physical passions forbidden them in the Protestant north.

"Seemed to find," however, is the critical phrase. The Australian historian Robert Aldrich looked deeply into the homosexual mystique of southern Italy in *The Seduction of the Mediterranean,* his delicious romp through the lusts and fantasies of German and English aesthetes during the last 250 years. "Homosexuals," Aldrich points out, "rarely could conceive of themselves outside art and literature, outside the culture created by the Greeks and which appeared still discernible (and could be experienced) in the Mediterranean. For those in the cultured classes, homosexuality *was* literature and art;

sex was transformed into an aesthetic act." From the mid-eighteenth century forward, as the specter of the industrial marketplace brought order and discipline to the urban denizens of the north, these gentlemen sought to recall and to resurrect what they believed to be classical ideals of beauty and proportion found in nature. If urban commerce and concomitant Calvinist theology sought to rein in and temper unbridled nature, these men of the gentried classes, educated in the ethics and aesthetics of the classical era, looked into their own natures and found a reflection of the finer, purer love that united Greek men with adolescent boys. They saw in that erotic bond an exquisite grace exemplified in the unblemished bodies of eighteen-year-old boys, but more, they saw in the classical relations of the *erastes* and the *erameno* a code of ethical proportion that could justify and give guidance to their homosexual longings.

And, of course, they found the flesh. In the paintings of Caravaggio, lustrous and ripe with desire. On the ceiling of the Sistine Chapel, where Michelangelo draped pubescent boys across every spare hillock. In the poems of Michelangelo written to his own beloved Cavalieri. And on the streets of fishing villages or in the fields of peasant farms where impoverished families were all too eager to offer their sons' services to the rich Northerners.

Boys and young men born into poverty and confronted with opportunity easily dismissed the moral pronouncements of distant archbishops (themselves widely known for their taste in comely lads). For those who exist on the boundary between survival and sacrifice, the body is always the last defense and sex its most versatile tool. If Northerners like Norman Douglas or J. A. Symonds saw in these "Praxitelean youth" the physical vestiges of Ganymede and Apollo, the young men saw something decidedly more tangible: the promise of food and shelter. At a time when vast numbers of their brothers and cousins were shipping off to Ellis Island to find a future in sweatshops and factories, these boys found a method of survival more or less at home, which, on occasion, even offered warmth and affection.

This highly embossed erotic moment that brought peasants and aesthetes together was surely not accidental: it was a moment made possible by the laws of Malthusian population movements and industrial invention. Rich and poor families alike no longer required that sex be at the service of making more worker-children to till the estate. Desires heretofore suppressed, or hidden away in the stables, could be expressed in a seductively soft landscape where neither church nor state exercised much control over personal behavior. Law in the Mezzogiorno was, and largely still is, a charming fiction, subject to the exigencies of family necessity. Even so, there were forces at work besides the desperation of the poor and the crippled fantasies of the Romantic rich that helped to shape how ordinary people looked on the uses and delights of the flesh.

On December 31, 1781, William Hamilton, then the British minister to the Kingdom of Naples, sent an extended letter to the British Royal Society entitled "On the Worship of Priapus in the Kingdom of Naples." Lord Hamilton reported that in the city of Isérnia, in Abruzzi, was an annual celebration of the "Feast of the modern Priapus, St. Cosmo." Priapus is the ancient Roman god of the phallus, symbol of procreation, fertility, and life force, which was also identified in Greece with Dionysus and Pan and in Egypt with Osiris. What seemed to shock (and stimulate) Lord Hamilton was that the fertility rites and phallic worship associated with Priapus had been thoroughly reproduced into Catholic feast ritual in the name of Saints Cosmo and Damian. The fair lasted three days. Describing one of those days, he wrote:

> The relicks of the Saints are exposed, and afterwards carried in procession from the cathedral of the city to [an ancient church]. In the city, and at the fair, ex-voti of wax, representing the male parts of generation, of various dimensions, some even of the length of the palm, are publicly offered to sale. There are also waxen vows, that represent other parts of the body mixed with them; but of these there are few in comparison of the number of the Priapi. The devout distributers of these vows carry a basket full of them in one hand and hold a plate in the other to receive the money, crying aloud, "St. Cosmo and Damiano!"

As though this were not evidence enough of popish corruption, Hamilton went on to point out that elder canons of the church sat inside the vestibule selling entrance to Mass at a price of "15 Neapolitan grains." And more. When the women would present the waxen phalluses for sale, they would offer up pleas: "Blessed St. Cosmo, let it be like this" or "St. Cosmo, I recommend myself to you," parting their lips to kiss the inert organs. Later, in the service, the priest would go to the altar with a vessel of St. Cosmo's oil to give "the holy unction"; those townspeople with physical ailments would then "present themselves at the great altar, and uncover the member affected (not even excepting that which is most frequently represented by the *ex-voti* [translation: impotent men presenting their penises for treatment]); and the reverend cannon anoints it saying, *Per intercessionem beati Cosmi, liberet te ab omni malo. Amen.*"

"The oil of St. Cosmo," Hamilton noted in concluding his report, "is in high repute for its invigorating quality, when the loins, and parts adjacent, are anointed with it," adding that 1,400 flasks of it were distributed during the feast celebration.

Poor Hamilton. Throughout his letter his tone ricochets between the shocked ethnographer—an Anglican man of letters—and the prurient voyeur—the other side of Anglican men of letters. (And all the while his wife was conducting one of the most infamous affairs of the era with Lord Nelson, admiral of the British Navy, under his own roof.) Nor was it altogether by accident that Hamilton came to learn of the Feast at Isérnia. He had been collecting phallic artifacts and symbols for some years, having "long ago discovered, that the women and children of the lower class, at Naples, and in its neighborhood, frequently wore, as an ornament of dress, a sort of Amulets, (which they imagine to be a preservative from the *mal occhii*, evil eyes, or enchantment) exactly similar to those which were worn by the ancient Inhabitants of this Country for the very same purpose, as likewise for their supposed invigorating influence; and all of which have evidently a relation to the Cult of Priapus."

Sir William's justification for his inquiries into the priapic was to provide "fresh proof of the similitude of the Popish and Pagan Religion." By the late eighteenth century Britain was already well advanced in its archaelogical pillage of ancient artifacts, including like items from Pompeii and Herculaneum. He eventually contributed his collection of stone erotica to the British Museum. The proxim-

65

ity of pagan ritual, indeed of pagan gods and goddesses, to the Catholic saints (now regarded as synchronism in Brazil, Colombia, and the Caribbean) was an old issue for the post-Reformation Christians of northern Europe. Such corruptions had long been cited in political and military struggles waged by the Protestant powers against the Vatican and its allies. Rather than risk internal crisis and embarrassment over these anomalies, the Church has for the most part chosen to remain silent and not condemn these lightly shrouded reminders that pagan fertility rites crudely linked to the Greeks, the Romans, the Etruscans, and even the Egyptians still persist beneath the Church's robes.

Now, two centuries after Lord Hamilton's inquiries, the alert visitor walking the streets of Naples still finds phallic images scattered everywhere—not least among the saints. They are not homosexual per se, but they are unmistakable celebrations of male sexuality. San Raphael watches over the harbor, traditionally carved with a fish in his hand. Fishermen ask him for protection and good fortune. But a fish, in Naples, is not only a fish. Pregnant women, or their mothers, also pray to San Raphael, kissing the fish he holds out in his marble hands, for his fish, symbolically and also in crude street language, represents a phallus, and it carries the power of fertility. There is also La Smorfia, the encyclopedic Book of Dreams used to interpret the numbers in *tambolella,* the vaguely mystical lottery game played like bingo by the poor of Naples. Certain *tambolella* numbers carry clearly sexual connotations; the number 29, for example, always indicates good luck and stands for the penis even though the precise phrase listed in La Smorfia for number 29 is "father of the child." Mothers of baby boys born with apparently large penises will pass the infant around, kiss the little dick, and boast of its size. (A friend in New York was startled when a young third-generation Italian-American couple proudly reported their pediatrician's prediction that their son was certain to have a large penis.) As Neapolitan boys grow up and form street packs, penis comparison is universal; the one with the biggest dick gets called *capòcchione*—technically "big head," but all the kids use the word to mean "big dick." Even in the tourist shops in recent years, one of the hottest-selling counter items is a palm-sized calendar, called La Pisella, illustrated with famous photos and paintings of well-formed penises.

The most blatant of all the "pagan saints" is the patron saint of Naples herself, San Gennaro, or in its anglicized form, Saint Januarius. In A.D. 305, San Gennaro was beheaded at the order of the Roman emperor Diocletian in one of the last major persecutions of mystical Christian cults. According to legend, the saint's followers captured vials of blood spurting from his arteries and preserved it for what has become the annual "miracle of San Gennaro" (celebrated in New York as well as Naples). The ritual, called "the menstruation" by some, carries its own fertility aura, for three times a year, in December, May, and September, a vial of the saint's dried blood "liquefies" as a sign of good fortune to the city's people. A failure of the blood to liquefy bodes all manner of ill-fortune. The failure of the miracle in 1943 was accompanied by the eruption of Vesuvius and in 1980 by the most severe earthquake of the century.

These pagan pentimenti of a time before either modernism or Christ perfume the ordinary ambience of Neapolitan life to a degree that North Americans, or even northern Europeans, can seldom imagine. As much as we may look to the Greco-Roman culture as the cradle of our civilization, the artifacts—and the behavior, the beliefs, the psychology they imply—are visceral and ordinary in southern Italy. They sit side-by-side with death-cult skulls and purgatory shrines on nearly every urban block in the city's center. More than visual curiosities for blocks of camera-clicking tourists, they shape and color the preconscious memory of each child born here, linking a panorama of departed bodies and spirits to the details of everyday life, all the way down to the bronze fertility horns men and women wear around their necks and the baudy phallic references that punctuate so much of Neapolitan dialect.

■ ■ ■

I first met Claudio at the dinner party with the magnificent gnocchi in pesto. But it wasn't until more than a year later, when I'd come back to Naples a third time to explore the exuberant world of the *femminielli,* that Claudio became my friend. This time we met at noon, in the lobby of the extravagant Hotel Vesuvio, where President Clinton and the so-called G-7 leaders had gathered in 1994 to plot the fate of the industrial world. The Vesuvio is also said to be the place where the great Caruso spent his final days.

Claudio is an architect. His manner is as plain and unaffected as his business card, which displays his name, address, phone, and a line drawing of a bare electrical lightbulb. He has agreed to be my guide and interpreter for the coming week because he is not exactly a full-time working architect. No one and nothing in Naples is exactly who and what he seems to be. Twenty-nine, he is still finishing his studies, designing and restoring houses, offices, and apartments, sometimes for free, sometimes for off-the-books money, mostly for friends. I am paying him a translator's fee, and right now he can use the money. He is also intrigued at the prospect of taking an American writer on an erotic tour of this most perverse of Italian cities.

We step outside the hotel, and though the day is sunny, a sharp January wind has churned the bay with whitecaps. He produces a blue, knit watch cap, the same sort the weathered fishmongers wear as they warble out their competitive selling songs along the narrow back streets. He pulls the cap down over a wide, fair forehead, just to his eyebrows, which are thick, straight, and set wide. I look twice at him and he is transformed. A moment earlier he had been a bohemian student-architect whose bushy, dark hair tumbled down across his shoulders in a rambunctious, curly ponytail—an easy model for one of Botticelli's young squires. Now, with this soft blue woolen bowl covering his head, he could indeed pass as the fishmonger's helper or as a sailor or as a petty camorra cigarette hawker. The only discordant detail is a strange pendant hanging below his neck on a leather string: a clear glass sphere suspended in a silver clip that he describes as his "empty globe."

The trick of experiencing Naples, Claudio tells me as we start walking up past Opera San Carlos, the grandest opera house in Italy and by night the parade ground for the grandest and most beautiful of *femminielli* prostitutes, is always to be watching for what might happen, on any block, at any moment.

I already know a few things about the *femminielli:* that like Brazilian transvestites, they are renowned for their beauty; that they have largely displaced women prostitutes on the streets of Naples; that they are thoroughly integrated into the infamous Quartieri Spagnoli and other central-district neighborhoods; and, so I have heard, they frequently live with their families, occasionally having been raised by their mothers as boys in women's clothes. Almost none of these assertions would be possible in most American cities, I explain.

We climb up the hill from the Opera, above the Via Toledo, which until the Spanish took control of the city in 1504, formed Naples's southern wall. On a small square where the Friday produce market is closing up, we amble into a cycle shop. A man wearing a light blue sweater and work pants is crouched down beside the yellow Vespa he is rebuilding. Another fellow is working on a motor a few feet away. The first man in the blue sweater says hello and extends his wrist, broad and flat as a board. His hands are too greasy to shake. His eyes are as black as his short gel-combed hair, and he returns every glance full and strong. He is maybe twenty-three years old, and his name is also Claudio.

"I just met him three or four weeks ago, at a party here in the Quarter," my Claudio, the architect, has told me as we walk up to the wide shop door opening onto the square. "I think he can tell us a lot about the Quartieri if he wants to."

The problem today is that Claudio-the-mechanic's girlfriend (probably his fiancée, we decide) is at the shop, a smartly dressed, probably professional woman in a white blouse, blue blazer, and a Catholic pendant. Claudio explains that I want to learn about the routines of traditional life in the Quartieri including, among other things, *tambolella,* the ancient, mystical bingo-style game that women play late at night. He sends us off around the corner to ask for an old woman who might invite us to a *tambolella* party. Along the way I notice plaques commemorating the victims of the cholera plagues of 1832 and 1884. Several more people direct us in several more directions, and one elderly woman seems ready to pepper us with any imaginable story we'd like to hear until we are eventually laughed off as simpleton outsiders who ought to know better than to ask about *tambolella* at lunchtime.

We return to Claudio-the-mechanic. He exudes warmth and sexuality, but his girlfriend is still there, and it's hard to talk. So we hang out. At last he takes her off to her house and returns. The re-built Vespa with a long afterburner exhaust is his pride. "It'll do 175 kilometers easy," he boasts. That's almost 120 mph. On a Vespa.

The two Claudios, it turns out, had exchanged more than small talk at the party a few weeks earlier. They had groped each other and begun a mutual masturbation that didn't quite work. Too many people; not the right setting; maybe not enough interest on Claudio-the-mechanic's part.

"It's something that happens," my Claudio tells me as we're killing time. "It's not at all uncommon. Two friends who began wanking each other off as adolescents, the way all boys do, can do it again off and on well into adulthood. They're really not homosexual. It's just a friendly way they relate with each other.

"You can do it by yourself," he says, "but it's better with another boy."

Claudio had stopped by the other Claudio's bike shop a few weeks after the party, and it was clear the mechanic had not been offended. My Claudio still wonders what might happen with the bike mechanic, under the right circumstances, perhaps even today. Gradually he walks the younger man out of the shop to explain that we're interested in meeting *femminielli,* particularly a *femminiello* he once met who calls herself Anastasia.

The mechanic is a bit puzzled, maybe even a little embarrassed. But he agrees to take Claudio on a fast bike ride through the Quartieri to point out where we might look.

"I never went with *femminielli,*" he swears as they ride down the street.

"Come on, don't bullshit me," Claudio answers. "Every kid in the Quarter's gone to *femminielli* at least once or twice for a blowjob."

"Okay, sure," the biker admits, "but I never went for sex here in my own neighborhood with a transvestite." Fast and discreet, he gestures to a couple of black, metal doors. "There, and there," he tells Claudio, whizzing past. Then, around the corner, he indicates another *basso,* with a wooden door and window. This one, Claudio-the-mechanic thinks, might belong to Anastasia. Each apartment, called a *basso,* is a ground-level studio almost always furnished with a king-size bed in the center and a few chairs and tables, which, in warm weather, convert the streets into a procession of public living rooms.

We set out on foot through the grid of narrow passageways that the Claudios have just spun through on the Vespa, but once we're fully inside the Spanish Quarter, we face the same problem as Dorothy on the road to Oz. Each street is twenty feet wide and looks just like the other. Plain stone buildings of burnished and faded ocher are laced six stories high by clotheslines laden with shirts, sheets, and underwear. Only the slope of the hillside offers orientation.

"Just here . . . I think," Claudio says. We turn a corner, then another. "No, there were two black metal doors. Then . . . around the corner . . . a wooden door, and a window. You see, there are not so many wooden ones."

We find no wooden door. No Anastasia. Anastasia was the *femminiello* he seemed to remember. Should we ask in the street? "Why not?" A man and his wife are closing up their produce cart, like all the other vegetable sellers.

Falling into Neapolitan, Claudio lets his voice slide into the back of his throat. The ends of syllables disappear. A rough, jazzy rhythm loops the strange words together.

"*An-a-stas-i-a. An-a-stas-i-a? No. No. O, sì. Sì!*" The wife understands that Claudio is asking about one of the *transvestivos,* one of the streetwalkers. Yes, she says, just down the block, up two more short blocks, then left.

We begin to retrace our steps, but it doesn't seem right. We stop at a pastry shop. The proprietor, thin, severe, his hair thinning, his tie properly knotted, feigns total ignorance of any such people in this neighborhood, then acknowledges reality and gives us more directions.

We turn a new corner.

"That's it. Right there!" Claudio exclaims. "Don't you think? It's wood."

We knock at the half-open door. A person steps forward. Even though the sun has gone away to the upper stories, the daylight is not kind to her face. Her lips are thick and slightly bulging, her jaw a bit puffed with no trace of beard, and her thinning strawberry hair falls forward, straight, an arrangement of hopeful bangs.

Claudio, with a smile to melt the executioner, speaks first about Anastasia and where she might be. No, there is no Anastasia here now. Yes, perhaps before, but that was two, three years ago.

She introduces herself as Lea. Her eyes are suspicious, of course, but gradually she warms to Claudio, all the while keeping a quarter glance on the tall, pale "American writer" standing beside him. Claudio explains something of our general quest to talk with and learn about the *femminielli* of the Quarter.

Lea says nothing about herself. But certain things are obvious: Her breasts are real, and full. Her skin is fair, though worn. She is at least sixty, perhaps several years older. Her faded-pink-and-cream-striped tights betray a swelling more akin to a codpiece than a maidenhead. Inside the *basso* I can see that the king-size bed is neatly made. Above it are several sentimental prints and photographs.

"Come back at five o'clock," she advises. "Everyone gets together next door, upstairs, before getting ready for work. It's a kind of gossip hour, and you can explain what you want. Ask for Marilene."

The Quartieri Spagnoli, which has the only regular grid of streets in Naples, was built early in the seventeenth century as a garrison for the troops of the Spanish viceroy, newly installed to rule over the Kingdom of Naples. Naples then was one of Europe's largest cities, a center of art, theater, music, and home to Italy's second university. By the outbreak of the French Revolution, it held more than four hundred thousand people. A quarter of the population lived in squalid penury, stuffed into dark hovels more akin to caves than houses, "lying like filthy animals, with no distinction of age or sex," in the words of one contemporary. The Quartieri lay just beyond the city's western wall. It has always had a seductively unrespectable character marked by a passionate, celebratory sense of neighborhood. Orange peel, cinnamon, garlic, and dog shit fight for olfactory dominion, and travel writers rhapsodize about how bel canto song was born in the competitive pitch each produce seller belts out to passing customers. *Ah-rannn-ji, lee-MO-ni, fee-NO-ki-o! Ah-rannn-ji, lee-MO-ni, fee-NO-ki-o!* Colorful, it is also dangerous, for the Quarter is ridden with drug dealers, burglars, purse snatchers, and petty bandits, the trades that have fed the center city since before the Spanish arrival. Tourists are told not to enter, as are American soldiers. When they landed in 1943, American sailors were told the Quartieri was strictly off-limits, so of course they quickly became the streetwalkers' best clients.

Claudio wants me to see and feel the nuances that separate each small district from the other, from the Quartieri to Sanita just north of it, to Montesanto near the University and on eastward through Centro Antico, where the streets were laid out by the Greeks, and then into the genuinely dangerous slums of Forcella. The deeper we go into the poverty zones, the clearer it is that men and women exist in separate worlds. Old men in black and brown, wearing woolen caps, play cards in the alleys. Old women tend to chores and laundry and children. Men speak to other men. Women to other women.

The separated power of man and woman hangs palpable, as though the residual molecules of each refuse to mingle. Not out of hostility for one another. This is not the bashful deference of Ireland, where young women blush and turn away their faces. Women walk these streets with a sturdy, and yet feminine, stride. The feeling is more like walking over the stones of an old battlefield where the truce continues to guarantee the terms of trade. It is friendly, respectful, even jocular, but unlike in Venice or Paris, where even the poorest couples caress, men and women here seldom seem to touch.

We stop at one of the city's oldest *pizzerie,* where a meal costs two dollars; only men sit at the long, wood tables. Loud and boisterous in their gestures, these men touch each other easily. They grasp their mate's thigh, knead his forearm, massage his back.

I understand nothing of their deep Neapolitan dialect and ask Claudio to eavesdrop, but he has nothing to report. It is ordinary workmen's talk: the job, the car, the wife, the shortage of money. Intimacy, at least casual public intimacy, is a male preserve and seems to have no need of women.

We wander back into the streets, aimlessly filling the afternoon until our return appointment with Lea's neighbors. Small shrines cut into stone walls are everywhere: shrines to favored saints, shines to the dead, clay figures being consumed in the flames of purgatory, amulets and angels hanging above their uplifted eyes, fading photos of departed family arranged behind them. We enter a small square where a relatively large and new shrine to the Madonna has been built above a pool composed of artificial stones. Coins layer the bottom of the pool. A single goldfish floats stationary just above the coins. Asleep.

A man of perhaps fifty-five approaches us. Speaking English, we draw attention. We compliment him on this most gloriously kitsch shrine we have seen. "I built it as a shrine to the Madonna for the miracle of my son," he tells us, the beginning of a long story. His son, thirteen, had cancer and seemed sure to die. Miracle, the boy is healthy now. And so the shrine.

As we leave, Claudio thanks the man and crosses himself.

Walking back to Lea's and the daily gathering of the *femminielli,* I tell Claudio about Lord Hamilton and the priapic amulets he found around the necks of poor Neapolitans centuries earlier. We stop at one of the shrines that has a flat surface, and I draw him some pictures of the amulets, with rings and protruding phalluses. He has never seen one, save in the illustrations from Pompeii. They seem to have disappeared, though a great many people do still wear the golden (brass) curved horn, itself a good-luck and fertility sign. At a cluttered old tobacconist's shop he buys me one.

"I am an *ateo,* an atheist," he tells me. Still he has been drawn to the world-famous religious processions that are so common on the islands and the little towns of Campania. Once on Ischia, where now he is redesigning an elegant house, he stumbled upon a feast-day celebration. The whole town was out walking and singing. He decided to join in.

"It's not so hard if you watch and listen. But most important, I didn't want to break the energy. There is a special energy you feel in these celebrations that moves from one person to the next." As he tells me the story, his eyes dart continuously after attractive men, and women, we're passing on the street. Many are people he knows. Others are only what he calls "possibilities."

"If I'm in a church or in a procession, if I don't sing, too, then the person who is standing next to me will stop singing. And the energy will be broken. I think you even find something like that in the disco sometimes. If there is someone just standing when everyone else is dancing, someone just watching and not moving, you feel it. It's a break."

These processions and feast-day rituals, like the priapic rites of St. Cosmo, long predate the arrival of Christianity. I want to understand more about how Claudio, an atheist, a modernist, an educated, cosmopolitan man, feels them. Instead, he changes the questions.

"What kind of man do you like to have sex with?" he asks me. We have talked about sex all afternoon. I tell him a bit.

"I want to make a ritual," he begins. "A sex ritual with men. A kind of orgy. But with rules. Of course, there must be a director and a victim."

"What kind of victim?"

"A sacrifice. A victim to be sacrificed."

"And how will he be sacrificed?

"That will be the decision of the director. The problem is that no one knows how to begin to do sex. We all want to wait for the decision, for someone to decide."

We walk along in silence for a while, climbing up, toward the Quartieri Spagnoli. "It could be a woman even," he says. "It might be better if the director is a woman who will tell all the other men how to perform the sacrifice."

He turns to me. "What do you think you would like to be: the director or the victim?"

"I think the journey of the ritual is more mysterious for the victim. No?"

"Maybe."

"Of course," I add, retrenching a bit, "I'm not sure what you mean by 'victim.' If it's symbolic, or how physical the sacrifice is."

"You must be a little afraid if you are the victim. That is the mystery of the ritual. And the energy. Not to know what is going to happen."

■ ■ ■

"It was such a beautiful house I had, before the [1980] earthquake," Lea begins. "A truly beautiful house." We are back in her *basso*. Cycles, noisy cars, and shoppers rumble by outside her door.

We had stopped in for the five-o'clock gossip hour next door, at Marilene's, who is determined to leave the streets and become an actress-performer. Her manager, a six-foot-three-inch blonde with broad shoulders and ice cream breasts named Carlotta, was there, along with Antonella and Valerie and Sorissa. All *femminielli* in their twenties or thirties who work the streets, a few of them down at the Opera San Carlos. Except for Germana, a real woman from down the block with her daughter and her three-year-old grandson. We listened and laughed and explained ourselves and were invited to return, but it was really Lea, they told us, whom we ought to talk to. Lea, who was the original, who was the first *femminiello* in the Quartieri, who had slept with the great movie directors in Rome, who had appeared in their films, who had warmed the beds of the black-cassocked men of the Vatican.

Lea's suspicion has evaporated. We crawl like cats onto her great bed with its faded spread of pink and blue wildflowers. Her pesky, yapping Pekinese hops up, too. Lea's voice is as husky as a stevedore's, as provocative as Rita Hayworth's. It's been a long time since anybody has asked Lea for her story.

"I was the first. The first in Naples," she wants us to know. In fact there were other transvestite hookers in Naples, one famous *femminiello* named Coccinella, or Lady Bug, just after the "liberation." The legacy of female men is fundamental to the Italian story, wrapped into the myth of Pulcinella, the masked hermaphrodite, who bore children from the hump in his back and gave birth through his anus. Plastic Pulcinellas are on sale at every trinket shop in the city.

But we are here for Lea's story, Lea's myth. In the flutter of a lash we are inundated with photographs of a younger, beautiful Lea, a Jean Harlow Lea, a Leslie Caron Lea, tempting and irresistible, on holiday in Barcelona, playing at the beach, performing at wedding parties, dancing before the movie camera, a Lea born with the name Carmello, tousle-haired boy from the port city Taranto, in Apulia, during the Great Depression, in the time of Mussolini, and reborn, moth from chrysalis, after the Fascist collapse, as the flamboyant, shimmering, sultry vamp of the South.

"I was the only one," she repeats, remembering the immediate postwar years. "All the others were *prostitute,*" by which she means real women. "But I was better with the Americans!" she boasts. "So the others, the women, they came to me to find out how. Ha! Ha! Ha! Ha!" Her laughing rolls up from her plumpness and her pride.

The American boys bankrolled Lea in the beginning just as their bosses in the CIA and the State Department and the Pentagon were bankrolling new labor unions to rid the city's docks of Communists and were organizing secret financial agreements with the Vatican and the formerly Fascist industrialists to keep favored political parties in power. Not that Lea's sailor boys understood much about their greater mission—any more than they understood what really lay between her legs.

"When I'd meet one of your American soldiers with a big dick," she says, widening her eyes, shifting into streetwalker English, I would tell him, 'No, theees iss too beeg 'cause I got leetle poosy.' Then when we were done, the soldiers would all say, 'No theees is beeg poosy!' " She slaps the bed and rolls out more laughter. She could always fool the boys, she says, because her anus is positioned farther forward than normal, and anyway, she always knew how to bind and pad her undergarments to keep dick and balls disguised. "It was an art not to be discovered by the Americans."

With the Italian men there has never been any need of such artifice. They never feel compromised by getting a blowjob from a transvestite or a gay boy. But with the Americans it is different.

The sounds of the street burst through the door as Valentina, another neighbor, enters, stunning as a young Sophia Loren. *"Buona sera, Lea!"* she sings out, extending her hand to Claudio and me. Soft layers of black silk gather up her full, golden bosom and accentuate her long, Betty Grable legs. She props herself up against the bed's headboard and joins the conversation about the tastes of American boys. Not much has changed in forty years, she allows. "If an American boy comes now, and he's alone, he's the best homosexual in the world. He knows who we are now. If he's in a group, though, they won't respect you at all. They sneer and poke fun at us and say nasty things. Then the next day, one by one, they come back on their own and want to fuck. And they want to touch you and wank you."

"Don't the Italians want to play with your dick, too?" I ask.

"Not so much. Maybe two out of ten. It's not a big question."

"And the Americans? How many of them want it, want to get fucked in the ass?"

"The Americans, they all want to play with your dick, and maybe three or four [out of ten] want it up the ass."

Valentina has a lot to say about the American soldiers, who make up a significant part of her customer base. The Americans genuinely puzzle her.

"Their minds are so perverse. That's why they act so butch even though so many more of them want to suck or be fucked." She pauses and adds flatly, "It's the hypocrisy. Like with your politicians. If there's a minister in the government that's married and he has another woman, and it becomes public, then he's out. It's the same hypocrisy your soldiers have when they yell and sneer at us in groups and then come back to us one by one alone."

The portrait Lea and Valentina draw of the Americans is brutal, but it is neither caustic nor angry. They like the Americans because they find that when the American boys are alone, they are full of goodwill and decency, seemingly incapable of the marvelous Neapolitan capacity for guile and duplicity—that self-conscious "two-ness" or doubleness that my friend Marcello confessed to me. Lea is instead disheartened, sad that the Americans continue to be so fearful of acknowledging their submerged feelings, so afraid of reaching down to touch their buried realms of longing and regret. She is puzzled about this country, this land of the free that lured away so many of her cousins and brothers and aunts and uncles, which yet remains so knotted up in puritanical anxiety.

I hear in Valentina's brief aside on contemporary American soldiers an echo to the great postwar Italian writer Curzio Malaparte. Malaparte, variously a young Fascist follower and an anarchic leftist, was an Italian Army liaison officer to the American occupation forces. He came to know and love the Americans. In his notorious novel, *The Skin,* which *Time* characterized as "a macabre tour of the gutters of wartime Naples," Malaparte captured the arrogant innocence of the American invasion as it replaced the wartime struggle for survival with the grasping hustle of greed, a time when the blank optimism of sunny-faced boys from Canton and Cleveland and

Columbus fed new levels of corruption in the Neapolitan soul. Malaparte describes one of the sweetest, most callow of the American GIs, Jimmy, a Midwestern insurance clerk who moves about Naples's squalid streets:

> Jimmy walked through those filthy alleys, in the midst of that miserable populace, with an elegance and a nonchalance which only Americans possess. No one on this earth save the Americans can move about with such easy, smiling grace among people who are filthy, starved, and unhappy. It is not a sign of insensibility: it is a sign of optimism and at the same time of innocence. The Americans are not cynics, they are optimists; and optimism is in itself a sign of innocence. He who is blameless in thought and deed is led not, to be sure, to deny that evil exists, but to refuse to believe in the necessity of evil, to refuse to admit that evil is inevitable and incurable. The Americans believe that misery, hunger, pain, and everything else can be combated, that men can recover from misery, hunger, and pain, that there is a remedy for all evil. They do not know that evil is incurable.

Then, as now, both Malaparte's and Valentina's Americans can acknowledge evil, and its offspring, suffering, only as a project for programmatic reform. They would go to the end of the sunset to fix the suffering but refuse steadfastly to acknowledge and experience it themselves for fear of the demons it might let loose in them. They would clean the streets, never having breathed in the fetid, sparkling richness of their odors.

And now, fifty years after the war, no longer blessed with cream-pitcher innocence, they would kneel before Valentina's cock, hungry and desperate to slurp it down, and testify the next day to congressional inquisitors about the incompatibility of faggotry and fighting. And so, to these Neapolitan men-women, there is something not fully human about the Americans. Not for a moment, Valentina says, would she exchange her life in the broken-down Quartieri Spagnoli for a life on the streets of New York or Las Vegas or Miami.

Lea asks me about the transvestites in America, how they are

79

treated by the police. Here Claudio, my Virgil through the rings of the Quartieri, is no help. What can I tell her? Yes, there is the triumphant success of RuPaul, the glammer-fab queen of sass-rap, sashaying through the talk-show, disco, celebutante circuit. And the fifteen minutes of fame visited upon the drag-vamps and voguers of *Paris Is Burning*. And the transvestite hustlers dodging the cops in New York's meatpacking district or along Santa Monica Boulevard in L.A. And the part-time, hormone-free queens who make up the drag shows and imperial courts of gay districts in big cities and small towns all over Dixie. Lea would not find an America laid out from the plain-style sermons of Cotton Mather and policed by the perversely prurient Jerry Falwell. Neither, however, would she find many friends like her neighbor Germana, the grandmother with the soft gray eyes, who wanders in and out of the apartment during our conversation.

"Yes, it's true," Germana says of the old days. "Lea was the only one working the street. It was good to have the *femminielli* here. They always watch for thieves. They'd keep track of what the children were up to, sometimes watch after them." What Germana doesn't say, nor does Lea, is that as the little boys grow up, the *femminielli* often introduce them to their first sex beyond masturbation. "We are the first ones where they get a blowjob, or even more," another *femminiello* streetwalker told us, "because they know us in the neighborhood, and their parents know us."

The *femminielli* are as integral to life in the Quartieri as the priests and the cops, who, Lea says, have always been totally respectful. As in the *femminiello* marriages. Sometimes these marriages are only a great party, an expensive show, like the 1992 marriage of Moira, filmed by RAI-2, the Italian television network. Moira and her wedding party took over the Quarter for a day. Banners hung from the clotheslines. Potted palms lined the procession way. Friends and neighbors filled the streets. A distinguished-looking gentleman walked Moira, resplendent in white silk and taffeta, down the aisle, giving her away to a handsome young Algerian whose mother cried as everyone threw rice at the couple. And then the couple toured the sights of Naples in an elegant leased Audi sedan. The day done, the narrator explained, "Everything except for Moira's emotions had been phony." The handsome Algerian groom, a hired actor, had gone home. His "mother" was an older woman, a neighbor from the Quartieri. It had long been Moira's dream to have a grand champagne wedding, the kind she often goes to as a lip-synching drag entertainer, and she had done it. It had cost her a fortune, and it was good.

Some marriages, however, are not phony. Sara, who lives next door to Claudio with her family, has never been a prostitute, and she proudly shows off her wedding band, evidence of her eight-year marriage to Pepe, a carpenter. One wedding in the Quartieri, Lea recalls, was between a man, by which she means a heterosexual man, and one of her transvestite friends; that time the priest even opened the church for a kind of truncated ceremony. "Sometimes," she explains, "the husband is an actual boyfriend. It could be a boy from the neighborhood, or maybe someone she has met on the street. Sometimes he could be gay.

"But for me," Lea confides, "the man has to be a married man. I like married men." She spots my confusion, adding that of course she does not "marry" such men, but she has had a number of long relationships with them—one for almost a decade with a famous scriptwriter, through whom she met the director Federico Fellini. At that time, in the 1950s, she lived in Rome and won several bit parts as an extra, the best as the blond, transvestite whore who, wrapped in a boa, runs alongside Marcello Mastroianni through the woods at the end of *La Dolce Vita*.

It is past seven o'clock, and politely, Lea lets us know that she must prepare herself for the evening. She no longer works the streets, but some regular customers still come to see her, even though she is well past sixty and there is only the slightest trace of the winsome waif Fellini filmed trailing Mastroianni to the sea.

■　■　■

"You are not Neapolitan. You have just arrived in Naples off an airplane. You cannot understand the way a Neapolitan is made—that a Neapolitan is both good and shit at the same moment. You have to stay in Naples seven, eight years to understand that somebody will get very close to you only with the idea of fucking you. They can

even kill you. And you don't even know why. Just because he needs something. Or just for *capriccio.*"

For kicks.

I am sitting on the edge of Claudio's bed, face-to-face with his old friend Mizzone, or Mizzo, a small-time camorra hoodlum who brokers contraband cigarettes by the truckload. It is nearly midnight, a couple days after our séance with Lea and her neighbors. Now it is time to talk to the men who go with *femminielli.* How, otherwise, Claudio has reasoned, should I understand the special place *femminielli* hold in Naples? So he and his buddy Ciro and I drive out to the edge of the city, where the poor from central Naples were housed in new, barren, concrete towers after the earthquake of 1980. Ciro is a middle-class gay man who works in tourism and publicity. He knows and has sex with lots of straight, working-class guys. They are not "tricks" who fulfill some rough-trade fantasy; they are genuine friends who invite him into their families, where more than once he has been adopted as a sort of extra son. By chance, we find Mizzo in a parking lot with his fiancée. He is taking her home. She lives with her parents, and he lives with his mother.

Sometimes Claudio and Ciro refer to Mizzo as O Nero, "the black one," because his eyes are dark and sunken. Mizzo is a small man who has power. Among his pals, he is the *capòcchione.* True to the title he also has an enormous dick—one of the biggest Claudio has ever seen—which wanders visibly beneath his trousers like a lazy, overstuffed python.

Claudio met Mizzo—slang for "cigarette butt"—seven years ago. Claudio was twenty-two. Mizzo was sixteen. They didn't have sex that night. Mizzo had missed a ride and had no place to sleep, so Claudio took him in. Mizzo was slight and boyish, a cigarette seller on the street. He had grown up on the streets. By the age of nine, long after he was kicked out of school for throwing a chair at the teacher, he tells me, he was already *scugnizzo,* street smart. By ten he had started fucking, the first time with a girl four years older than himself.

For a year, when he was twenty, "Mizzo was in bloom, really beautiful," Claudio has told me. Now, at twenty-three, his body has already begun to shrink. In another year or two, he will easily pass for forty.

It's not long before I realize that our "interview" is a two-way game in which Claudio is the referee. I am an opportunity for Mizzo as much as he is a subject for me. But he doesn't know, yet, what sort of opportunity I might be. Maybe only for knowledge. Maybe money. Maybe a free blowjob. A master *scugnizzo*, he is also a master analyst. He is not alone. We have also picked up his friend Max, nineteen, a fair-faced boy with a boxer's build who's already served four short terms in jail. Mizzo and Max, it turns out later, have a wager about the American writer. Mizzo thinks I'm a *ricchione*, a fag; Max says no, that I'm just some weirdo intellectual sort with a perverted curiosity.

Early on, a cigarette cut with hash passes through the circle. We sit on two single beds that serve as couches in the corner of Claudio's studio, Claudio on one of the beds, Mizzo, Max, and Ciro on the other. Max laughs a lot and allows Ciro to stroke his neck gently. Max and Mizzo know lots of *femminielli* who live with their families out in the towers but work the streets downtown. Sometimes they have sex with the *femminielli,* but, they boast, they never pay.

Max has a story.

"Once I went with a guy and took him out. Almost killed him.

"I was standing there on the street, hanging out, and this guy comes up in a nice car. He was old. He even had a beard. I took him around to a parking lot. Then he started to do his business.

"I just wanted to steal the fag's car. I could've killed him right there. But"—Max laughs the sweet laugh of a high school boy—"he had my prick in his mouth. He might have bit me." The hash is doing its job: Max, then Mizzo, then the rest of us fall into giggling laughter, a laughter that is all the more grotesque for the three of us who are fags. We laugh for the same reason we laugh at the poignant sight gags of Keaton and Chaplin. We laugh at the absurdity of the situation, at the image of vulnerability that we, like Max, have all experienced, alone with a stranger whose lips and tongue make us moan with pleasure even as his sharp teeth encircle and scrape our engorged flesh. And we laugh because we are horrified at the sweet face of this boy and his brutality. He takes a sip of wine and continues.

"After I came, I started hitting and kicking the guy. I was wearing these big steel-toed shoes. I left him in the parking lot. Then I got away with the car and came home, but I was afraid that maybe I'd killed him. So I left the car on the street."

I wonder how real Max's story is, if he's told it for effect, because he thinks it's what I'm looking for, a hash-fantasy remake of the murder of Pasolini, starring Max of Naples. In fact, the story seems so offhand, so much like a ten-year-old torturing a cockroach, that Claudio and I believe him. It's one of several "crime" tales Max and Mizzo rattle off about purse snatching and stolen cars. It's then, too, that I realize Mizzo and Max are using *femminiello* in a very Neapolitan way, to mean any homosexual person, not just a transvestite, which is how Claudio and Ciro and I are using it.

Mizzo wants to tell me a *femminiello* story, about the time an air force lieutenant offered to buy him away from his mother. Mizzo was a boy selling cigarettes in the street.

"How much can you earn a day?" the lieutenant asked.

"Seven or eight thousand [lire]," Mizzo told him.

"I'll pay you that much and more. Don't worry." Then the lieutenant went with Mizzo to his mother's house and offered her 40 million lire to take the boy away and keep him. "My mother was going to kill him," Mizzo says proudly. But her reaction wasn't only maternal protection. Mizzo's father, who had been a camorra cigarette broker, had disappeared, run off with Mizzo's brother's wife, and Mizzo and his mother had taken over the business as partners. "She couldn't [sell me]. I was the one earning the money in the family. I was making one hundred and fifty thousand a day."

"Wait, I thought you were only getting seven or eight thousand," I started to ask, confused. But the numbers were not the point. The story was the ruse, the *scugnizzo*'s gambit. Mizzo had lured the lieutenant, led him on, and trumped him. He'd "fucked" that fag, a man three times his age, and more still he'd trumped his mamma: even at nine years old he was the man of the house, the *capo,* whom she depended upon as her "partner."

These stories are all part of the dance of our interview, the presentation that Mizzo and Max are mounting, their way of testing who I am, of evaluating what sort of "investigator" I am. I want to return to the "real" *femminielli,* to the men with penises and breasts and pretty dresses that they have grown up with. Earlier, Ciro has advised me that they are both vain about their looks and that I should appeal to their vanity.

"Why," I ask, "do kids like you, good-looking straight guys, go to a *femminiello,* to a *transvestivo?"*

Mizzo takes another draw on the joint and watches me. "Why do I fuck with *femminielli?* Because it's an *ingrippo.* It's something that possesses you." Something that rolls around and around in your mind and you don't let it go.

Max shrugs his shoulders and Ciro begins to play with his ear. "Because someone is looking for something new," Max says, and drifts off. But Mizzo isn't finished.

"You've got options with a stranger. You take some hash, take a blowjob . . . you let yourself go. You've got a good deal."

He continues to stare at me. "If Americans start fucking the way we do in Naples, America will explode. In Naples, everybody fucks a lot."

"What if your brother were a *femminiello?* Would your family accept him?"

"If he's born that way, what can you do? Of course. You can beat him, but it won't change the fact that he'll become a woman."

I ask Max what he would do if his oldest son became a transvestite.

"If you could do something to make him normal, I would try. But if not, I could accept it."

"In Naples," Mizzo breaks in, "we accept *femminielli.* Why don't you accept *femminielli* in America? In Naples we say, you know where you're born, but you don't know when you'll die."

"What if your son brings a boyfriend home?" I ask Mizzo.

"Impossible! If he's a fag and he reaches a certain age, he can go off on his own. If I don't accept the boyfriend of my daughter, how can I accept a boyfriend of a son? Anyway, by the time you're fifteen, it's time to take to the street, so how do you bring someone home?"

I want to press him. "You and Ciro are close friends. What's the difference between Ciro and other *femminielli?*" Before Claudio can translate my question, Mizzo, who's been whispering to Ciro, draws his face up to mine, no more than three or four inches between us.

"You. Are you getting hard listening to these things?" He holds his gaze and I meet his eyes, waiting for Claudio's translation.

"No," I answer honestly. "Not at all."

Only now am I beginning to understand the dance between Mizzo and me. I had supposed he knew I was queer, but Claudio has not told him and I haven't had occasion to give it away. Later Claudio explains that it is a matter of respect, that nothing would have happened between us if it had all been laid out in advance. When we listen to the tape of the conversation, I hear Mizzo ask Ciro, "He's a *ricchione,* isn't he?" Ciro feigns ignorance. "Nobody can make me believe that he's a normal guy." At the time, Claudio translates none of this, and I go back to my earlier question, "What's the difference between your friend Ciro and other *femminielli?*"

Mizzo's face hardens. He turns to Ciro. "So he knows about us?"

Ciro nods.

The burnt-brown skin tightens around Mizzo's eyes. "There's a lot of difference. Because we can spend a week together as friends, and no sex happens. Then it might happen that we do have sex. If sex happens, it's a second level of importance to friendship." He extends the index and middle fingers of his left hand and draws them across his right wrist, a gesture of the blood-rich strength of real friendship.

"If I come to your house and all you want is to have sex with me, then I won't do it, I won't fuck you, because I won't respect you—because I respect friendship first. The friendship must be the link. If you are a friend, a real friend, it's not important. Then, there might be a *qualche cosa.*" Something could happen.

Mizzo has exposed himself, and he has exposed his friend. Ciro is as a brother to him. He is not "a fag" because your brother is not a fag. A fag is a man unworthy of respect. He is a man who has demeaned and degraded himself. Sex between two men who respect each other is only sex, a progression of intimacy from a slap on the butt, a squeeze on the arm. It does not matter now that Ciro feels no offense. There are obligations of respect that Mizzo feels to Ciro, especially before me, an American with money to fly on airplanes and ask perverted questions about his relations with his friend. Again, he addresses me head-on.

"Now that I said what I really think, would you fuck fag?" Even as I wait for the translation, I hear the leer in his voice. "Whether or not you go with gays, don't you have the desire for it? In your guts, when you are back home in the States, don't you really want a queer? Don't you think of a man going down on you?"

"Of course," I answer, still the witless interviewer who hasn't understood the wager Mizzo and Max have about me, who hasn't altogether grasped this tango of mutual respect.

Mizzo slaps my hand and tosses his head toward the dopey Max. "I was sure you would say that! I could have cut my dick off!"

Mizzo is finished. He has trumped both me and Max. He is still the *capòcchione*. He has figured me out and he has lost all respect: I am just another faggot, a foreign pervert *borghese* who has come to gaze stupidly on the baroque world of Neapolitan life, who cannot possibly understand what it means to be shit and to be the best all in the same moment. Now he is tired, bored with this game. He has better uses for his time. He tells Claudio that it's rude for them to let me, as a visitor, go home alone in a taxi, that at least they must walk me to the taxi stand.

The three of us, Claudio, Mizzo, and I, pull on our shoes and jackets. Walking across the courtyard parking lot, Claudio explains that Mizzo and Max have decided they want to have sex with him and Ciro. It's been some years since Claudio and Mizzo have screwed, though Ciro sees Max regularly. All this explicit talk with the strange American has churned them up, made them horny. The whole taxi gambit is only Mizzo's polite way of getting rid of me so he and Max can get blowjobs from Claudio and Ciro.

■ ■ ■

A drizzly mist falls as we say goodnight and my cab pulls away from the Piazza Dante. There are two ways to go from Claudio's place to Marcello L.'s beautiful apartment on the Via Tasso up above Mergellina Harbor. One requires winding through the Quartieri past Lea's home, up to the top of the ridge just below the San Martino Monastery. The other is to proceed down the broad Via Toledo to the Opera House, where Lea's younger girlfriends command the sidewalk life. Each night I make my way back across the top by taxi; each morning I walk down the Via Tasso and the pedestrian stairs, along the elegant shopping streets to the Piazza del Plebiscito, to meet Claudio for a coffee at the Café Gambrinus. A century ago the Gambrinus was favored by writers and artists in stiff collars. Today it is frequented by businessmen and tourists in the day, by Valentina and her friends in the night when they want relief from promenading about in their four-inch spikes.

As distant as Marcello's world seems from Mizzo's and Lea's—distant by class, by taste, by education—Claudio, who moves between these worlds, is leading me to see how closely linked they are. Claudio and I first met, he reminds me, at the gay dinner with the fabulous gnocchi—long before I'd learned that *gnocchi* was an off-color term for the female sex organ. Claudio grew up in a grand hillside house just a brisk walk around the hill from Marcello's place. He learned the city's streets by foot, and it is by foot that he still moves through them. Our way—his way—of moving about is not by the names of the streets. He seems to know the names little better than I do. We move on visual cues: shrines, vistas and lights, the textures of paving stones small and grand, glimpses of arched stairways inside the courtyards of baroque palaces. I could say that Claudio, an architect, is a visual man. But that doesn't quite explain it. He knows the city and its routes the way a farmer traces his property lines between twisted tree trunks and piles of rock. Maps are an abstraction superimposed over the vibrant spirit of the place, and that spirit inhabits Marcello L. as surely as it inhabits Mizzo and Lea.

This way of moving through the city brings me back to an exchange I had with Marcello L.'s friend Marcello D., the designer of fanciful glass. I'd mentioned to Marcello D. that my boyfriend and I were going to spend a few days in Venice. His face, an easy blend of Mastroianni and Bogart, softened in delight. "Ah, my heart is in Venice. Yes. But, still, I am a man of Naples."

What could it mean, I'd wondered, to say without irony, "I am a man of Naples"? Could any American say in good faith anymore, "I am a man of Los Angeles" or "I am a man of Chicago"? It's not the same as saying, descriptively, I'm an Angelino or a Chicagoan or even a New Yorker. Maybe a certain class of people could still say that they are Savannahians or Brooklynites and mean something more than their mailing addresses, but for most of us the link between our character and the spirit of the place we inhabit has become a fanciful nostalgia.

The next time I see Marcello D., I bring him back to his earlier offhand remark. He is amused. In fact he is frequently amused by my questions. "You know the Latin concept of genius loci?" he asks me. "That is the big difference between you Americans and us. I think in America you have lost that idea, you have lost that spirit of place." If I am to understand the meaning of sexuality in his life, and how it differs from the American notion of "gay identity," I must understand this notion of genius loci. First, he wants me to know that while he is absolutely militant on the defense of civil rights for gay people, *being* gay is meaningless to him. As with Marcello L., Marcello D. returns to his family.

"Two or three months ago I told my mother I was a homosexual and that I have a certain kind of life. I told her that I have *una storia* [literally "a story," but colloquially "a relationship"] that has lasted fifteen years." He takes a draw on his cigarette, studying me in much the way Mizzo did, clearly curious about the hidden presumptions I've brought to the conversation. The difference is that this time the terms of "normalcy" are reversed. Marcello D., charming, urbane, literate, has seen my earlier book on gay Americans; we have passed time together in exclusively gay settings. Nominally, we understand each other's position. Were I in America, this familial coming-out story would almost surely have moved on to a series of episodes about secrecy and hidden sexual longing. But that is not where Marcello D. is going.

"When I was young, sixteen [in 1972], I left the house. It wasn't a question of homosexuality. My father, who was a policeman, raised me in a very tough way. We were always 'arm wrestling' over everything. My whole way of life was different, and my need was to find my own life. When I was seventeen, my friends and I formed this club, KLIK, the Committee for the Freedom of Expression and Communication." There were guys and girls in the club, but the strongest rapport was among the guys. "They were tighter . . . and so something 'homosexual' was probably going on in the club. There were subliminal messages, and slogans like 'freedom of the body,' but no one would say, 'I love you, I want to touch you, I want to suck your dick,' though probably each one was thinking about it."

"Did any of them turn out gay?" I ask.

A new smile breaks on Marcello D.'s lips and turns into a characteristic laugh. It begins in his throat, then tumbles down through his body like a rubber ball bouncing down the stairs. Taking my arm in his hand, he makes a smaller laugh and says, "The question is a little stupid.

"I think a better question is, 'How many of these old friends know that I am gay?' Most of them, probably. I guess that some of them are gay, but no one says, 'Yes, I am homosexual!' "

I hear my American activist friends crowing, "See, still in the closet! He cannot be open about what he is and who he loves!" But Marcello D. means to take that American position straight on—and move beyond it.

"Twenty years ago in KLIK we felt a passion, but to be in a club doesn't mean they all believed what they were saying in their slogans. Who knows? If all [this talk about free communication and freedom of the body] had really been true, I'd still have relationships with these people. We had a poster from another club and its theme was homosexuality. It said, 'To touch oneself is good.' And there was a French magazine we all read. It had a comic strip with this guy whose penis got bigger and bigger and bigger. He wrapped it around his legs. He formed a lasso. He tied it in knots, and he jumped rope with it. I was at home with my sister in her room and we were laughing and laughing at these strips when my mother comes in. She saw what was going on and called my father. Of course, he ripped up all the papers."

The point, Marcello D. wants me to understand, is to keep alive the passion for *experiencing* the body, to feel alive inside your skin, not to live inside your family's religion or inside slogans about your body and your skin. Giggling with his sister at drawings of the lasso-length penis, agitating with his friends in KLIK, he found himself in radical opposition to the conservative Catholic values articulated by his parents, just as he now rebels against what he regards as the consumer-lifestyle slogans of the gay movement. Again, he talks about his relationship with his father. The more his father pushed him to be a conventional, tough, macho male, the more rebellious he became until, finally, he left home, set up his own house a few blocks away, then began living with a boyfriend. While he and his father never talk about "being gay," he says his father has clearly known it for a long time. Once, when he and his boyfriend were both sick in bed with a high fever, he called his mother, who quickly made a giant pot of soup and dispatched his father to bring it over.

"My father asked me, 'Who sleeps in this room, who sleeps in that room?' I said, 'Sometimes I do, sometimes he does. It depends.'

"I was standing there in my pajamas. My boyfriend was in bed. And there's this photo of the two of us embracing, on the beach in Jamaica. So, my father picked up the picture, looked at it, and said, 'Hmmm. Well.' Very simple and with great effect.

"Now, if my father has some trouble about my brother or his parents, or some personal problem, he speaks with me about it. Only with me, not my brother [who is straight and married]. My problems now are not about my family. They are about my life. His problems are about his life, and our relationship is very sure, very open."

There is something almost cinematic about this fevered exchange between father and son over a pot of soup and a night-table photo, as though it were an idealized coming-out dream. Perhaps it was that, but for Marcello D. the coming out had little to do with homosexuality and heterosexuality. Instead, it concerned the oldest issue of fathers and sons: establishing mutual respect within the family for the independent routes each has taken in his life. Even his recent coming-out confession to his mother was not so much about sexuality.

"My homosexuality," he says, "is neither the starting point nor the point of arrival for me—and it's not the address of arrival." Rather, he supposes, his homosexuality is a natural consequence of the route he has taken to find his life. Telling his mother fulfilled a personal need to declare his adulthood, much, I suppose, like a marriage announcement or the birth of a child in a heterosexual context. "I wanted to create a distance from my family, an appropriate distance to watch and see what was going on emotionally between us from a more adult perspective. I wanted *to be seen* by my family." Coming out to his mother was a gesture of closure meant to register the independence of the life he conducts in his household.

When he looks at the contemporary gay movement, Marcello D. finds little of the personal, social "liberation" he has sought in his own journey. "The gay liberation movement now," he protests, "is the television way of life. It is a consumer style, a big business of gyms and sex clubs, S&M, M&S, cha, cha, cha. It's all a great mystification.

"Homosexuality and heterosexuality don't exist. There doesn't exist an identity common to everyone. This homosexual model of life isn't a liberation. It is a limit to the personal experience of each of us. I'm not homosexual twenty-four hours out of twenty-four. I'm not a designer twenty-four hours out of twenty-four." Raising his eyebrows in a new smile, he adds, "I'm not nice twenty-four hours out of twenty-four. The risk today is living the ideology of life rather than the experience of life."

To mistake the model for the experience (to confuse the menu and the food, as an American friend puts it) is surely not the particular burden of the gay movement, Italian or American. It is, Marcello D. would say, the particular burden we all face in contemporary consumer society, where we accumulate concepts and slogans *about* experience instead of living inside of experience, where we spend thousands of dollars and hours sculpting ourselves into models of erotic attraction in place of touching each other in direct erotic engagement, where under the slogan of "coming out" we confuse primal tensions of intergenerational autonomy with phantasms of sexual identity. In the most profound way, it is about the loss of genius loci, the loss of an integral aesthetic of place, and our progressive inability to live inside the skin of the places we inhabit.

Genius, to the Romans, was something like a guardian angel, but more enduring. Genius accompanied families from one generation to the next, passed at death from father to son. As a father lay on his deathbed, his son would stand close by, awaiting the final breath. Then the son would cover his father's mouth with his own, thus capturing the elder's breath, and his genius, to draw it into his own lungs and there preserve it. The passing of breaths, in which genius was thought to reside, was the ultimate act of male passage. That is how we might see it. But it was more, because the genius permeated, guarded, gave guidance, to the entirety of the family. Then, too, the Roman family was not what we mean by family, for among citizens, it included the whole enterprise of the household: husband, wife, children, critical and beloved friends, as well as personal servants, aides, and retainers. Individual family members also seem to have had additional personal geniuses, but the family *as an institution* held its own greater genius.

The possibilities for conflict were deliciously complex—just as were the bitchy battles of the gods. Genius as an animating force was not, however, restricted to families and individuals, for physical places might also be possessed of their peculiar genius—be they the pleasure spas of Pompeii or the sacred caves of the Cumaean sibyls or even a hillside or a neighborhood within a town. That genius of place, or genius loci, left its spiritual, aesthetic, and characterological mark on the people who lived there, and with the other genii lurking about, it further personalized an individual's relation to fate.

Genius persists throughout the modern Mediterranean, usually rendered as a spirit world of superstition and sorcery. In her account of village life in Calabria, *Torregreca: Life, Death, Miracles,* the American Italophile Ann Cornelisen described how her neighbors wore an array of amulets and called on witches and spirits to protect them from the effects of the evil eye. There was even a rustic, medieval hill town near her village whose name no one would dare speak, referring to it only as Quel Paese (That Town) because to utter its name was sure to bring bad luck on the speaker. In a similar vein, an editor at *Il Mattino,* the Naples daily, told me about the time that his housekeeper spent an entire day breaking into tears. When he at last asked her what had happened, the woman explained that her daughter was approaching the end of her pregnancy and had no donkey. No donkey? he repeated. Yes, she answered. Unless she could find a donkey that would lick fresh grass from her daughter's pregnant belly, the yet unborn child could not be protected from the evil eye and might enter the world afflicted. And then there was Max, the young tough who was carrying on a sometime affair with

93

Ciro, who told me he was about to get a big break. A milk-processing plant had offered him a job. How, I asked, could a nineteen-year-old kid get such a job in a city with 30 percent unemployment? "I went to a friend of my family who is a witch, and he told the plant manager that he should hire me." At first I assumed "witch" was a euphemism for a camorra fixer, but no, Claudio explained. All sorts of people, bosses and workers, consult witches when they make important decisions.

And then come the *femminielli,* who hold their own peculiar place in modern Neapolitan mysticism, displayed nightly on the city's UHF television stations. During the eleven-o'clock news report, the stations present their own version of *tambolella,* the popular bingo game. Just as on *Wheel of Fortune,* the hostess is a beautiful woman. Instead of spinning a wheel, however, she dips her hand into a bag of numbers, picks one, and holds it up for the viewers to see. Next she turns to La Smorfia, the ancient Book of Dreams, to interpret the numbers. The *tambolella* interpreter examines the numbers as carefully and as intricately as professional astrologers read the calendar and the stars. She takes into account strange events, like the birth of triplets or quadruplets, reported homicides, or storms. Each sign or event has its own number. The reader's skill is in understanding the relations between numbers, how they affect each other, their relation to the number of the day, the week, the year. Of course, the beautiful woman who draws and interprets the numbers is not really a woman: she is always a *femminiello.*

Vanna White with an eight-inch penis, spinning the Wheel of Fortune, is a strained image for American television, but then neither the Wheel of Fortune nor Atlantic City roulette is quite the same as *tambolella* and the Book of Dreams. In a city like Naples, where a third of the population is perpetually unemployed, hustling money off the books, looking back to a five-hundred-year legacy of plague and cholera, fate is not the same as a betting man's chance. Centuries of conquest, supplication, and subversion of the conquerers have earned the Neapolitans their reputation for fatalism. But it is not a fatalism of defeat, as the Germans, the French, and the Spanish each came to learn. Neapolitan fatalism, *rassegnazione,* includes a wily respect both for fate and for those who have special knowledge of how fate works. The special place reserved for *femminielli,* I came to realize, speaks to that history, its resultant fatalism, and perhaps most, to a fascination with mystery and knowledge.

■ ■ ■

One morning in May on my second stay in Naples, Pat, my American interpreter, and I went to see Dominico Scafolio, a noted anthropologist at the University of Salerno who has spent much of his life studying the myths of Pulcinella. Scafolio's apartment occupies a few rooms of a once grand seventeenth-century palace. Around the apartment, hanging from the wall, propped up on tables and desks, was his collection of ancient phalluses. Some were small, clay casts, not unlike those Lord Hamilton reported seeing two hundred years earlier. One double-ended phallus had seven heads attached to it, indicating the seven lives of Pulcinella. A wooden phallus, suspended from a string, was more than a foot long, painted red and blue. On Scafolio's desk, there sat a devil in flames whose penis grew brighter and brighter toward its head. Still another seemed to be a face with a cap under which protruded a phallic nose supported by round, testicular jowls.

The acceptance of *femminielli* in Neapolitan life is not so hard to understand, Scafolio explained, because the *femminiello* is in effect Pulcinella incarnate, a genuine man-woman whose excitement resides in his/her physical mysteries. At a mythic level Pulcinella was loaded with the signs and symbols of fertility and recalled the primordial tribal dream of male parthenogenesis, in which a man is the first human, who himself gives birth to the first child. The myth of Pulcinella is an almost universal story—whether told in the Sambia men's secret rites of passage or in the biblical account of Eve's emergence from Adam's rib—that suggests an atavistic longing for exclusive male bonding and solidarity. As Mizzo, the camorra cigarette broker, put it, to go with a *femminiello* is an *ingrippo,* a magnificent obsession, that touches the mysterious and still transpires within the exclusive world of men.

Yet why should the *femminielli* be favored as interpreters of the *tambolella* lottery? Because in a game of fate, those who have been touched by mysterious forces, who show the physical signs of mystery, are presumed to have special understandings. "Traditional Neapolitans," Scafolio said, "believe *tambolella* is regulated by some type of providence, not pure luck, that the rules of the lottery *can* be known by experts. Experts are people who have rapport with the beyond, and they are characterized by some sort of anomaly, like the hump on the back of Pulcinella. These are the so-called signs of God, because having something wrong with them grants them exceptional power, rapport with the beyond and with death. Homosexuality is seen as such an anomaly, an abnormality affording people with special powers." He corrected himself. "No, not all homosexuals, only the *femminielli,* the *transvestivos.*"

These mythic *femminielli* and the *femminielli* who satisfy Max and Mizzo on a horny night seem like very distant cousins. I remember what Max said when I asked him why he has sex with transvestites: "It's like a fantasy. You take some hash, you get a blowjob. It means you let yourself go." But isn't a fantasy, at some level, a way of gaining "rapport with the beyond"? To say that Max or Mizzo go to *femminielli* in search of a mystical experience pushes the point too far; nonetheless, in the violent day-to-day life of petty street hoods, to have such a matter-of-fact fantasy encounter with someone who carries a mother's breasts and somewhere inside a brother's mind, someone whose body has once experienced the tactile pleasures that you feel, seems very much like a journey into the beyond, out and away from the deadly dead-ended-ness of the street and the family. Further, as a number of Italian writers have pointed out, the transvestite traffic proliferated only after the Italian government closed the nation's brothels in the late 1960s, depriving heterosexual men of the ready sex through which they demonstrated their dominion over women. In the game of face-saving and respect, where little boys are taught from the crib onward to top their adversaries, what could be a better trump than for a husband to leave his wife at home with the kids and go out for the night with another guy who has bigger breasts and shapelier legs than she does? That, in fact, is what many men said on camera in Pier Paolo Pasolini's famous 1963 documentary about sex in Italian life: close the brothels and men would turn to homosexuals.

On television or on the streets, the *femminiello* promises a voyage into the fantastical beyond, a beyond that is both antique, pre-Christian, mystical, and that is here, present, today. What the accidental arrangement of chromosomes gave to ancient Pulcinellas, hormone tablets provide today. Fifty years ago, *femminielli* held secret "delivery" parties during which one of them would have a doll with an enormous dick strapped to her crotch, would writhe through the motions of labor, and would then deliver the ultraphallic "baby," which would be passed to her rough, macho "husband," the whole episode a direct reenactment of the Pulcinella story. Today, Lea and Valentina dismiss those parties as old-fashioned traditions. Today, medicine gives them beautiful women's bodies, and they carry cell phones to book their clients. Still, the shadow of the myth is as close as the sea, as ordinary as new mothers boasting about the size of their babies' pricks. The shadow of the myth informs ordinary memory and lends aesthetic structure to the events of everyday life revealed as the peculiarly Neapolitan genius loci: it undergirds and reinforces the ubiquitous sense of doubleness, the recognition that truth is never as simple or as direct as we would like it to be, that the sacred is inseparable from the profane, that redemption is dependent upon evil, that no soul has a single address, that identity is the most banal myth of all.

Giuseppe Griffi, whose novel about Neapolitan transvestites, *Scende giù per Toledo (Going Down Toledo Street),* drew the attention of my friend Pat's traveling companions on her train ride down to Naples, writes of this special spirit in plainer terms. Griffi's novel recounts the story of a young transvestite from the Quartieri, Rosalinda Sprint. At the beginning of her career, Rosalinda presents herself to the grande dame of the *femminielli,* who goes by the name of Marlene Dietrich. Rosalinda is looking for guidance in love and work. She asks Marlene Dietrich if she never gives herself for love.

"Love has nothing to do with it. Aaaaaaaaah, you are really naive! If you look for love in this work, you are fucked. You have two asses, this is what you must remember. Two asses!"

"Two asses?"

"One day you will realize it, you will feel it coming out from the deep one underneath the external one, like a secret that unravels itself. The external ass is the one that the others want, and you can give it away thoughtlessly. You can build your fortune on it. Your real ass will be revealed only by the one who will be able to reach it—the one who will be truly yours."

t h r e e

Tools:

Outness, Place,

and the

Aesthetics

of Desire

Tools were the first question.

Which tools would be necessary to break through the cemented-up brick wall covering the mouth of the fireplace? My parents had sealed off the fireplace fifty years earlier, during the Depression. Fireplaces are pretty, but not sensible or efficient; so they replaced it with a fuel-oil heater to keep the house warm. Since childhood I'd always wanted to reopen the fireplace.

I'd imagined marvelous mysteries stashed away and covered with soot just beyond the masonry, fragments from the time when both the house and the newly planted apple orchard were full of romance. Crystal chips of the hollow-stemmed champagne glasses my father told me he had once thrown against the burning logs. The missing brass andirons that had been handed down from some obscure Scottish ancestor. Or maybe lost pages of poems he had written in the twenties (his twenties), when he lived in Provence with his first wife, before his romantic spirit had been broken with her death and the Depression's arrival and the stark reality of living cold winters alone in that converted log house on an isolated hilltop in eastern Kentucky.

I'd imagined lying on faded Oriental rugs before the fireplace, snuggling, caressing, recalling earlier delicious evenings on the wet paving stones of the Place de la Concorde, when love was fresh and the future infinite and apples were not just a crop, but poetry.

In just a few weeks Gene would arrive from New York for the holidays. My father's first wife, Betty, had come from "back East" (well, Pittsburgh, but they'd met back there, when she was a Smithie and he a Yalie). Various aunts, uncles, and cousins who'd moved East would visit or pass through during my childhood, opening up vistas of excitement, intelligence, and enchantment. (And, yes, one even brought me my first original-Broadway-cast recording.) But the house itself, a pleasant two-story, three-bedroom building framed around a central cabin of twelve-by-twelve poplar logs, was a hazy place where the images of exotic cities were clouded in bittersweet memory and too much cigarette smoke.

Gene's arrival would be more than a confirmation of our then new relationship. We'd just finished two weeks of exploratory vacation together, driving through the English countryside of Somerset, then staying with friends of mine in France. We'd broken all the standard advice against embarking on foreign travel too early in the affair, and we'd survived, more tolerant, more appreciative of the temperamental quirks that come with middle age. Not only was it clear we cared about each other, we enjoyed each other. His arrival for the holidays, in the place where all the childhood emotions evoked by Christmas had been born, would finally break open all the old entrapments I'd felt there as an adult gay man.

I wanted the fireplace to be ready.

I'd never before spent a night in this house, my father's house, with a boyfriend. To make it right, to restore its capacity for romance (and, I suppose, to release my own capacity for romance), I had to exorcise the dusty spirits of defeat and obligation that had settled into the logs, to open the firebox and let them escape up the chimney with the smoke of burning applewood. Not that I wanted to erase my father's memory from the place, or the memory of his first wife, or of my mother. Their traces are indelibly preserved in scores of household artifacts: a small, blue Rookwood vase; the heavy black-walnut desk; several framed pieces of brightly colored, crewel stitchery. By opening the fireplace I wanted only to release the torpor that for too long had left no room for lovemaking. (Already, on a reporting trip to Central Asia, I'd bought my own Oriental carpet to cover the floor before the fireplace.)

The original hearthstones were still in place, soft, polished, gray rectangles half-covered by a utilitarian wall-to-wall rug. The fire-place itself was grand—nearly five feet from one side to the other, large enough to crawl inside if you bent your knees and lowered your neck. A thin cement frosting, painted gray in the fifties, masked the opening.

I took an old claw hammer and tapped. The eight-pound sledge-hammer I'd borrowed from a neighbor seemed unnecessary.

A crack formed. Then another. I slipped a wood chisel into the cracks and twisted. The tired cement came loose in great, crispy flakes, exposing an inner wall of superhardened, yellow firebricks. A few more taps and a little more chipping against the mortar with a broken screwdriver, and the first brick fell free.

Breaking through proved easier than I'd imagined: the wall to the firebox was stacked only one layer thick. A quarter hour later a dozen more bricks had given way, forming a ruin of broken corners. I peered through the hole. No misplaced andirons. No broken champagne glasses. No bundled sheaf of forgotten poems. Only dried-up oak leaves and fragments of birds' nests. (As a child I'd loved running into my parents' bedroom early in the morning to press my ear against the cool, summer chimney and listen to the swallows chattering.)

The chimney man finished his work in short order. Gene found the house intriguing but jumbled. "It doesn't have to look like a col-lege dorm room," he quipped. Before he left, we'd rearranged the odd assortment of downstairs furniture, he'd built a new bookcase, and more than once we'd anointed the Armenian carpet before the fireplace with the requisite amount of fevered writhings about.

Two years and more later, the opening up of the fireplace remains an essential "coming out" ceremony. Like Marcello D.'s conversation with his mother, however, it was not precisely a gay coming out—even if my sense of sexuality was deeply implicated. Opening the fireplace was a way of opening myself to the place that had made me and of opening it to another person, my companion, who at least occasionally inhabits that place. Opening the fireplace was not an explicit verbal declaration, nor was it a metaphorical gesture. It was a direct inquiry: a use of my hands to touch, to probe, and to physically restore the aesthetic intention of the room. While the blockage of the hearth in some ways recalls an array of blocked family expressions, sentiments, and affections, that is an insight a posteriori, a psycholiterary elaboration on something that is much, much simpler. Had the great hole never been sawn out of the logs to make a fireplace at the end of the room, then the room would not have missed it. Before they became our house, these poplar logs had formed a plain, mountain cabin, its joints sealed with a local clay stucco. But my father had bought the cabin, numbered each log, dismantled and transported the logs to the flat sassafras grove several miles distant where the house would stand; there he made new cuts for new windows, new doors, and the new fireplace, then reassembled the logs as the simple home where he and his wife would build their lives.

The new house was carefully sited: its front windows looked out, southward, over orchard fields that fell down to the road and beyond across the fading blue ridges of distant mountains; two west-facing windows on either side of the fireplace spilled the tangerine light of sunset onto the floor and walls, reflections in spring and fall of the flames that lapped the firebox. The fireplace was the mouth through which the soul of the room breathed. As a child I would never have put such words to my objections to the cemented-up cover: I simply thought it looked like an ugly scab.

We might have peeled away the grainy scab thirteen years earlier when after a fire we had to rip out all the smoke-saturated interior walls of the house. That was the first I'd ever seen of the enormous, hand-squared logs behind the drywall. The fire (started by a dropped cigarette or a lightning ball; we never knew which) had been hot enough to melt my father's college tennis cup and bring bubbles to glass table ornaments. His three thousand books, their spines roasted away, fell apart at touch. But the logs, cut from virgin poplar at least 150 years earlier, paid scant attention. A thin, black char, no more than a few inches long, crusted one or two of them: they refused to burn.

I recall clearly the wet, June afternoon that I saw the logs. Along with my brother and two neighbors who worked at the orchard, I had been using crowbars to pry loose the gypsum boards and the remains of a three-bay, floor-to-ceiling bookcase. There's a blood-thirstiness that comes of ripping a house apart, however sad the circumstances. I would jab the sharp point of my long black bar into the gypsum to collar a nail, then snuggle the V-crotch of the bar close under the head and press. At first, for a part of a second, the layers of old paint and paper that were the gypsum's skin would resist; but inevitably, the skin cracks. A bowl of tiny plates squish into the gypsum grains and my arm feels its triumph. The nail, fifty years asleep, its hairline bonding grooves well wed to the fine fiber of the poplar, is unmoved. My arms, extended above my shoulders, relax, but not so much as to lose the bar's hungry hold on the nail. I pivot it leftward around the shaft and press again, spreading the broken bowl of cracked paint and gypsum. The nail remains in place. A third time. A third position. The crowbar's mouth bites the nail a millimeter farther down its neck. Nail and poplar send a gut-groan into the wet air. But nothing more. Both arms rebel against the sustained overhead prying. I bring the bar back down and pant. I will prevail against nail and wood and gypsum, but they will be sure that I know it. Nail and wood will shriek, as their predecessors have all day in the face of my revenge, and they will let go of one another forever.

Nails discarded on the floor, I set the crowbar aside, spread my arms, and curl my fingers around the edges of this last remaining sheet of wall. Off it peels, easy as a wet Band-Aid. Nothing is left but bare, gray logs, their curing cracks exposed to daylight for the first time in half a century. They are the hard-muscled skeleton of the house, and I can go no deeper.

Seeing the logs, touching their hardness, running my fingers over the soft-sharp edges axed by some unknown mountaineer contemporary of my great-great-grandmother, I felt what I can only call the spirit of the house and the spirits of the elements that had made it be a house. Even *spirit,* however, is not quite the word, for *spirit* now has too much a New Age fragrance to it—like a sinsemilla séance in Mendocino County. I would say I experienced the soul of the house, but *soul,* too, bears a religious perfume. What I knew was that the lay of the logs, the lateral, sidewise energy they expressed, thrusting across the length of the room even as their stacked strength held up the floor and roof above, gave a certain sense to the rough, red-brick proscenium that was the face of the fireplace. Together with the wide-open eyes of the doors and windows to the south, the east, and the north, they made a coherence. They formed an aesthetic unity.

To recover the aesthetic integrity of a place—of a room or of a table within that room or of a hillside upon which that house and its rooms and its tables reside—is to release the beauty that is inherent within the place. By revealing that inherent genius of place we find pleasure and thereby open ourselves to the beauty within ourselves. That is the sort of experience I think we are looking for in our "coming out" rituals. Coming out, we examine, excavate, and reveal aesthetic form within our lives. We relax the barriers between our aesthetic imagination—our fantasies—and the experience of our senses—skin, flesh, heart—and become suffused with sublime wonder. We begin to touch the form of our desire.

But what is "form"? By form I mean the way in which I perceive and organize beauty within myself. When I run my fingers down the grain of the poplar logs, how do I make sense of the tactile sensation of my skin against wood? How do I interpret the movement as pleasure in being connected to a beautiful room? How does the touch of skin to wood release a rain of pigments in my mind that intensify the hypnotic effect of apple logs burning blue and orange against the brick, which in turn releases erotic arousal, which then in turn enables me to feel rooted to the room as a sacred zone of fulfillment? The technical organization of form—how we cut the logs to allow light to fall across the room in such a way as to reveal the alluring texture of the hearth—is the technique of art. Art, or the reach toward art, is what propels us into life; or as Nietzsche said, art is "the affirmation, the blessing, and the deification of existence."

When I drape my thigh across the haunch of my lover and slide my lips down toward the small of his back, I experience my movements, I experience the connectedness of our movements, in incomparably different ways than I did some years earlier when I brought a casual trick into the very same room, organized and furnished the way it was at the end of my parents' lives with the fireplace bricked up, the heat supplied by a propane stove. The difference is not only that one was a lover, the other a trick, and it is not merely the sentimental effect of a warm fire burning in the fireplace. Now, with my lover, I have in my mind, sometimes conscious, sometimes not, the stories of this room, of its construction, of the all too obvious fantasies that each of its makers applied to its construction, of the recurrences and disappearances of those fantasies, loaded and focused through memory and heat of flame as I run my thumbs through the loops of his Levi's and pop open the brass buttons of his fly with my teeth. As the story of the room has shaped my submerged dreams and desires and brought form to the erotic engagement of this moment, so the intercourse of this moment, the intercoursing of our two lives on the firelit rug from central Asia, becomes a new episode in the story of the room. We are as Borges's aleph, the invisible crystal that absorbs the splendor of all past stories and projects the panorama of all future stories. Touch the story of the room: enter the room's story.

■   ■   ■

I have come out to the story of a place, and as with all comings out, I have become more deeply implicated in the place. It is no longer the same place. Others who enter it, use it, inhabit it, will be affected—if I take my responsibilities seriously. I have left my marks on its physical form: because the fireplace is open, the currents of convection have changed; moist air is exchanged with dry in new patterns; because of new dampers atop the chimney, swallows no longer nest inside in spring, and subsequent children will not hear them squawking in their parents' bedroom; because the fireplace is centered at the sunset end of the room, the room has recovered a focal point that encourages intimacy and flirtation and exchange: you enter and see instantly the potential for devilment. The room itself seems to be coming out as a playground for mischief. This coming out has nothing, in fact, to do with sexual identity, about gays or straights, and everything to do with nurturing the impulse to spontaneity and the respect for memory. Still, something queer has taken place in the restoration of the room, but that something queer isn't gay. The remake of the room feels queer because it opts for the erotic over the utilitarian. Queer because it seizes sex from behind the bedroom door and throws it onto the center of the living room rug.

Queer because it asserts an aesthetics of eroticism and pleasure as essential to the fulfillment of the room's possibility.

Let me be clear: while I use *queer* in an erotic sense, I do not mean gay or homosexual, or even the purely sexual. The erotic moment is not about orgasm; it is about the lure of human beauty that releases pleasure. What feels queer in this room is the gradual disruption of the depressions and the defeats that over fifty years came to characterize it: my father's loss of his beautiful and gifted wife, the collapse of his youthful dream of himself as a poet-farmer, the economic collapse of the Great Depression and the isolated retrenchment that came in its wake, the expectations born of a second marriage and the bitternesses that flowed from it, the ever inward withdrawal that came with age and then old age and wheelchairs and disease and death. And then a decade of emptiness that made the room and the house into a vacation dormitory. The renewed sense of erotic possibility within the room, the tapping of that earlier aesthetic design that valued another sort of (heterosexual) eroticism, lets loose in me an electric tingle of queerness. I feel a connection to a mischief that never totally disappeared. Restoring the setting for mischief (my homosexual mischief), I enter into a delicious transgression against the defeat that was so palpable in the cemented-up face of the fireplace. And I, a queer, make a pact with the older "straight" erotic spirit that was there in the beginning, when the poet and his wife were young and full of their mischief.

In an essay entitled "Cosmos," the writer and Jungian analyst James Hillman writes of our moral obligation to restore beauty to a place of centrality in daily life. Hillman argues that beauty, eroticism, and pleasure are integrally intertwined and essential to our survival.

> Unlike ancient Egypt and Greece or modern Bali or the bird-feathered, body-painted "primitives" of Papua, New Guinea, our culture just can't accept aesthetics as essential to the daily round. The prejudices against beauty expose our culture's actual preference for ugliness disguised as the useful, the practical, the moral, the new, and the quick. The reason for this repression of beauty is nothing less than the taproot of all American culture: puritanism.

You see, taste, as the word itself says, awakens the senses and releases fantasies. Taste remembers beauty; it enjoys pleasure; it tends to refine itself toward more interesting joys. Puritanism would much rather focus on hard realities and moral choices that you have to suffer through and work for. But for me, the greatest moral choice we can make today, if we are truly concerned with the oppressed and stressed lives of our clients' souls, is to sharpen their sense of beauty.

There is nothing homosexually queer in Hillman's essay, but I would argue that his call for a renewed deification of beauty, of aesthetic primacy in ordinary life, speaks to the most vital part of (homosexually) coming out. To come out in endorsement of pleasure as the reason for existence, to see pleasure as an inherently human response to beauty, is a reenactment of the most vital thing we do when we celebrate the homosexual potential of our lives.

If I use "coming out" to mean more than a conventional declaration of sexual orientation—as in "Hi, Mom! Hi, Dad! I'm gay"—it is because I think the phrase is a muddier notion than we usually acknowledge. Since the gay liberation days of the 1960s, gay Americans have focused on the act of "coming out" as the social and psychological cornerstone of the movement for social equity and personal self-worth. A life of denial, we have argued, is a form of personal self-imprisonment that reinforces the collective abuse of homosexual people: to live "in the closet" is to live a lie. Each year gay Americans celebrate National Coming Out Day. There are even handy, multistep programs on how to do it: how to come out at work, how to come out at home, how to come out at school, how to come out to your priest. In a nation where self-help sections of bookstores take more space than the politics and religion shelves, one should not be surprised. But the more time I spend with people who are not white, middle-aged, middle-class men, the more I am led to share the question posed by David Mills, the twenty-five-year-old San Franciscan I wrote about in chapter 1: Toward what are we coming out? What is the object of this flourishing ideology of "outness"? Does it speak only to our short-term appetite for self-declaration, or is "outness" a dialectical journey, a path toward be-

coming? Does it nourish our primal human hunger for aesthetic coherence in our lives, or does it reinforce our all-too-American tendency to see the world (and ourselves) in Manichaean terms of good
and bad, honest and dishonest, truth and lies?

I go back to the question of form.

If you have just come out to a reporter as an "an openly gay man,"
that reporter's readers will likely *form* a picture of you. First, white—
because the published and televised images of gay Americans are almost universally white. Second, middle class and an active member
of "the gay community." The picture probably also includes certain
corollary suppositions: probably you belong to a gym where many
other members are gay; probably you spend or have spent many
hours in bars or discos; probably you place a high priority on eating
at restaurants; and almost certainly, you own several pairs of Levi's
jeans, likely 501s. The data that *form* this picture are the data that reporters and consumer merchandizers have in mind when they refer
to "the gay community." Look at the images of most of the advertising in successful gay publications. Notable exceptions aside, their
underlying assumption is that, having "come out," gay men have re-
*form*ulated their lives in such a way as to enter this "community," a
community that is both in a place and in the mind as an aesthetic
ideal. Go to Chelsea in New York City or West Hollywood in Los
Angeles and you will find it, complete with a recognizable "aesthetic"—as dictated by the designers at Klein, Hilfiger & Versace.
Residents of these communities may legitimately protest that many
people there don't fit the image—Puerto Rican families in Chelsea,
Hasidim in West Hollywood, gay men in both places who don't go
to gyms. The fact that they must protest their independence from
the hunked-up Calvin Klein image only demonstrates what aesthetic power the image has over public perception and our consumer habits. These are the primary images of the contemporary
"out and proud" gay man even though few of us bear any resemblance to them. The same could, of course, be said for any fashion-
model marketing, from GQ to the *New York Times Magazine*. We are
not and will not become the people whose rags we buy. To confuse
our lives with the baubles we buy, to believe that they will deliver us
our dreams, is to become a commodity fetishist. In a culture like

ours we are all of us, at times, commodity fetishists—even the eco-
logically minded consumers of Chinese herbs and organic fruits.

But for gay people the issue is deeper still. We have built a movement that has united politics and identity with style, for style is by
definition the manner in which we present ourselves. It is our exte-
rior, the form of our presentation to the world. And it is critically
important to us, now, in the last third of the twentieth century, because we have been the forward edge of homosexual people who
would not keep our erotic truths hidden. We have argued, correctly,
that the suppression of our desires has oppressed us as human beings.
In art, fashion, and daily life we have until very recently suffered the
subordination of our sexual aesthetics: we have been told that what
we find beautiful is pornographic, therefore shameful, therefore
ugly. To free ourselves erotically, aesthetically, we have necessarily
constructed a politics of display, and that display, that "outness," is the
evidence of our value.

The growing trouble I have with our language of "coming out,"
and even more directly with the word *out,* is that it fails to deal with
the dynamic quality of identity and form. To say that I am out
("out" is what I *am*) implies a specific erotic aesthetic. There is "out"
and there is "in." Having made a public declaration, I have joined
with all the other happy "outs" who can be identified and labeled
according to the form of our common aesthetic identity. I am a bear
or a boy or a daddy or a buff hunk or a grunge queen; subcategories
include pecs man, buns man, dick man, top, bottom, pierced, tied, or
hot-waxed. I turn to the personals section of my local homo catalog
and find my form. Yet, of course, none of these fantasy forms touches
the dynamic, contradictory, always shifting form of my actual aesthetic attractions.

The question of aesthetics here is not a minor linguistic fixation,
especially for people driven by homosexual desire. Already by acknowledging and acting upon homosexual desire, I am in rebellion
against our society's dominant program of human beauty. Almost
every body image I have seen on television, billboards, magazine
covers, even calendars for machine tools, has laid out an aesthetic of
what I as a male should find beautiful and attractive in a human being. By seeking my erotic satisfaction in the form, the behavior, and

111

the spirit of other men, I have placed my response to beauty on the line—first to myself and then to others. I have had to make a conscious examination of what sort of human beauty most gives me pleasure; I have had to throw over the beauty codes my culture has given me. I have had to participate in the discovery of beauty, and it is that exploratory participation that has enabled me to find the beauty that brings me pleasure.

A declaration of "outness" itself is but the simplest, crudest variety of participation. As a statement of witness, self-declaration may have value, but declaration itself does not lead us to the engagement through which we find the art of our lives. The fact of my "orientation" is not in itself dynamic; it speaks nothing about how sexuality is a "participant" in the form of my life; it gives no necessary direction to my passions, my dark desperations, what brings me joy or sorrow, how I fall (or fail to fall) in love.

Participation is active, ongoing, and necessarily unfinished. Participation depends absolutely on another person (or persons) who is similarly unfinished. As a participant I am incapable, ever, of arriving. I cannot then ever *be out,* because as soon I have arrived at that point, I have become a static thing and am no longer moving outward. To be engaged with the beautiful, I must act: that is the requirement of engagement. I cannot stand in the river and be *of* the river because the form of the river that gives it its particular beauty is its movement. If the river ceased to flow, it would be a lake, which has an altogether different aesthetic configuration; beautiful as the lake may be, I do not experience its beauty in the same way I experience the river's. To the bacteria of my stomach, to the microorganisms that will one day consume my rotting flesh, I may seem to be a lake. But as a living human, I am moving and continuously incomplete so long as I am engaged with other human beings. It is not that my sexual interest is moving back and forth between some homo-hetero binarism, like a bisexual Ping-Pong ball. It is that the expression and meaning of my desire—which is almost exclusively for men—is in continuous flux in response to new dreams, new goals, and new experiences: now for nurturing, now for adventure, now for accomplishment, now for contemplation. The love that I find, the beauty that I see, the pleasure that I experience, cannot stay still. I can only *be* out once I have been laid out on the slab.

At best "out" can only be a method of aesthetic exploration: a form of journey into the emerging design of ourselves. But even then, *outness* as personal method suffers a fatal flaw. As soon as I tell you, "Now I am out, and yesterday I was not," I have betrayed my memory, because each day I can make the same claim, and the truth of the new declaration will forever falsify the previous day's declaration. With each declaration all that I shall have done is elaborate a web of falsity, for in fact yesterday's life is still present in today's experience. I cannot kill my past any more than Hitler or Torquemada or St. Paul could erase theirs. If I make love in my father's living room, my memory of the room when it was his is present in the touch and passion of my lovemaking today. However much we declare ourselves reborn and "out," the demons of the past do not disappear in the salvation we promise ourselves today.

Only if I can use *outness* as a point of balance, a fulcrum, to explore the inside of my dreams and declarations am I likely to touch the aesthetic design of all my declarations, am I likely to know how and why I chose the particular path of declaration that I have: the declarations of love, the declarations of loss, the declarations of power, the declarations of terror, the declarations of faith, and the declarations of despair. *Outness* ceases to describe my identity; instead it is a method of becoming, a method of inquiring and of acting, which then forms a new basis of new inquiry and new action: a state of relentless journey.

As a political "program," however, *outness* is deeply problematical, for while it promises the satisfaction of fraternity to all those who are "out," it offers no collective action, no design, that would take the "out" into further exploration. It contains neither program nor dialectic. The problem shows itself most clearly in the act of "outing," where declaration is turned to accusation in a radical tactic of queer rage. Were outing merely a theft of authority over another person's life, it could nonetheless be justified. Would we not have destroyed Himmler and Stalin by any revelation we could have found if it would have saved their victims, if it would have relieved us of our complicity? There is always the occasion in which an individual sacrifices authority over his life.

But outing as a tactic of expressive rage reveals the emptiness of "outness" as an end in itself. In the name of liberation the outer seizes the mystery of desire and seeks to reduce it to a single label of identity. The outer may have justification: hypocrisy, oppressive power, threats of violence exercised by the one to be outed. But the act of outing, of conferring *outness* on another human being, has nothing to do with liberation; its intent is containment within a labeled category; its object is the destruction of the very thing that makes life worth living: the beautifully unfolding mystery of discovering who we are to become. Its pedigree is fundamentalism, and like all fundamentalist creeds, it takes the universal human longing for place and self-recognition and calcifies it into dogma.

To take a popular outing case consider two actors who have long been the objects of homosexual fantasy: Richard Gere and Jodie Foster. For years when I lived in Los Angeles, I would hear tales of Richard Gere jogging through Beverly Hills with his boyfriend until they reached a secluded grove, whereupon Gere would pull up his sweatshirt hood, trot on into the shade, and passionately kiss the boyfriend. Since her student days at Yale, Foster has been on every most-famous-dykes-of-Hollywood list. It goes without saying that for two such widely admired personalities to reveal their homosexuality would help to "normalize" homosexuality in the nation at large. (I'll leave until later my reservations about "normalization.") Young men and women could cite them to their friends and parents as clear evidence that queers can be talented, attractive, and successful. The political value of demonstrating that "we are everywhere" is unmistakable; the more "straight" people become accustomed to the ordinary presence of "queer" people, the less likely they will be to hold bigoted attitudes toward them.

But beyond that first, crude (and essential) step of self-proclamation, where does this politics of outness take us? Toward a new ethics of the uses of pleasure? Toward a reevaluation of the hierarchies of gender privilege? Toward a reimagination of intimacy and commitment in our relationships? Toward a better comprehension of power and desire in our sexual emergence from childhood? Or does it give us only the quick, thin rush of group identification followed by an equally quick rush to establish our own new normalcy where new "perversions" are either denigrated or ignored—pain and bondage, child sex, cross-race and cross-gender theatrics, recreational and Dionysian revelries—any one of which may be distasteful to many or most of our "out" membership.

As a tactic "outness" is quick, direct, and effective, but as an ideological or even a strategic program, "outness" is empty. It offers no particular linkage between our relations as human beings (politics) and the mysteries of our psychic selves (our aesthetic coherence). Scrambling after celebrity icons and second-rate bureaucrats, we seek to magnify their homo grandeur, and by extension our own. We claim we are excavating the psychic lodes from which they derive their art and influence. In fact, like all the other celebrity siphons and tabloid gossip hacks, we are only sucking away at our stars' complexities, at their nuances, their contradictions, their protean profiles, desperate to feed our own hunger for personhood, until drained and out-of-date as icons for the next generation, they would be cast aside as camp queens of the sorry past. Richard Gere as Rock Hudson as Mommie Dearest. Finally we are left in the usual vapid American politics of the preoccupied self.

And what of the outers, those who would usurp the aesthetic journey of their brother-sister icons? Are they untouched by their own actions? At the first level, the outer reaffirms his own out status: as a queer he is asserting his privilege to identify another member of his clan. (I say "he" because I suspect it is not accidental that most of the practitioners of outing have been men.) If his action puts him in some jeopardy—if, say, he were an unknown hustler who had taken Jesse Helms to bed—he may even be sacrificially heroic. But by reducing the object of his rage to a neat, categorical commodity, he also turns the process on himself. If I can expose the hypocrisy of my enemy by revealing that he is one of my own kind, then inevitably I have identified myself as one of his kind. If his most important characteristic is that he is as I am (though in hiding), then I am as he is. The critical dynamic of my political action is to label, but my label has a double adhesive, and I can make it adhere to him only so far as it adheres to me. I, too, have contained the limits of my

desire and disrupted the ongoing journey of my outward exploration of desire. I have subverted the promise of my own *outness.* I
have become a counter-icon: the commodity queer.

I bear down on outing and *outness* not out of a clear hostility to
the tactic or the object. I, myself, engaged in outing several years ago
at National Public Radio, when I reported that the Reagan administration was relying on a group of lightly closeted gay men to raise
money illegally for the support of the Nicaraguan contras. For me,
then, the issue was threefold: the hypocrisy of a homo-hating government turning to gay men to finance a highly sensitive covert op-
eration; the fact that one of those gay men contributed to a gay hate
campaign; the obvious nepotism when subcontracts were let to
lovers of the principals. Were a parallel story to appear again, I would
still report it. But I have no illusions: my object was and would be to
disrupt both their policies and the integrity they had established between their policies and their lives.

As with the famous English homosexual spies who worked on
the KGB payroll, as with J. Edgar Hoover's apparent homosexual attachments, these covert bagmen for Oliver North derived an excitement, a certain frisson, from their doubly closeted dance with
power that may even have fed their erotic imaginations. My object
was to expose and disrupt their work because it seemed to me politically debased, a corruption of democratic practice. My technique
was not merely to criticize their policies, but also to fracture the aesthetic coherence they had established in their lives: to turn their personal codes of beauty and desire against what I took to be their
deeply dirty work. In doing so, however, I was inevitably subverting
my neutral stance as a dispassionate journalist. To my colleagues I
was employing special knowledge that I as a homo possessed, and I
was exploiting my standing as a homo to make a revelation that
would have been taken as bigotry were it done by a heterosexual reporter. I was not merely outing myself at work—that I had done
years earlier—but I was using my professional, journalistic tools to
engage in a broader cultural conflict about the place of homosexuality in a political arena dedicated to its benign suppression.

From that point forward, of course, I was perceived to have "an
agenda" (never mind that others, not least editors and correspon-

dents panicked about their children's sexual meanderings, also had their own agendas). That perception of my agenda was not, however, restricted to my nail-biting straight colleagues. For as I learned on the promotion tour of *Culture,* my outing of the contra bagmen had given me a modest iconic status as well. Frequently, gay reporters or reviewers would identify me as the whistle-blower on the gay contra story. For them I inhabited a particular profile that, while not false, was more cartoonlike than true.

To be rendered as a cartoon is the curse of a society where politics has become an exercise in image declarations, the insight that made Andy Warhol famous forty years ago. Cartoons, being two-dimensional, possess only an outside. They have no "interiority," no integral aesthetic, no soul. By dwelling on *outness* as our destination, instead of seeing it as a technique of examination, we glide into hopeless solipsism, relinquishing the recognition that we are each made of a vast set of closets within closets. The act of coming out, if it is to have any meaning, must move beyond declaration and use declaration as a way of moving into the labyrinth of secrets that form memory and expectation in our lives. It is into those closets of experience that I find the power to imagine an outwardly moving life.

■ ■ ■

Like many homosexual men, I cherish and am aroused by the curtains of secrecy that surround sex. My arousal comes not only from being shrouded by the curtains, but it also comes from pulling the curtains open (or having them pulled open). The easy vernacular of *outness,* however, leaves no room for shrouded, furtive, disguised sex. Sex, and especially sexuality, must be open. Yet the landscape of our desires tells us something else, something we see in public-sex playgrounds all over the world. Tunnels and labyrinths—in the shrubbery at San Francisco's Lands End, beneath the feathery fens in Boston, along the darkened corridors at New York's Zone DK, inside the moveable passageways of Washington's Cinema Follies—lead us into the altars of our imagination. I go into the darkened corner, find myself wedged between bricks and bodies known to me only by the touch of skin unseen, and I am grasped in a collective disappearance. My knees dissolve and I descend, as in a re-curring dream of a free-floating, weightless elevator moving ran-domly through the walls of an enormous building. Head to breast to navel to groin, and I am engorged by the flesh of another's flesh, re-leased from the contingent aloneness of my life, all limbs my limbs, all heart one heart.

It is a fantasy, and it is real, and it is wrapped in the secrecy of night. Epidemiologists are understandably disturbed at my vision and my confession. Even if I am not opening myself to HIV and AIDS as I open my mouth to all these random tongues and body parts, I am exposing myself to legions of unknown other microbes. The epidemiological record is incontrovertible. We exist now in a viral village of global disease exchange in which the abyss of the anonymous orgy carries unprecedented dangers. Viruses and bacte-ria that only a decade ago lay neatly isolated in remote towns and villages glide across the globe in first-class comfort. Challenged by new environments and medications, they mutate and hatch out new disease, often untreatable and unrecognizable. As I merge myself into the sweet grip of a dozen others, and a dozen dozen of their others, I take myself to the biological brink. Not only do I take myself to the abyss, but I make my body a conveyance through which un-known agents track their way into unknown other bodies. I become an altar of secrets: secrets whose (microbial) nature I do not know and whose destination I cannot specify. I become the abyss of the unknown. For that (sublime) reason alone, I, like any abyss, become yet more attractive, more alluring to those others drawn to the dark secret. I am the escape from the floodlit world of *outness*.

At a meeting in New York's Lesbian and Gay Community Ser-vices Center during the winter of 1995, the renewed threat of the microbial abyss exploded with volcanic force. The meeting had been called by a group of respected writers and activists concerned about the resurgence of HIV infections among young men. AIDS had just become the nation's leading cause of death among young men, and young men, by all reports, were the very people who were exposing themselves to HIV infection.

Police the bathhouses and the sex clubs! one group demanded.

Those clubs that permit penetrative sex should be closed, if necessary by the government. Gird our loins against the intrusion of the state! answered a larger, counter group. Most of the most painful, emotional debate centered around the role of government: should the state be brought in to force closure of those clubs that refused to bar unsafe sex practices, and, if it was brought in to regulate the sexual terrain of gay men, would that lead to further repression, further policing of sexual practice? Or would the presence of the state only press sexual men further into the secret closets of sexual abandon— alleyways, piers, warehouses, and the like? Should "the community" voluntarily mount its own boycotts of those clubs that failed to bar unsafe sex?

The debate was not new. It has recurred regularly since the arrival of the epidemic, first in the mid-1980s when many, many gay bathhouses shut their doors. The telling detail about this debate, however, concerned doors. Should those clubs that still provided cubicles with doors be allowed to remain open? Those with doors, both the owners and the activists agreed, could not be effectively monitored; locked behind the doors, men would be free to forget their rubbers and the virus could hop from body to body like ticks in August. Pull the doors off, turn up the lights, and anal intercourse could easily be blocked by house monitors. Not only would the sex club be eliminated as an easy vector of infection; symbolically, patrons would be discouraged from putting themselves at risk in their own bedrooms. The sex clubs could then use their semisacramental status to encourage wider behavioral norms for the very people most drawn to sexual adventure. It is a classic example of tribal or communal mobilization in which the temple is transformed into a meeting house where vital threats to community survival are addressed.

Proponents of the plan seemed genuinely perplexed, however, at the passion expressed around the matter of doors. No one wanted the state to regulate queer people's sex lives, they insisted. No one wanted to close any sex clubs. And in any case, only five of New York's forty-eight sex clubs—all old-fashioned bathhouses—had such doors. Since everyone in the hall was in apparent agreement

that anal sex without rubbers should not be condoned in any public place and should be discouraged even in private, why would such
minimal sacrifice to personal freedom in the midst of a medical crisis be so threatening? The answer, I think, goes well beyond anal sex;
instead, it is about the power of secrets in a world where individual
lives are subjected to relentless scrutiny, judgment, and regulation.
Doors and video parlors are but metaphoric sentinels to a vital
dream world, the territory of Persephone, that essential zone of secrecy, where terror lurks beside beauty and we find the sublime
power to imagine and reimagine what is sacred in our lives. It is not
that the orgy booth itself promises passage to the sublime, but that
by eliminating it in the name of health we give over authority to
well-meaning managers who seem to have no sense of the sublime—theirs, ours, or anyone else's—and who seem incapable of dis-
tinguishing the sacred from the sordid. Of course in this era we are
dancing at the abyss when we enter the sex club. That dance is the
very thing that leads us there, and it is our moral obligation to make
all those who enter with us aware of their own proximity to the
abyss. The managerial ideologues who would close them down re-
trench in horror, but the specter of the abyss behind the door is the
very best reason to shelter and celebrate the sex club, so that those
who dare to may touch that which is most sacred in themselves, that
which is at greatest risk: the awareness of what it means to be alive.

The secret and the sacred have long been intertwined, Sissela Bok
writes in *Secrets,* her study of ethics and secrecy. While the secret is
not necessarily sacred, sacred places are nearly always swathed in
some fog of secrecy that combines a sense of doom and longing.
When we go to the altar, we present ourselves to the unknowable
and we are quickened; we may be saved or we may be sacrificed.
Fear and expectation swirl about in us—if we believe. The invisible
secret inside, outside, beneath, and above the altar vibrates from the
core to the edge of our being. We touch destiny and know that we
are alive because we are so proximate to the awareness of our in-
escapable death.

Secrecy houses the magic in our lives, a truth we all learn in
childhood games of make-believe and hide-and-seek. "I've got a se-

cret" gives us an alluring charm—whether we're on the playground or a TV game show. And, as the German sociologist Georg Simmel wrote, our secret promises us entry into the beyond even as we go about our ordinary daily lives; it "produces an immense enlargement of life: numerous contents of life cannot even emerge in the presence of full publicity. The secret offers, so to speak, the possibility of a second world alongside the manifest world; and the latter is decisively influenced by the former."

My childhood secrets were as innocent as the stories I made up "talking" to the wild squirrel that ate my bread crumbs out behind the barn and as invasive as phony questions asked after discovering mislaid "adult" letters. One of the delicious secrets I remember from childhood began with my sixth-grade history book. Sixth grade (age twelve) was when we studied "ancient history" from a text that contained line drawings of naked runners and discus throwers. At night I would come home and quiz my father about famous Egyptians, Greeks, and Romans. He thought I was developing a healthy interest in history. In fact I only wanted my parents to buy me books with more naked men in them. The gambit worked, but I never shared my secret, and the reason was not only fear that looking at men was somehow wrong. The best part was that I had maneuvered my parents into giving me something they never knew they were giving—which only intensified the excitement I derived from looking at the Olympian images. In the same way, I would get especially aroused looking at etchings of brawny, half-naked angels in my grandmother's family Bible precisely because the Bible—and angels—supposedly had nothing to do with sex.

Simmel goes further into the electric charge of secrecy when he examines its double, betrayal. Secrecy of necessity resides at the wall of betrayal. He writes:

> The secret . . . is full of the consciousness that it *can* be betrayed; that one holds the power of surprises, turns of fate, joy, destruction—if only, perhaps, of self-destruction. For this reason, the secret is surrounded by the possibility and temptation of betrayal; and the external danger of being discovered is in-

terwoven with the internal danger, which is like the fascination of an abyss, of giving oneself away. The secret puts a barrier between men but, at the same time, it creates the tempting challenge to break through it, by gossip or confession—and this challenge accompanies its psychology like a constant overtone.

In these few lines Simmel captures the terrifying wonder of homosexual conquest (although he was not consciously writing about sex at all) and its calculus of betrayal. I read the passage and am propelled backward to the early 1970s to an evening of secrecy and betrayal aboard a train called the Southern Crescent.

The Southern Crescent sweeps south from Washington through Charlottesville, Greensboro, Spartanburg, Atlanta, Birmingham, and finally New Orleans. The Crescent, which now rattles behind Amtrak engines, was in those days the last of the grand passenger trains, the gem of the Southern Railroad. The Southern Railroad: "Covers Dixie like the dew."

Every Friday night the Crescent's great green diesel engine turned its wheels toward the Potomac, hauling behind a dozen coaches stuffed with the working refugees from Carolina, Georgia, and Alabama, black mothers and their children heading home for the weekend. Every morning there were fresh grits and biscuits on the dining-car table. Ham steak was sliced thick. Eggs were creamy rich.

I rode the Crescent often, at least once a year, to visit my brother's family in Asheville. Even when I couldn't afford a roomette in the sleeping car, I never denied myself dinner in the diner or a drink in the club car. There were too many stories—like the grandmotherly ex-schoolteacher who made a modest fortune cornering the market in concrete highway dividers, or the airline mechanic returning home to help his octogenarian father bury his septuagenarian mistress. Or the adventuresome young men who fell under each other's spell in the coded secrecy of the open club car.

It was summer. July, I think. The air conditioners in the thirty-year-old cars labored loud. I had finished dinner and just stepped through the vestibule into the club car. A young man with a Brueghel face, wide and full of shadows, had secured a perch off to the side of the bar. His hair was straw blond, protester long. His drink sat next to him in the peculiar pedestal made especially for trains, a double steel ring that kept the glasses from tumbling and contained a silvery ashtray in the center. I put my drink in the pedestal next to his, and as one does on trains, I introduced myself and shook his hand.

Jimmy was his name. His grip was firm and full, as it should have been in a bar full of porky white men smoking cigars and talking politics and baseball. But we both thought we knew we'd let loose the grip a mite too slow.

Jimmy was on his way to Atlanta, where he lived in a group house. In Berkeley it would have been a "collective," but in the South mostly people just lived and worked together. Jimmy did civil rights work and antiwar organizing, and sometimes he helped out on the famous underground paper *The Great Speckled Bird*. He knew some people I knew or knew of. I bought him another beer, and as I sat down, our knees brushed. Then he did the same for me.

We knew by nine-thirty what we needed to know about each other. We never uttered a sexually insinuating word. We spoke about politics and about freedom and what it meant to live freely and not only to talk about the ideology of freedom. We pressed the toes of our shoes against the legs of each other's crinkly green upholstered chairs and bounced a quiet rhythm.

"I could get a roomette," Jimmy told me when the barman wandered off for a moment.

I nodded and offered to throw in half the cash.

Neither of us had enough to get a roomette on our own, and I had to buy a bus ticket the next morning between Greenville and Asheville. The Crescent got into Greenville at 5 A.M. the next day. It couldn't be a long night.

No one had seen or heard this mutual faggot seduction that was going on right beneath their noses. At least I thought not when Jimmy followed the bar steward down the corridor and asked him about renting one of the roomettes at the opposite end.

The steward was a thin man of at least sixty. He looked Jimmy up and down with a single glance and shook his head.

"I knows just what you two are up to and it won't be happening in my car," the steward said. Flat. Sure, he'd sell Jimmy a space, but he better not have any idea that that other fella or anybody else was going to go inside with him.

Jimmy signaled with his eyes that there was a problem and walked on back to the next coach car. He'd gone ahead and paid for the roomette—after all, he wasn't about to accept the steward's accusation—and was ready to give me the ticket. I proposed another drink thinking perhaps the steward might wander off and we could both slip into the roomette unobserved, but the steward was on guard. There was no hope for sleeping together, and the sexual tension grew unbearable.

A little past midnight I stood up, as though going back to my coach seat. The steward was beyond earshot.

"Three cars back," I told Jimmy quietly, assuming he would know to go to the men's rest room. Then, at normal voice: "Nice talking to you—have a good trip."

Our sex lasted until nearly two, bodies twisted and contorted and dripping with sweat in the tiny locked men's toilet stall of the third car back, wilder and more exuberant than would have been possible in the bar-car roomette. For his part, the steward hadn't the least interest in where Jimmy had gone for all that time, so long as it wasn't in his car. Before we parted we kissed until we'd drained ourselves dry of kissing, able to stand only against the support of each other's weight. Jimmy, who had six more hours of Crescent ahead of him, took the roomette.

When I tell this story of seduction on the rails, I usually get one of two reactions: (1) wow, are trains really that hot? or (2) that's why everybody has to come out, so gay people can snuggle together in their own roomette as openly as straights. Most interesting is who expresses the two reactions. Usually the aroused excitement comes from men over forty-five or under thirty. Those who hear it mostly as a tale of repressive discrimination came of age in the 1970s at the height of post-Stonewall gay activism; to them it feels like nostalgia for the good old days of the closet. I feel both sentiments myself as I tell the story, but my excitement comes from the tension of secrecy. As a citizen I must demand equal access to public facilities and safety from physical harm. At the same time I neither can escape nor would want to relinquish the powerful place of secrecy in the erotic game.

By secrecy I do not mean privacy: privacy concerns protection from intrusion; secrecy connotes hidden, parallel dreams and agenda, and as Simmel notes, secrecy is surrounded by betrayal: "The secret contains a tension that is dissolved in the moment of its revelation. This moment constitutes the acme in the development of the secret; all of its charms are once more gathered in it and brought to a climax—just as the moment of dissipation lets one enjoy with extreme intensity the value of the object: the feeling of power which accompanies the possession of money becomes concentrated for the dissipator, most completely and sensuously, in the very instant in which he lets this power out of his hands."

That evening in the Crescent club car produced a progressive escalation of secrets. First were the two secrets Jimmy and I held from each other as strangers in a supposedly "straight" setting, the secrets of our mutual desire, wrapped in the necessity of "betrayal" (confession) to each other if we were to make contact: how long to let the handshake linger, how to read the tension in the palm, whether to look directly or guardedly at each other as our hands parted. Next, how to confess the position of desire: how tough, how sweet (how top, how bottom), how ready, how reticent, how reckless, how trustworthy; and the matter of language: which references, literary like Whitman and Wilde, pop like Dean and Garland, political like GLF and Stonewall, horny like Mastroianni and Newman; and body language: how slowly to let the tongue cross the lip, how openly to look and avert the eyes, how firmly to rock a foot against the other's chair. Then, the barrier between us betrayed, how do we carry forward our merged secret: Do we act to consummate or relish the glow of unrealizable anticipation? Do we open up our secret language to those around us to feel closer to the flame of exposure (and the pride of our disguise)? Do we contrive with authority (the steward, and above him the conductor, who has the power to put us off the train at midnight in the next whistle-stop) to provide us a place where our bodies can join the secrets in our words? Finally, discovered by (betrayed to) the steward and denied that roomette, do we raise the stakes of our secret even higher by disappearing together into the tawdriness of the toilet stall where we know that discovery will bring certain expulsion? Each betrayal constructs a new secret, and through the progression of secrets we each learn about the soul and character of the other.

These are the kind of nights human beings remember, the kind of nights that lead us into the secrets we keep even from ourselves. We open them, like sealed fireplaces, not as declarations of the degree of our "outness," but as outward-bound journeys into the zone of our becoming.

four

The

Way

of

Some

Flesh

A week before Christmas, 1993, I found myself with my friend Sean at a restaurant in Washington, D.C. Sean spent his early twenties in a monastery before turning secular and hitting the noisy, bumptious, ultra-ego world of Washington broadcast news. Despite his steady professional success in the news trade, he had begun to contemplate returning to the monastery.

"I have no time for solitude in my daily life," he told me, no time for the vital moments of clarity that had ordered his earlier monastic life. Because of the timing of broadcast deadlines and the antic nature of the daily news spin, he found himself progressively divorced from more primal daily rhythms, from witnessing and acknowledging what a day really is. Before, in the monastery, the celebration of each day had been codified in the vespers service. Unlike the fixed daily deadlines of news, vespers is the fluid marker of the day's completion, driven not by a clock but by the trajectory of the sun, the length of the shadows, the imminence of night. The implications of the word—vespers, taken from the Roman word for evening star—were joyous, reflective of a fragmentary, early Christian hymn that told of the happiness that came in seeing the light of God reflected in the vesper star.

Sean and I continued to talk about the tension between monastic rhythms and news rhythms in the back of a taxi that was delivering us to Washington's tawdriest sex bar, a place called La Cage aux

Folles. La Cage, which is noted for providing happy evening moments to congressional staff, military men, and lobbyists, features
buff boys naked down to their boots, undulating their limbs atop the
club's two long bars. A certain discontinuity struck me about our
conversation and our location.

At first flush I supposed this sex temple—really a sex-fantasy temple—to be one of the polarities Sean was examining for himself,
inasmuch as he takes the vow of monastic celibacy seriously. Flesh-
pots and news deadlines on one side. Silence and prayer on the
other. But that was only the most superficial way of reading the
evening.

Later as I would replay in my mind the tableau of Sean, me, and
the other customers sitting on their barstools and the young, beautiful men dancing on top of the bar, I began to contemplate what Sean
had told me about the qualities of happiness that the vesper star
brought to the faithful. As much as the star shifted in the heavens, it
was a continuous companion in the Mediterranean night, a beacon
from God that night was not death and a reminder that the physical
world and the celestial world were connected. That interconnected-
ness of the physical and the celestial, of the flesh and the spirit, derives from the pagan religions of Greece and Rome. Though the
early Christians may have claimed vespers as their own, they took it
from the rituals of pagan belief, which never separated the physical
from the celestial or the human from the spiritual.

When Sean suggested our evening outing, I expected to find just
another gay bar overlaid with a porno pastiche. Naked men are not
altogether exotic in gay bars. As I observed Sean, however, I saw in
him an unusual contentment. Though he was single and looking for
a boyfriend, he seemed more delighted than hungry as he watched
and touched the dancers. Absurd as it sounds, his monastic impulses
seemed to make more sense to me there, at La Cage, than they did
when he was barking out orders in the newsroom. Of course, as
readers of Boccaccio and Chaucer will recall, bawdy escapades are
not entirely absent from the monastic life. For as much as the
monastic impulse is to withdraw from the transactions and relationships of the secular world, the monastery often insists that its brothers immerse themselves in the physical experience of being on the

earth, of touching the soil, crushing the grapes, wrapping the cheese, cleaning the filth. As much as any human institution, the monastery requires ritual immersion in the physical simultaneously with personal removal from the world. To be in a state of contemplative solitude is not to withdraw and sever the spiritual from the physical, but to order and contain the physical in celebration of the continuity between spirit and flesh.

I do not know how many of the men sitting around that bar stuffing bills into boots on Christmas week would talk of any spiritual or cryptoreligious intimations at La Cage aux Folles. I do know that for Sean the periodic taxi ride to La Cage takes him into a territory that is both physical and spiritual. To project a bawdy house as a zone of spirituality may strike many readers as a scurrilous blasphemy—a confusion of cheap thrills with sublime ecstasy. But it is the common proximity of the sublime and the tawdry—of the sacred and the profane—that loads sex temples like La Cage with their spiritual charge. The contact that humans make with one another in the darkened corridors and along the red-lit bar tops becomes so powerful, so provocative, because, in almost all cases, fully intimate exchange is impossible. Physical contact is so strictly ritualized, so repetitive, and so protected from the confusions and obligations of conventional intimacy that there can be only a momentary arc, a flash, of synaptic connection. Surrounded by the most crass, market driven of settings, where even now the police might raid at any moment, exposing all present to ridicule or ruin, we are offered the possibility of losing ourselves in raptured contemplation of the sublime.

By the sublime I don't mean the merely beautiful, although of course only the most conventionally beautiful men are chosen to dance atop the bar. Unlike the figures on a Grecian urn, these men are not preserved in timeless eternity. They are momentary. They will be replaced. The hardness of their bodies will soften; their market strength will sag. They may, in only a few years, compete with their current customers for space on the very same barstools. That is the dark terror that resides within the contemplation of such vital, gorgeous young bodies, and it is key to the rapture that sometimes unites the watcher and the watched.

Watching them, watching Sean, watching myself inside the flesh temple that is La Cage, I realized, too, that we were worshiping in a peculiarly American place. American not because it is a sex bar. Sex bars litter the world. What makes this dive in the shadow of the Capitol so American is the transcendent expectations its customers have brought to it: the expectation of a momentary release from the shame Americans feel about pleasure; the common assertion that a sex bar is a "community institution"; the search for a self-revelation—a true if hidden identity—in the rapt adoration between dancer and fondler. Here, by night, a "true identity" can show its face and know its name and feel, for a moment, a connection with a spirit that is greater than self, that looks back to the myth of the reborn American in a new-made world, that finds in the dear love of comrades the visceral touch of God.

I. Intimations of the Sublime

As I grew up, my own early spiritual sensibilities were at best a fuzzy-focused pantheism expressed in the color, taste, texture, and grandeur of the oak trees, tobacco plants, and autumn apples we harvested each year for our living in Kentucky. My father shielded us from the local organized churchery and itinerant preachers who peddled Bibles up and down the highway. He was not antireligious, but he found more hate than love in their fire-and-brimstone oratory. And so, aside from a few months when I accompanied neighbors to their church and learned the tunes and lyrics to the basic gospel hymns, I was, and would still be considered, a heathen.

Despite the obvious evil that has been committed in the name of religion, especially of the Judeo-Christian-Islamic variety, I have never felt hostile to the religious impulse. Perhaps perversely, I have even felt sympathetic toward the ecstatic Christians, for I suspect that their obsession with the uses of the flesh constitutes a tacit admission of the fundamental connectedness of flesh to spirit (NB the scandals of Jim Bakker and Jimmy Swaggart, the ongoing reenactments of Elmer Gantry, the operatic tale of Susannah)—just as I suspect that many of my secular, straight liberal colleagues would neutralize all mystery about sex and spirit by relegating it to the realm of passionless hormonal chemistry. The first step to spirituality comes in contemplating the mystery, not in resolving it.

The matter of mystery in ordinary life recurs frequently in talks with my partner, Gene. Some summers ago he began putting out a garden in his long, narrow Brooklyn backyard. He starts, as many city people do, in February. He pours over seed catalogs, looking for exotic flowers and gorgeous vegetables. He awaits the arrival of the crocuses in March, then watches to see how long it will take the squirrel (who has spent January and February scavenging bird seed) to gobble up their blue and yellow petals.

Unlike many Park Slope yuppies, Gene doesn't put out his garden in order to have his own fresh, organic vegetables. For the dinner table he's generally happy with Pathmark's produce section. Gene's garden is sacramental. It is, to him, a mystery that the Park catalog packets of rattling grit that arrive just before the crocuses bloom should be transformed, by his hand, into promiscuous zucchini, curly lettuce leaves, and goofy cosmos by August. When, during the first winter I lived with him, his first seedbeds failed to germinate, his faith in the process seemed shaken, as though his own life and health were somehow put in jeopardy by his failure to germinate new plants.

"There's nothing very mysterious about it," I would say. "You overwatered the seedbeds, just like I told you you were. Seeds probably rotted."

I had been planting or helping plant gardens in our heavy, yellow Kentucky clay since I was seven years old. You wait until warm weather, till the ground, cut a row, drop the seeds, cover them up, and hope for rain. Usually by July or August you get plenty of squash and limas and pole beans, tomatoes and corn, cabbage and cucumbers. We never had magnificent gardens, but we generally had plenty of fresh things to eat. The notion of starting in February with tiny seeds carefully sown in high-priced potting soil would have struck us as so much silliness. Gardens were work, not mystery.

Of course, the most compelling mysteries are the most quotidian, the ones we accept sunrise to sunset as articles of faith. If we continue our ordinary work successfully all day long, we call it technique. And technique can be learned. But to those who look on the crinkled lettuce leaf as evidence of grace and coherence in this world, the technique is itself infused with grace. The beauty is not merely the leaf but the orchestration of acts and observations and new acts that have caused the leaf to rise there, covered with the sweat of morning dew, safe from the decaying slug that was salted to death the night before.

Like Sean, Gene responds to the rhythms of nature, rhythms that can reveal the force of the sublime just as fully as the destruction of earthquakes and floods. Their reflections have also drawn me to reflect on the actual "religion" of my early life, where acres of barren, winter orchard turned out thousands of tons of apples. The apples themselves were not altogether free of religious taint. Not only were they the Christians' forbidden fruit, but we also sold them in violation of Christian law. As with most orchards, our biggest sale day was Sunday. We earned most of our year's income on a dozen Sunday afternoons of autumn as people drove up onto the mountaintop from miles around to buy them—except for the preachers, who would choose them on Sunday and pay for them on Monday.

At the time I took the preachers' actions as plain evidence of religious hypocrisy. In retrospect—now that all the blue laws have disappeared and the supermarkets are busy on Sunday—I suppose they were preserving the ritual rest of the Sabbath. If they could persuade themselves that they were not transacting business on Sunday, then most likely they could experience it as the easy, relaxing autumn outing it also was. To come to the orchard along with hundreds of friends and neighbors was to enjoy a picnic of the senses and to appreciate God's or nature's multiple bounties and beauties. To a degree, and though it provided our family livelihood, the collection and presentation of the harvest was a seasonal vespers, a marking of the inevitable closing of the growing season and preparation for the dark months. Unlike all the other fruits, the apples these country people bought would last them through the winter until the sun returned.

That sense of persistent continuity, linked to the marriage of sun and earth, expressed in the fecund, drenching beauty of spring bloom and the terrible wrath of hailstorms and earth-cracking drought, remains my fundamental liturgy. It is not nature as a placid, benevolent, or curative force. The ecology of creatures that live in the fields and the orchard is brutal and rapacious, a predatory dance of fruit and leaf and insect and fungus. There are no pacifists in the natural liturgy. Nor is there denial of concupiscent appetite. To contemplate it fully is to enter the territory of the sublime.

The sublime moment, as the Romantic poets recorded it, is the moment in which we see ourselves at one with the awesome, majestic, and ultimately unknowable power that drives the exquisite beauty of nature. Unlike prayer to the personified Christian deity, the sublime blinds us with the fact of our humble inseparability from that force; it reminds us that we are neither more nor less than any other organisms in an infinite food chain busily eating itself to death—descendants of amoebas, waste of viruses. Yet paradox of paradoxes, the same sublime comprehension that so reduces us can also release us into an ecstatic joy for our inclusion in the infinite. In the territory of the sublime, terror guards beauty, just as it did for the poet Shelley, who, when gazing in awe at the face of Mont Blanc, wrote that he was consumed with "an undisciplined overflowing of the soul" and dwarfed by "untamable wildness and inaccessible solemnity."

Even that crotchety schoolmarm of eighteenth-century German philosophers, Immanuel Kant, was not immune to the lure of the sublime. The experience of the sublime, he wrote, is "brought about by the feeling of a momentary check to the vital forces followed at once by a discharge all the more powerful, and so it is an emotion that seems to be no sport, but a dead earnest affair of the imagination." We are hit, as we experience the sublime, by a shattering recognition of a presence vastly greater and more powerful than ourselves, a presence that takes all that we have conceived in our minds, that consumes our minds and presses us beyond what our minds can contain. We are left in the infinite, which our finite faculties cannot order.

Kant considered how we experience the churning sea in a storm: "The broad ocean agitated by storms cannot be called sublime. Its aspect is horrible, and one must have stored one's mind in advance with a rich stock of ideas, if such an intuition is to raise it to the pitch of a feeling which is itself sublime—sublime because the mind has been incited *to go beyond the senses* [emphasis mine], and employ itself upon ideas involving higher ends." The horror of the tempest is not itself sublime: first comes the jolt of terror at our incapacity to order the boundless beauty and savagery displayed in nature; but we can only touch it and render ourselves sublime when we return to the security of intellect witnessing the tempest, erecting in our minds a method of comprehending a sensual experience that overcomes our senses, generating the metaphors that transport us beyond the finite limits of the fragile flesh. We are like the anxious airline passenger at takeoff who stares down the terror of his imminent destruction and instantly senses the lift of the air rushing over the plane's wings as though he were himself in flight. We comprehend ourselves as being simultaneously out of and at one with time.

To feel the force of the sublime—perhaps Christians would say to feel the force of God or the Holy Spirit—in observed nature is a commonplace experience. Our poets and painters have left us a clear and easily read legacy. When that is not enough, there are always earthquakes, monumental floods, and volcanic eruption, chromatically packaged and pumped onto our videoscreens. We feel dwarfed, or at least we witness those who were dwarfed by it.

Recognition of the sublime is an act of the spirit: though it requires that we fall back on reason, on intellect, to avoid drowning in nihilistic despair, the communication of the sublime is spiritual. It is a common way of knowing that is beyond the adequacy of words, as the words of the finest poem are only vectoring approximations—metaphors—for the poetry that resides inside and just beyond the poem's words. To those of us raised without formal religion, or for those of us who have rejected institutional religion, this common witnessing of the sublime opens up the possibility of a spiritual zone. That spiritual insight, however, requires neither an altar nor an earthquake.

To look only outward, toward natural disasters or the regeneration of gardens and the annual fruiting of orchards, feels incomplete. It is finally the queer body, my queer body, that has led me to experience the sublime within myself.

When finally as a young man I began to figure out what sort of sex my body wanted, I was fortunately free of the usual internal taboos that the church and synagogue system had stamped into most people I knew. I had no trace of moral abhorrence at the prospect of men mating with one another. But I could not, until much later, integrate the morally neutral fact of same-sex desire with the apparent biological imperative of complementarity between the sexes. Whether expressed in the Eastern terms of yin and yang or the hormonal distributions of estrogen and testosterone, the natural world seemed to revolve around the interrelation of sexual opposites. The same-sex erotic option seemed to represent a refusal to engage in the most integral dance of life, the will to regenerate, nurture, and continue the species. Fundamentalist Protestants and Jews, as well as doctrinaire Catholics, of course, make a similar argument, asserting that Old Testament prohibitions are a reflection of nature's (and thereby God's) laws.

The mystery that eluded me—and which the Christians refused to acknowledge at all—was how our animal natures consistently produced homosexual eroticism, generation after generation, millennium after millennium, throughout the range of species. Not that I saw abstinence as an answer; I actively pursued erotic, homosexual adventures. It was the realization of unity between my flesh and spirit that eluded me.

An event in the summer of 1988 brought me closer toward resolving the impasse.

I had taken the summer off from my NPR work and was living in Oakland, California. Gay San Francisco was just beginning to emerge from the darkest terror of AIDS—a generally unstated fear that everyone would be wiped out. The passionate, sexy resurgence of "queer" activism hadn't yet arrived, but a rebellious militance around AIDS had displaced the defensive despair of the mid-eighties. There was an air in the streets redolent of late-sixties exuberance, but better than the sixties, when my own sense of sexual displacement had seemed inadmissibly frivolous, we as queer people were at the center of a national cultural battle with life-and-death consequences. AIDS had moved the gay discourse from the sentimental to the sublime. For the first time (and arguably very belatedly) I had begun to figure out how to apply twenty years of professional technique to the examination of my own existential condition. And I was in my tenth month of chronic, painful muscle spasm in the lower back.

The original pain and muscle seizure had happened one afternoon the previous November as I sat down at my desk inside the Washington NPR office. Moments earlier I'd been in a yelling match with a colleague I liked and respected. It was one of a seemingly endless series of pointless, bureaucratic battles and power struggles that had become commonplace and that led many fine staff members to quit, or at least to depart the home office for foreign assignments on the opposite side of the globe. I had come to the Bay Area both to exit the company's stifling atmosphere and to confront the gay story I had so long avoided. But the pain persisted. Chiropractic, acupuncture, diet modification, Alexander technique, better posture, and regular exercise had not released the clenched muscles that lashed the lower vertebrae in place.

Then one evening the pain dissolved and disappeared as though by magic. The curative technique was absurdly simple: I allowed myself to be penetrated by a man who, for a variety of reasons (including the fact that he wore multiple layers of condoms), I judged to be safe. The act took place at seven in the evening. My near yearlong muscle spasm was gone by midnight.

When eventually I told my secular, materialist friends how my tense, compacted muscles had responded after taking this man into my body, they would say simply, "What a marvelous technique! I'll ask my chiropractor about it." Few, however, saw any "spiritual" meaning to what had happened. They preferred a straightforward neurokinesiological explanation: the sex felt good, the other man's hips and penis probably stimulated new muscle groups, and therefore I had been able to relax my back more effectively.

Missing from the neurophysiological explanation, however, is something we all know about back pain: in many, if not most, cases it is symptomatic of profound psychic stress. In my case, much of that stress reflected standard midlife aspirations and obligations. However, to an equal if not greater degree, the power of the AIDS epidemic had been pressing steadily closer. During the previous October, shortly before the muscle seizure, the AIDS quilt had come to

Washington and filled the Ellipse behind the White House. At the network, none of the editors considered it worthy of a story until some of the gay staff convinced a weekend show host to do her own essay. Nor did I feel capable of producing my own story: my own losses, though they were still few, felt too personal, too precious, to be converted into journalism. And yet by failing to merge my personal concerns into my craft, I felt even more surrounded by the bleak horror of the epidemic, more guilty for not bringing this collective gay story forward in my own gay voice.

The relentlessness of the epidemic had equally powerful effects on sex itself. Sex had become wrapped in disease. Penetrative sex had become both metaphor and method for death's invasion of our lives. Many men I met that summer told me that since the advent of AIDS they had tightened down all their sexual contact. No matter how much they had loved to be fucked, they could no longer imagine such sensual release of their bodies. Actual intercourse had disappeared from the screen of conscious consideration.

For five years I had not had receptive intercourse. As I lay there, looking upward at the man who was about to enter me, examining all the calculations I had made of who he might be, at who I thought I was, at the weight the act would carry for both of us, I felt the unbearable jolt of our presence. Like Shelley gazing upon the face of Mont Blanc, I had been propelled by the act into a sublime and timeless moment "where silence and solitude were vacancy."

For most males raised in the Judeo-Christian tradition, the initial experience of being penetrated is profoundly disordering. It is a challenge to one of the most fundamental principles by which we have been taught to know ourselves as masculine. But then to dress penetration in the terrifying imagery of the body's own rot and decay, precipitated by the particular penetration of an unseeable virus, opens us to the possibility of touching all the unknowable terrors and beauties of nature.

Unlike the work of any other microbes we know, the attack of HIV on our immune systems reveals, in reverse, the technique by which we remain alive. Its genius is that *it* does not kill us; instead it builds a theater of our own flesh, from which we watch as participant-observers the spectacle of dying, the chemical, electrical,

and physical disconnections that offer us up to our countless preda-
tors in the food chain. In AIDS we experience ourselves being eaten
by the force of nature. As the ordering of cells that gives us life
degenerates into the disordered material of our prey, we find ourselves revealed as merely exquisite pigments in a palette whose shape
we cannot see. At best we are witnesses to our own oxidation, neither good nor bad, moral nor immoral. Denied the capacity to order our experience or know our fate, we have only one choice: to
witness or not, to be penetrated by the experiential wave washing
over us or to stand aside, blind, dumb, and untouched.

II. Civic Spirit

As surely as this epidemic has brought us to the eye of nature's God,
it has also surrounded us with a public spirituality that contains the
sublime. I cannot think of that act of physical penetration in the
summer of 1988 independent of that broader collective experience,
which resulted in what I now see as a second "coming out."

I had been open about my sexuality for many years, with friends,
with family, and with colleagues. I had occasionally reported for
NPR about gay and AIDS matters. But my "sexual identity" had re-
mained incidental to my work and to most of my social life—as it
was for most journalists and political people I knew in Washington.
Once I began to integrate those identities, I inevitably became more
than a witness.

Like thousands of others, I found that I had entered into a bargain
of faith. Unable any longer to insulate craft and technique from the
material of our own lives, we propelled ourselves into a double dialogue, using our skills as writer-journalists to interrogate our lives,
looking into the intimacies of our lives to interrogate the quality
and shape of our work. We initiated the painful, tedious process of
acknowledging that as professional observers we cannot be separated from our duties as human beings. We are human observers
both of ourselves and of the world by which we are surrounded.

By observing (and coming out is a public self-observance) the
queerness of ourselves, we inevitably change how and what we observe in the world as well. Those things we cause ourselves to see—

love, bigotry, deceit, courage, chicanery—change because the way we see and hear has changed. The distanced language of heterosexual convention that we once employed to separate our observer selves from everything queer becomes unusable and is replaced by terms of ordinary intimacies. Adjectives of the exotic become nouns of a new normalcy. We learn to drop medico-criminological terms like *homosexual lover* or *avowed homosexual* or even coy but obtuse phrases like *longtime companion*—all of them flags to "straight" readers that something strange is coming.

Why presume, after all, that readers are straight, or incapable of understanding direct description? We grow gradually comfortable integrating the language of ordinary life—*boyfriend, girlfriend, partner, lover,* or even camp usage like *girlfriend!* for buddy—into the common narratives of storytelling. The consequences of those linguistic acts are, in the most precise sense of the word, *spiritual:* as we alter the spirit with which we see and present ourselves to the world, we alter the spirit with which others observe us, and that in turn alters how we see them. It is like mastering a second language that gives us ideas and insights that do not exist in our first language, or the physical triumph of training our bodies to undertake a perfect catch, a graceful dive, or a powerful throw. Not only have we learned something new, but we have also changed ourselves in such a way that we are no longer quite the same persons we were before. The moment in which we recognize that we are changed, that we can no longer stand outside ourselves, is the moment in which we acknowledge ourselves as *inside* a transforming common spirit that we cannot control, any more than we can hold back the force of a rolling ocean wave. At that moment we arrive at a sublime comprehension surely as powerful as Kant's tempest or the face of Shelley's mountain: we can no longer retreat into the alienated, internally divided selves of our pasts.

The act of observing ourselves in the world we are observing constitutes more than simple self-consciousness—for in the end any outsider's dream is about losing self-consciousness, losing the "otherness" that makes us feel like a class of perpetual outsiders. It is a dialectical process with ontological implications. It is not a single act. We cannot will it to be so. The words that we speak to present ourselves do not settle who we are so much as they raise questions about who we are becoming: closeted last year, "bisexual" last month, gay today, queer next year, fabulous forever. Otherness cannot be absolute, because the normalcy itself—white, American, male, straight—is ever more in flux. And once we have embarked upon the journey, once we have seized the words of "ordinary people" to tell the stories of queer people, we have marked ourselves as the subverters of normalcy and we cannot regress to who we have once been.

That realization became clear to me not while I was covering AIDS but in the aftermath of the 1989 earthquake in San Francisco. I had arrived about eight-thirty on the day after the quake as part of the NPR coverage team. The city was blanketed in darkness. No streetlights burned. No traffic signals flashed. Hotel porters held candles at their doors. Traffic, what there was, inched into and through each intersection. Atop Twin Peaks I found a handful of people, most of them strangers to one another, gathered beside lanterns and campfires, reading stories from Dashiell Hammett, Frank Norris, and Jack London. Their emotions were raw and tender, and they sought to draw the spirit of their city into their skins by reading aloud the words of its most cherished writers.

I drove down the hill, through the Castro district, along Market Street toward the barely silhouetted Ferry Building, its flagpole toppled into the dome. I turned onto Franklin Street and stopped for a moment. Two bearded men sat on a motorcycle across the way in an empty lot. They had their helmets off. They held their legs astride the seat to hold the cycle upright. The driver let his head fall forward, as behind him his buddy rubbed his palms deep into the driver's neck and shoulders.

I filed a piece the next day on the mood of the city, shaped around those two scenes. The report won praise from colleagues and listeners. But from the managing editor, who posted daily comments about the news programs, came a mixed reaction. Nice mood piece, he remarked, "but," he went on, he thought the "gay" bit at the end was unnecessary. Nowhere in the piece had I described anyone as gay or homosexual, though it was a reasonable inference about the men on the cycle. Besides, I wondered, in a city where gay men make up 10 to 15 percent of the population, why should it be startling to incorporate a gay tableau into the story?

Only some years later did I realize that what was most disturbing about my report was its lack of labeling, its failure to hang a "gay" sign around the bike riders, to warn the listeners, to remind them that, well, yes, "these people," too, are part of San Francisco. By simply showing the intimacy between two men in ordinary descriptive language, contextualized not by sex or by AIDS but by the stresses of common catastrophe, I had normalized these men. I had made their touch, their pain, equivalent to the touch of a mother and her daughter or a sister and her brother, or a man and his wife. Still worse for a "mainstream journalist," I had failed to mark off distance between me the reporter (the representative of the presumably straight listener) and the exotic, disturbing queers on the bike. I had, in the eyes of the managing editor, crossed a line, after which I could no longer be trusted to see and describe the "ordinary world" as "normal people" would. By presenting queers as normal people, I had become abnormal, queer, and at the deepest level unreliable. In time, I have come to see that his never fully articulated judgment was correct: my reportorial eyesight had developed a queer refraction, and that queer refraction was emblematic of an internal transformation of spirit.

Such transformations of spirit, of course, are not restricted to writers and journalists. The experience of collectively witnessing that which before had been unspoken, that is, telling the stories of lives free from conventional demonization and disguise, alters both our lives and our subjects' lives. We do become collectively "reborn." Still more importantly, the incipiently queer individuals coming of age today are qualitatively, developmentally, and existentially different from those of us who were coming of age twenty-five years ago. The "coming out" experiences of today's adolescents, surrounded by a rich literature of queerness, is not comparable to the experiences of my generation "coming out" at age thirty after years of denial during which most available "homosexual" literature was either pornography or abnormal psychology. In the act of crafting a collective story, we have brought into being a public spirit, which, willy-nilly, has irrevocably reshaped who we are and how we comprehend our place in nature and in society. That public spirit, I suspect, is peculiarly American.

III. AMERICAN RELIGION, GAY IDENTITY

Whenever I encounter queer people from other lands—Brazil, Italy, northern Europe, especially East Asia—I almost always find a fascinated amusement with the communitarian spirituality of the American gay movement. They are not startled to find a spiritual element in homosexuality: the notion of special powers being linked to a body with special capacities, of Neapolitan *femminielli,* of Zuni berdache, of Indian *hijras,* of Condomble spiritual leaders in Brazil, is nearly universal. What surprises them is how American gay activism has cast a spiritual, often almost religious, character over what is essentially a *civic* movement for human rights. "How is it," one of my Italian friends asked me, "that a country premised on the separation of politics from religion should build a movement for sexual freedom that is so full of spiritual overtones? You talk about coming out like your preachers talk of being born again."

Village Voice writer Richard Goldstein addressed that question several years ago in an essay he called "Faith, Hope and Sodomy." Recounting the last century's treatment of homosexuality as first a crime, then a psychosis, then a politics, Goldstein argued that it was precisely America's peculiar history of politics and religion that has shaped the gay project: "What sprouted at Reading Gaol, from the depths of Oscar Wilde's despair, has taken root in the American dream. A condition has become a community: a movement is becoming a faith." Goldstein's musings drew heavily on Harold Bloom's remarkable book *The American Religion.* Like many students of American culture, Bloom reminds us how profoundly American life continues to be shaped by our religious origins, how suffused in religion we are even in our most secular concerns. "Freedom," he writes, "in the context of the American Religion, means being alone with God or with Jesus, the American God or the American Christ. In social reality, this translates as solitude, at least in the inmost sense. The soul stands apart, and something deeper than the soul, the Real Me or self or spark, thus is made free to be utterly alone with a God who is also quite separate and solitary, that is, a free God or God of freedom."

Nearly four centuries after the pastoral utopians settled in Virginia and the Protestant radicals dropped anchor off Provincetown, our most fundamental understanding of personal freedom and common spiritual being still echoes our ancestors' project. The sermons and debates that launched the American errand in the wilderness recur, altered and in new language in today's critical debates: in our search for a proper relation to the environment, in our struggles over property rights versus public welfare, in our anxieties over a stagnated national vision and moral renewal. Our sense of sexuality and identity is no less weathered by that past; indeed, I think, the very notion of a "sexual identity" owes much to the peculiar notion of American identity itself, an identity that arose from our first and most radically utopian enterprise among the Puritans of the Massachusetts Bay Colony.

Puritans, for most of us, have become a pejorative metaphor for the loathing of pleasure. The metaphor is apt. The Massachusetts Puritans abhorred the worldly body as an evil thing, "a varnisht pot of putrid excrement," in the words of the famed colonial poet and missionary Edward Taylor. To ridicule the Puritans as grim prudes alone, however, is to miss their importance for America as a nation and for Americans as individuals—hetero, homo, or otherwise. The central contest in the American psyche then and now, the Puritans well understood, is between individual and community—in ecclesiastical terms, between the *exemplum fidei* and the *sola fides:* to see each person, each soul, as the individual expression or example of the godly community (the community of saints) even though each individual's experience of God was absolutely internal unto herself. Socially and politically, the Puritans were a repressively communitarian people, even communistic in their insistance that individual ambitions and prerogatives must be subjected to the values of community welfare. Yet the communitarian dream was continually shaken. Since the true church was to be found not in a building administered by a hierarchy but within the spiritual communion of saints touched by God, the potential for individual heresy was constant. Innumerable crises and heresies did break out as the Puritans went about constructing a New Jerusalem of the New World. Most centered on the individual's capacity for direct experience of God, his ability to make personal spiritual communion and to find redemption (what we might call wholeness) within that communion—a belief that the Calvinist insistence on predestined election strictly precluded.

The idea of the New World has become such a commonplace to us from our elementary school history books, we forget how potent, how radical, a notion it was. This New World was not merely a new geography where the Pilgrims could be free from "religious persecution." As historian Sacvan Bercovitch writes, the New World was *providential*. The existence of a New World was demonstrable evidence of "God's overarching, inviolable plan" in which every individual, every community, every event, occupied its own place "within the scheme of salvation." Man in the New World—and it was always *man*—was both the guardian of God's handiwork and the reflection of Christ's will. He and His kingdom were one. There could be no separation of self from the noble experiment, from the mission of God. If the pioneer's fortune fell, it was because he had separated himself from God's mission, and he had to be "reawakened" to reclaim his mission. If John Winthrop's "citty on a hill" declined, it was because "the citty"—the community—had lost its unity with the redemptive mission. Each new mission, each new utopian expansion and rebirth, religious or secular, became an exercise in the recovery of that singular idea of self and mission. That idea, deeply buried in the bedrock of our national myth, cycles over and over through our cultural, historical, and spiritual lives without respect to ideology or ethnicity.

Self and common destiny came to be interlocked for the emerging Americans in ways their European cousins could not conceive. Across the Atlantic, French, Spanish, and British rulers had only begun to define their own ideas of nationalism in rivalries over territory and in internal conflicts among monarchs, nobles, and traders. The ordinary subjects of the kingdom could hardly see themselves as a people united in a transcendent vision that would enable them to divine their common future according to the laws of providence. The king—and if not their king, another country's king—was the final authority against whom one carved out a space of freedom. God and the crown were all-powerful forces outside the individual's personal life. They were forces to be feared and revered, forces from which a stableman or a shopkeeper or a noble might win redemption.

Yet finally in neither the Protestant nor the Catholic cosmology did most humans see themselves as possessing God. Certainly they did not see themselves as manifest evidence of God's mission. At best they were foot soldiers in battles beyond their understanding, and they had learned well that the churches were firmly aligned with the competing political powers. Only radicals—Enthusiasts, Levelers, Diggers, mystics who claimed guidance from an "inner light"— dared to find God inside themselves. The notion of finding God inside yourself, of actually being a part of God, was breathtakingly dangerous to church and crown alike. Such people were heretics— as much to the Puritan radicals in the New World as to the entrenched authorities of the Old World.

If the Puritans succeeded in suppressing the "inner light" heretics on theological grounds, however, they still were captive of the Calvinist commitment to individual enterprise. Possessed by the certainty that America was God's kingdom, they came to see it as their duty to exploit the kingdom and make it fruitful, for in its fruitfulness was the evidence of its godliness. Successful personal enterprise was a sign of God's providence. Lacking the restrictive power of the crown or of a universal church, and confronted with the boundless opportunity of the frontier, the young Americans were let loose to construct the freest, most rugged commercial markets in the world. By the time the Revolution had succeeded, and the Lockean ideas of a secular state had helped bring about a government divorced from any single religion, the Puritan vision of an ecclesiastical America had lost out to the deeper force of individualism that lay at its core.

"Commerce, commerce, commerce!" exclaimed a prominent European traveler as he sent back reports of the young American republic in the 1820s. A century earlier the great revivalist preacher Jonathan Edwards had written in *Images or Shadows of Divine Things:*

"The changing of the course of trade, and the supplying of the world with its treasures from America is a type and forerunner of what is approaching in spiritual things, when the world shall be supplied with spiritual treasures from America." Independent and prosperous, the New Americans understood well that the source of their treasure was nothing less than nature herself. Prosperity linked them to the resources of resplendent nature. Both stewards and exploiters of the godly kingdom, the New Americans were more still: they were of this boundless natural frontier. As it flourished, they flourished. Its destiny was their destiny. As they were of God, so was it. There sprang, in Sacvan Bercovitch's phrase, "the myth of America," giving birth to an American Adam in spiritual unity with the place of his making. Even, finally, for those who were not properly Christians, the unity of God, man, and nature had become inseparable. Or as Emerson, the greatest of our nineteenth-century philosophers, saw it, "The continent we inhabit is to be physic and food for our mind as well as our body. . . . The Genius or Destiny of America is . . . a man incessantly advancing, as the shadow on the dial's face, or the heavenly body by whose light it is marked. . . . Let us realize that this country, the last found, is the great charity of God to the human race."

Emerson, the transcendentalist, saw in the secular transformation of the Puritan project a rebirth of human possibility that exceeded the strictures of Christianity or politics. The American Adam, what he called "the young American," would regenerate the whole of mankind, become "the home of man" where "new love, new faith, new sight shall restore [creation] to more than its first splendor." Out of the Puritan mission had emerged the fundamental faith that remains with us today: self-reliance.

There in that essential regeneration of the world is what Harold Bloom calls the true "American Religion"—the religion of gnosticism, at once experiential and absolutely internal, inside each individual, containing God and contained by God. Bloom, too, turns to Emerson and his famous Harvard "Divinity School Address" and his vision of Christ as the "one man [who] was true to what is in you and me. He saw that God incarnates himself in man, and evermore goes forth anew to take possession of his World." In the American Religion, God does not create man, Bloom argues, because we are older than creation; we are God in that God inhabits our truest spiritual reality. The act of making America, therefore, is and has been an act of spiritual imagination whereby we save ourselves *and* the world—at least all that world that would join us in realizing our rebirth. To realize the rebirth as a personal rebirth of the God within us is the essence of the *American* journey, or as Bloom puts it, "*Awareness,* centered on the self, is *faith* for an American." Bloom traces the rise of what he calls the ecstatic, gnostic religion throughout the nineteenth century in the triumph of the born-again Southern Baptists, the Mormons, the Seventh-Day Adventists, African-American Pentecostalists—all of whom in different ways experience God directly within themselves. To quote the gospel lyrics, "He walks with me and He talks with me, and He tells me I am His own."

The whole of Christianity, of course, is dedicated to a theology of personal salvation. What Bloom points out is the American genius for finding the divine within the realization of personal identity. The Puritans, the Calvinists, the genuine Presbyterians or Methodists, the Catholics, could never honestly reduce God to the expression of essential personal identity: but that is exactly what happened to my Kentucky neighbors when finally, during campground revivals, they were "saved" and declared themselves "born again." They experienced a euphoric, ecstatic communion with God in which was revealed their innermost self, a self that could not be seen by the unsaved, a "little me" inside the "big me" in African-American parlance, that led them to know that they had been saved and had joined the kingdom of God. In their salvation lay all salvation; the surviving dictum of the American vision is universal redemption: a reborn America will bring about the rebirth of all humankind.

That was—and remains—the essential errand in the wilderness: a New Jerusalem that will be a light unto the darkened world. To make that reborn self real was no less than to realize, to *become aware* of, the identity of the newly reborn soul. Unlike the conventional Christians, Bloom notes, the American Religionist *experiences* awareness directly—in trances, in tongues, in dances, in visions. The body, however denigrated it may be in sermon, is present at the emergence:

> The American finds God in herself or himself, but only after finding the freedom to know God by experiencing a total inward solitude. Freedom, in a very special sense, is the preparation without which God will not allow himself to be revealed in the self. And this freedom is in itself double; the spark or spirit must know itself to be free both of other selves and of the created world. In perfect solitude, the American spirit learns again its absolute isolation as a spark of God floating in a sea of space. . . . Salvation, for the American, cannot come through the community or the congregation, but is a one-on-one act of confrontation.

Change the words *American* to *gay man* and *God* to *sexual identity.* Only when he has permitted himself the freedom to see and experience his sexual identity free of the identities foisted upon him by the world will the gay man's true identity be revealed to him. Then he will understand his innermost being, his identity, as an emanation of the force of nature (love [God]) that permeates the universe. I use *gay man* consciously here because the ecstatic revelatory language of "coming out" seems so overwhelmingly male in the American experience. While the great majority of contemporary lesbian writers and activists speak of the importance of being "out," women's coming-out stories seldom seem to carry that explosive, almost evangelical power that marks the declarations of American gay men. From porno stories to high polemics the parallels in language and emotion between stories of coming out and being born again are so stunning as to be unmistakable.

One of the plainest, most powerful, most poignantly spiritual coming-out stories I have ever heard is recorded by Steven Zeeland, who for many years has been interviewing soldiers, sailors, and Marines about their same-sex experiences. Alex was a twenty-one-year-old Marine corporal, half-German, half–Native American, from northern Wisconsin. He was at Camp Pendleton, California.

Alex told Zeeland that he was attracted to women and started having sex with women at age nineteen, but he generally felt empty and degraded by the experience.

> **Alex:** My sexuality awakened pretty late. There were sexual desires, but that was always limited just to dreams, or very brief daydreams or fantasies.
> **Zeeland:** What were they like?
> **Alex:** [Pause] Earlier, it was—it was just me having sex with a hole. Just a hole. A human hole, but . . . it didn't have any gender. . . . They were just sex. Dry; no intimacy, no caring. Then there was coming, and that was it.

Later during Marine boot camp, Alex's fantasies turned toward older, very masculine men, but still he had no sex with men. At Camp Pendleton he developed a deep attachment to a fellow Marine, a buddy who shipped out to Somalia in 1992.

> **Alex:** I knew that I would have laid down my life for him. I was pretty sure that he would have done the same for me. We'd confide in each other. And when he went to Somalia, part of me—it was the closest thing I've ever felt to somebody like a lover, or mate, leaving. I was pretty tore up, because he was going off somewhere and there were people already getting killed. I volunteered, but my gunny said that I couldn't go because I was too important to be sent away.
> **Zeeland:** Did you have any further experiences with women?
> **Alex:** During that time? Yeah. . . . There's only one word to describe them. Bad. There were three or four instances, and each one was just as bad as the first time I had it. . . . I do still sleep with women, sometimes. And I've refined that now, to where it's on a personal basis. I sleep with women if they're nice. And it's actually nice to sleep with women, too, because they're a lot more feminine . . . But it still doesn't compare to sex with other men.
> I came out in May of '93. I was in an adult bookstore down-

151

town. I had never been in one before. They had all these girlie magazines, and I was looking through them. And then I noticed one next to it that was a gay magazine. I picked it up and went around to the other side, where you could see everybody that was coming in. There weren't that many people in the store. I started reading it, and my blood started rushing to my head. I started getting very sexually aroused. I had never felt such a rush of anything before. I bought a magazine that was wrapped in plastic; on the cover it had a big guy with boots on a forklift. I also grabbed a copy of [a local gay newspaper], too.

On the way back I was starting to think of what I actually did, that I had got a gay magazine, and I started punishing myself or whatever. How could I ever expect to be normal if I was to read things like this? I saw it sitting next to me, and it was inciting me to think even worse thoughts about me. And then something inside of me kind of stood up, and I started saying to myself, "This is me!"

Soon this voice in me became overpowering, and I just started feeling happy about myself, happy to just be me. I was laughing and yelling in the car, "I'm gay! I'm gay! I'm gay!"

I was euphoric. I suppose people going by—well, people do weirder things in cars, but I didn't care what other people thought. That was my gay . . . release. I knew that I was gay and I was going to be happy that I was gay because I had desired to have sex with males more than with females. I would say that that was the happiest moment in my life.

Like Bloom's gnostic Christians who fill up Baptist churches all over the South, Alex experienced an ecstatic conversion, an awakening that filled him with joy. His awakening, like that of the evangelicals, was not precisely about redemption. It was more like the Good News that comes of looking into your heart and finding Jesus' truth, that He is Love and He is ever present. The American Jesus, Bloom writes, is an agent of salvation insofar as he is the revealer of truth; He is "not so much an event in history for the American Religionist as he is a knower of the secrets of God who in return can be known by the individual. Hidden in this process is a sense that depravity is only a lack of saving knowledge. Salvation through know-ing the knowing Jesus, is a reversal wholly experiential in nature, an internalization of a self already internalized."

Being born again and coming out are ultimately acts of solitude that require public declaration. At its vital moment, each is a totally internal experience of awareness, later amplified and made commu-nal by sharing the good news with those others who have had the same experience and know within themselves how the truth has saved them. Each is a linkage of sublime awareness and spiritual union with others. Spiritual union, however, remains the required second step to awareness, as much for the newly out gay man as for the saved evangelical as for Emerson's young American who through "new love, new faith, new sight" would restore the world to "its first splendor." Evangelicals render their gnostic truth as preach-ings; gay activists render the revelations of identity into polemical manifestos. At the polemical level, nothing exceeds Michelangelo Signorile's "Queer Manifesto" in *Queer in America:*

> Everyone must come out of the closet, no matter how difficult, no matter how painful.
> We must tell our parents.
> We must tell our families.
> We must tell our friends.
> We must tell our coworkers. . . .
> Badger everyone you know who is closeted—your friends, your family members, your coworkers—to come out. Put pres-sure on those in power whom you know to be queer. Send them letters. Call them on the phone. Fax them. Confront them in the streets.
> Tell them they have a responsibility: to themselves, to you, to humanity.
> Tell them they have to face the truth. And tell the truth yourself.

No Mormon missionary, no Jehovah's Witness, no Southern Bap-tist preacher could speak more clearly, more passionately, about spreading "the Good News" of Jesus' personal salvation for all those who will be saved and born again. About sexuality, homosexuality, there is only one truth, and we must tell it, all together, and to each other, until no one is left who knows it and has not revealed it and been made free by it. As a strategy of spiritual politics, Signorile's manifesto is mint American: it is the same strategy the Mormons and the Witnesses and the Baptists have employed for nearly two hundred years in their bids to link collective personal identity with self-revealed spiritual truth. It works because it inspires us, and it inspires us because it touches a chord deep within our national myth regardless of our attachment to any formal religion: we can be free only when we have spoken to and confessed our identity with our one true and hidden self, a self that is nothing less than the manifestation of the American quest.

IV. THE EUCHARIST OF THE SUBLIME

So I return to the dancing boys at La Cage aux Folles and consider an American eucharist, a ritual revelation of the truth of the soul. Is it a blasphemy? Or is there a "numinous aura" that surrounds these sublimely beautiful dancers atop the bar as they are worshiped by the semicloseted bureaucrats beneath them? Are they latter-day American Adams who have turned the Puritan errand upon its head revealing that "varnisht pot of putrid excrement" as a luminous human body possessed of charismatic grace, radiant icons of Apollonian materiality, godlike summations of the visible world—to paraphrase a line from the writer Camille Paglia? Paglia is without doubt our consummate scholar-performer, an erudite if self-indulgent student of sexuality, charisma, and spirituality. She points out in *Sexual Personae* that charisma has long been associated with the divine, early Christians having used the Greek word *charisma* "('gift, favor, grace') for the gift of healing or speaking in tongues." But she takes charisma further to its roots, to the earliest Greeks— Odysseus "radiant with comeliness and grace," Achilles whose body emits "a blaze of light." Charisma, she writes, "flows outward from a simplicity or unity of being and a composure and controlled vitality. There is gracious accommodation, yet commanding impersonality. Charisma is the radiance produced by the interaction of male and female elements in a gifted personality. The charismatic woman has a masculine force and severity. The charismatic man has an entrancing female beauty. Both are hot and cold, glowing with presexual self-love."

Paglia's charisma is, she acknowledges, no different from *glamour,* a Scottish word signifying a magical "haze in the air" surrounding the desired or revered figure. But where does the light come from? Among the Greeks it was granted by the gods. Among the self-described charismatic Christians it is evidence of God's presence within. But among the queers in a honky-tonk dive longing to come out or just arrived?

Many of the closeted customers crowded in around the two long bars enter La Cage as a descent into degradation, a red-light substitution for physical intimacy they dare not admit into their ordinary lives, an hour of escape from repression and denial. Glamour is not theirs. But others experience a transcendence. One man furtively grips his palm around the sturdy calf of a young dancer, presses a greenback into his sock, and intensifies the impossible division within his life, numbing the spiritual energy of his soul, smothering the light of his awakening. Another touches his palm to the dancer's calf in a celebration of mutual joy, the toucher delighted by the young man's beauty, the dancer radiant in the beauty he imparts. The first man experiences a debauch, a profanity. The second experiences a sacred moment, a communion. The dancer is the same. No one else may know the difference in the two forms of touch, unless it is one of those rare evenings when the chance array of dancers and touchers is uncommonly special, and the realization of beauty overcomes fear, bathing everyone present in an unspoken awareness of charisma, and what was blasphemous before is made sublime.

five

Encounters

We have to understand that with our desires, through our desires, go new forms of relationships, new forms of love, new forms of creation. Sex is not a fatality; it's a possibility for creative life.

—MICHEL FOUCAULT
The Advocate, 1984

As he approached the end of his life, the French philosopher Michel Foucault gave a number of interviews on the implications of his work for modern sexual-liberation movements. Foucault's three-volume *History of Sexuality* had made him the most prominent living theorist on the relationship between power and sexuality. On his regular trips to the United States, particularly as a guest of the University of California at Berkeley, he was a frequent visitor to the flourishing gay demimonde of San Francisco—the bars, the baths, and the parks. He was, as his biographers have noted, especially intrigued by the city's South-of-Market clubs, places like the Barracks and the Cauldron, known for their S&M playrooms.

Foucault never made any effort to disguise his sexual interests or to hide the nature of his long relationship with the writer Daniel Defert in Paris. Yet much to the consternation of many gay activists, Foucault was reticent in presenting himself publicly as "a gay man." Americans have tended to regard that reticence with great suspicion, evidence that even a man with a global reputation harbored residual self-hatred. Yet as much as Foucault was drawn toward the urban gay meatracks of the United States, he was also deeply suspicious of gay politics and gay identity.

Foucault had spent his life examining how modern society worked to discipline and contain human beings as a means of maintaining public order. In his study of insane asylums, prisons, and the control of sexual behavior, he saw the cause of human freedom as pitted against the power of the state. And not just the brute power. The most insidious power, he argued, came not from the police and the prisons, but from the organization of knowledge. Through the schools, through the churches, through the media, through the imagery of consumer advertising, power asserts itself over the freedom of humans to imagine their own lives. What he called the power/knowledge equation was the method society uses to draw a line between the normal and the abnormal. Marriage was normal; cohabitation was abnormal. White European colonists were normal; Andean Indians were "savage" and therefore abnormal. Disciplined factory workers were normal; poet-wanderer-beatnik-bohemians were abnormal. Men who procreated with women were normal (in the nineteenth century); men who swallowed other men's semen were abnormal. For Foucault the history of power was, primarily, the history of ever-changing normalities. As he examined, somewhat eccentrically, homo- and hetero-erotic practices from ancient Greece up through the rise of the industrial revolution, Foucault tried to track the human response to the ever-changing rules of normalization, for in normalization he saw the suppression of the free imagination. To be free, he argued, was to resist. Resist the authority of marriage. Resist the authority of psychiatric normalcy. Resist the normalcy of routine work. Resist the validity of "heterosexuality." And resist the normalization of homosexuality.

Foucault found in homosexuality a marvelously rich source of creative resistance. What mattered to him about his homosexual desire was the freedom it gave him from the conventional geographies of intimacy. Friendship, normally defined as sexless intimacy, could be ecstatically sexual *and* fraternal. Yet the most profound physical intimacies, obtained in moments of total physical subjugation in an S&M game where the master had total control over the subordinate's survival, might have no "sexual" intimacy at all. To be free, he told his students and his readers, is to be cruel: to strip away all of the shibboleths of power and privilege hidden away in the ordinary routines of daily life, and then to dare to reconstruct with one another an ethics of mutual freedom that celebrates human pleasure and the unembarrassed, unfettered imagination.

Whatever his faults as an "amateur" and idiosyncratic historian, however much his inquiries were a cover for an exploration of his own life, Foucault synthesized what is for me the critical conundrum of the queer life: How do I make of my homosexuality a bridge of engagement with other people, other experiences, other imaginations, other ways of living. As an objective, *to be* "gay" feels no more appealing than *to be* "straight." The irreplaceable value of my journey through the queer geographies of the late twentieth century has been the peculiar engagement it has afforded me to intimacies I could have found in no other way, insights to human knowledge that could only be gained through the joint exercise of body and mind. Because our bodies are the final locus of our personal authority, when we put them at risk, when we put them at the disposal of other human beings, we have the chance (though not the certainty) of knowing the world in ways that polite, normal society would deny. Though I never went to war, that is, I suspect, what veterans recall when they confess quietly that their battle days were the most vital moments of their lives, the moments when *they put their bodies on the line.* To be *on the line,* to look into the abyss, where the rules of civil order have been burnt away, is to confront the sublime terror of being alive.

Foucault articulated for many of us the most sublime of homosexual lusts: not for the love of our own sex as such, but for an unquenchable, Promethean lust for knowledge of what it can mean to be alive. His mistrust of calling himself "gay," I think, was not fear of personal embarrassment or lost prestige, but that by adopting a category of sexual identification, he would have sacrificed his own ruthless quest for knowledge for the security of a new regime of normalcy. To be normal was to be dead.

As a traveler through the terrain of contemporary queer geography, I, like many gay men, have encountered an uncommon array of remarkable fellow travelers. These encounters have enriched my life, challenged my imagination, and forced me to question the nature of ethical obligation in modern society. What is unusual is that encountering such people is not unusual. Three of the most important people in my life have been Brandy Moore, Fred Hersch, and Bob Wingate. From Brandy I learned something about navigating between power and freedom. From Fred I learned to hear more clearly the relationship between art and identity. From Bob I continue to learn about the comedy of human categories. With all of them I have been touched by the resilience of unconventional love.

I. Brandy Moore

Brandy Moore and I met about ten o'clock on a Saturday night at a club in South Central Los Angeles called the Catch One. Chaka Khan was there, live in the spotlight singing in that deep, haunting, raspy voice about the waste and isolation of lives discarded in the barren, concrete canyons of America's cities. Two hundred and fifty, maybe three hundred people stood hearing her. We were stunned by the power of her voice, touched by the tender, bawdy words she had just said in tribute to the late Sylvester, the great drag, blues, and disco queen whose "You Make Me Feel Mighty Real" had gone gold as he was sliding toward death with AIDS. I was one of three white men there that night, the party night of the second annual Black Lesbian and Gay Leadership Caucus.

Brandy and I met about fifteen minutes after we noticed each other and began that gradual, cautious, lateral drift that is the mark of an anxious cruising maneuver. We stood side by side as Chaka sang, silent as all those around us were. Then I turned. We looked at each other. I had no words, offering only, "Whew!" and shook my head. Brandy, who in the subsequent years I knew him was seldom short of words, said only, "Yeah!"

Brandy and I found words to learn about each other—about what I, a middle-aged white reporter, was doing in this huge black homo party; what he, executive assistant to the Speaker of the California Assembly, was doing there, too; what it would mean that this striking six-foot-three ebony man in a tailored suit and handmade oxfords was calmly, openly leaving a black celebration with a white man; what it meant that three hours of talking later we would slip into his hotel-room bed together, holding each other, chaste through the night, and that the next morning, before he removed his shoes from their overnight stretchers, we would sit together in our stocking feet, under the heavy gray light of winter Los Angeles, and make an interview about the transformative power that the late Sylvester had had, showing white men and black men alike that we can all die of AIDS.

Brandy and I began to love each other that morning, though we were never *in love*. We never shared the same bed again. We had considered sex that first night. We made the starting moves as we lay together, but he took my hand away, in part because he was deeply, obsessively attached to a man in San Francisco, and because he knew that we could become more to each other than tricks at an out-of-town convention. In later years, as I visited or lived in San Francisco, we would see each other every three or four months, looking, as he would say, through the window into each other's life. The tension of possibility was always present, but I think we saw in that mutual looking that our passions were too volatile to sustain a modulated love affair, that friendship would not likely survive passion, and that friendship was more important to us than an apocalyptic romance. Rather, ours was a romance of constraints. Some of that romance was about race. Some was about disease. But mostly, my romance with Brandy was about the relationship of knowledge to power to dreams.

The first thing you had to know about Brandy Moore was his will to power. On our third lunch appointment I met him at his office, the San Francisco headquarters of Speaker Brown. Riding down the elevator of the old State Office Building, I made some casual remark about when he had "to be back." He smiled and in an almost patronizing tone said, "You don't know who I am, do you?" Who he was, he explained, was a key aide to the second most powerful politician in California, just behind the governor (and in the eyes of many, Willie Brown exercised more power than the governor). A liberal Democrat, Brown maintained a highly lucrative commercial law practice. His clients included a number of major corporations, many of whom he called on to supply food and beverages for the party he threw at the 1984 Democratic National Convention for "ten thousand of my closest friends." In the legislature Brown was ruthless in his rewards and punishments, banishing disloyal party members to dingy offices barely larger than broom closets, rewarding adversary Republicans who supported his bills with cherry assignments. Brown understood well that the gay vote in his home district could not be ignored, *and* he understood well that the black ministers of San Francisco and real estate interests were equally vital pieces of his alliance. Brandy Moore's job was to work with the gays, with African-Americans (he had been vice chair of the city's Black Leadership Forum), and to keep tabs on housing issues—which at times could prove troublesome for the downtown real estate developers who were Brown's friends and backers. At forty-two, in 1988, Brandy Moore was a player in one of the most envied cities in the world, employed by one of the most powerful black political leaders in the nation. Advising me of all of that on our way to lunch, he added, "And I make sure that everybody I work with knows that I love men."

We spoke about many things at lunch that day: about the unacceptable failure of the nation's black churches to talk about black men dying of AIDS, even though their choirs were being decimated by the disease; about the lethargy with which civil rights and congressional leaders were addressing the disease; about the equally dismal performance (then) of the leading AIDS organizations—San Francisco AIDS Foundation, AIDS Project Los Angeles, Gay Men's Health Crisis in New York—to develop aggressive programs in black and Latino communities. We talked about his own project to produce oral histories of gay black men and HIV, and how he never got the time to work on it. And we talked about sailing, about the boats he had owned and sailed on the Bay and in the ocean along the California coast. Not until several years later, when we began a series of formal interviews, did he describe the place that sailing held in his life, how a picture in a magazine had become an icon, helping to sustain the imagination of a queer black boy growing up in a world where all the power was held by straight, white men.

The place was Denver and Brandy Moore was Willy Moore. "My

mom used to collect *National Geographics* from these wealthy homes where she worked. They were my window on the world, and they were all neatly organized in my bedroom. I opened this magazine one day and there it was, that instant of awareness. Here's this beautiful boat, a four-masted schooner. It had a lot of black people on the boat, but it was the boat itself. It was black-hulled with white sails.

"I was eight years old, and I said, 'One of these days I'm going to own a boat just like that.' So, with that I began my search, looking for this boat, and ultimately I had a boat, a much smaller boat, with a single mast, built for myself."

How, I asked him, does the eight-year-old child of a cleaning lady living in Denver, far from water or boats or money, make such a dream? Though he didn't say so directly, the tone of his response, its soft, bemused quality, led me to understand that I'd asked a white man's question.

"Eight-year-olds don't think about that," he said. "You go to the candy store, see the candy, and reach for it. Often you get your hands slapped. Adults say, 'You can't have that. Learn to ask for things.' I saw this boat and that was the big piece of candy, and I said I'm gonna have it someday." He saw that I was still puzzled.

"A boat is about freedom. A boat is about power and control. A boat is about smooth things. All that kind of thing that entices you.

"And the sails. They were so powerful. All these big white sails and four masts. A four-masted schooner! Oh! I was just mesmerized. Still am."

Brandy's eyes went aloft just remembering the image. It became one of those moments when his poses and pretensions dissolved and he allowed me to see him directly. He looked at me dead on.

"How could anything so magical be a reality? I've been searching all my life since then for the perfect boat. When you're eight years old, when you make up your mind that you want something, you have no way of knowing how to make that happen. Somehow I was on the path and I just got there. When I was a kid, I just loved civics class. I can remember the book we had, gray and white, about the U.S. government. It had lots of black-and-white photos and documents reproduced. I wrote a paper about it and I got an A. It was at that moment that I said to myself, 'Someday I want to be a press secretary to a senator,' not knowing that my life track would take me right up to that door. I fulfilled that promise [to myself] . . . the same way with the boat. I saw this boat, which was unattainable I'm sure. But I didn't know that."

Race. Sex. Power. Money. All of those things were woven into the sailing life that Brandy Moore built for himself. Sailing was his oldest metaphor, but it wasn't only a metaphor. Sailing was real sensation: to feel the boat in the slot, when the jib and the main are trimmed exactly right on the wind, when the vibration of the rudder charges up through the helm into your wrists and your body becomes joined to the craft as it steals the power of the wind for its own purposes, tacking or jibing toward its own destination *against* the will of the wind. Sailing was its own end for him, *and* it represented everything that the larger world told him was supposed to be unavailable to "a little colored faggot boy." Sailing was display and carriage married to skill and qualification: the consummate sport of the navigator.

Navigation began early. The first time he ran away from home— and stayed away for several nights—he was six. Then at ten he snuck onto a train in Denver and made his way to New York, where he had an aunt and uncle living in Harlem. At fourteen he moved there to stay. Aunt Ruby, his mother's sister, was a pale woman, could pass for white, about which there had always been family war, since the rest of the family is dark. They resented Aunt Ruby her skin, her brass, and her position. Aunt Ruby was a registered nurse in the 1950s when there were very few black nurses. Ruby and Brandy's mother did not speak, but Ruby had always told the little boy when she decamped from Denver for New York that he could count on her if he ever needed anything. So at fourteen Brandy sent himself to New York for the second time and moved in with her: "I wanted to be a dancer, modern dance. I knew if I could get back to New York, I could be part of that, thinking I was the only one in the whole world."

Brandy never became a dancer, but moving to New York, having an aunt who helped him find a community center where he took dance lessons, reassured him that his life was his to navigate. Others in New York, a pair of white drag queens on the Upper West Side, taught him that he had to be tough and smart and full of sparks. It wasn't until he was twenty-two, in 1968, however, that Willie Moore found his name and the people who would begin to be "his family." By then he had already been to Vietnam, lived with a woman, had a child. Vietnam had taught him how many men were available for sex. San Francisco, where he settled after Vietnam, taught him that he could have sex with men and have a life.

"I came up here and I was tired of being one of the many millions of Bills in the world," he told me. "I didn't want to be a Willy, and I didn't like the way people said William." One of his new San Francisco friends was a well-known call girl named Brandy, who lived in Pacific Heights.

"One day I asked her, 'Can I use your name?'

" 'Oh, honey, I don't care what you do. It's all right,' she said. So I selected that name and made it mine."

Like running off to New York, finding his own name was a vital moment in finding the place of his identity—sexually and racially. About the time of our last interview, in 1993, Brandy's mother died. She was an alcoholic who had lived only into her midsixties and become a born-again Christian. She loathed her son's homosexuality. Brandy had long since stopped seeing his aunt Ruby after he became openly gay. As vital as they were in showing him the richness that the world offered, his family could not join him in either his social success or his sexual evolution. They became separated.

"I created my own family—gay men," he said. Still puzzling to me, though, was that his gay family was not only gay, but mostly white. His political work and much of his social service work in the city were among black people, but with a few notable exceptions most of his intimate friends were white. Certainly Brandy Moore was not blind to the racial divisions in San Francisco gay life—the bars and sex clubs that actively discouraged black men from entering them, the objectification of muscled black bodies as tricks but not mates. I had hesitated for several years about asking him why his lovers were so often white. Other gay black men I'd known who slept with white men simply spoke of taste. Brandy was startlingly candid. His choices, he said, were certainly tied up with the anger and struggles inside his large extended family, their expectations of

him, their battles with each other and the anger that bred in him—
"the stuff that builds you up and makes you finally come out, and I
don't mean come out just to say to the world I'm gay, but finally
makes you come out of yourself and be somebody, that makes you
know that you can create the name Brandy Moore, and it can mean
something.

"I was Will or Willy with my family. I still am. But I have no trust
in that. When anybody's growing up, you have to have a certain
amount of trust that they're going to provide you with safety and security. I didn't believe that with my maternal family. Once I discovered the magic of men, the [family's] security couldn't work for me
any longer. And I had to create my own.

"This means you're on a path to find a group of people who can
provide that security. It happened for me with men. It happened
best with white men. And why? Because I was exotic to them. That
exoticism is what makes me different. It makes you an object—yes.
But if you're smart, you can manipulate that to get what you need
out of life."

Brandy met his first great love, Robert, when Robert happened
by a smoke-shop kiosk Brandy was running in the Castro. Robert
was a successful white businessman in the marine-supply industry in
southern California. Brandy already owned a share in his first sailboat. He and Robert talked briefly. Robert rented a newly free
room in Brandy's apartment and, a year or so later, bought the house
that Brandy lived in for the rest of his life. At one point Robert
bought Brandy a custom-designed boat and helped support him
while he earned a master's degree, and later, after they had parted,
Robert bought him a sports car as a Christmas present. Brandy's
friends often had low incomes, but his boyfriends were never without money.

"I don't need to have to pay for some poor person," he told me
one day, adding, as he watched my expression, "That's not a nice
thing to say." I did find it crass, but I also wondered how as a young
black man in his twenties, beautiful but without credentials, he had
found his benefactors.

"I have always been very directed. I know what I need, okay. Why
should I, or anybody else, go out with people, or try to involve my-

self with people, who can't do anything for me? Why would you do that?" He was genuinely puzzled by my question. "If someone can't teach you something, or if someone can't take you somewhere, what do you need to be around them for? No dick is that sweet. No asshole is that delicious that you would give up your lifestyle to be with someone who couldn't offer you something."

"But what of those who have other things to offer besides money?" I asked.

"Like what?"

"Their art. Their spirit. Their work."

"But I would not be with them as lovers. I would be with them as friends. I used to go with a man called Paul, he's dead now. Paul was a beautiful man, but he didn't know where he wanted to go after a certain point. After I started making contacts in politics and government, it was easy [for me] to support him in going for the job as film-music critic at the local ABC TV [station], because I knew people who played in that realm. People had been looking at him distantly, but to me it was like, 'Paul, where do you want to go? You gotta move up to the light, up to the window, so they can see you. If you're gonna just be the mannequin in back, we got lots of those.' And so, he got that job.

"I've met a lot of men in my lifetime who couldn't make that leap. A leap of faith, if you will, in their own ability to get anything they want. I have never been bogged down by that leap of faith. I got that early on from the saying that my stepdad gave me: 'If you're qualified, you can get anything you want.'"

As he spoke that day, more brutally honest than I had ever heard him, Brandy forced me to look at the presumptions we make about love and romance, presumptions framed mostly by men with money, presumptions that romance and attraction are only authentic if they are unadulterated by power, ambition, and need. Most of our writers, lecturers, ministers—the people who have created most of our stories, plays, sermons, and moral fables—have until very recently been secure men of the middle class. Women, on the other hand, have always understood the pragmatic parameters of love. Generally precluded from holding positions of independence and security, women have known that love and romance are not neatly separated from primal longings for a secure place in the world. From the elegiac essays of Virginia Woolf to the Pop-Tart potboilers of Danielle Steele, women have told us that passion is never pure. Passion toward another human being is inextricably intertwined with the imaginary journeys we see in our lovers. The more deeply that passion touches our buried dreams and insecurities, the more powerful it becomes. Yet as liberated moderns we pretend publicly that these subconscious and subordinated considerations are merely crass holdovers from the Victorian era of calculated marriages. We pretend in our public talk of love that "marrying well" is a sign of selfish ambition. At least men like to make such claims. But such men frequently have the security to make the claims. Women, whose incomes remain a third lower than men's and who still bear the primary brunt of childrearing, have always been more candid with me: pheromones must even now be measured against a mate's ability to help provide a secure place in an insecure world.

Historian Stephen Kern writes in *The Culture of Love* about how love became transformed by the struggle for power at the beginning of the twentieth century: "In the course of a historical period in which women fought for and won concrete new powers from men in education, work, law, and politics, the battle of the sexes to triumph *over* each other overshadowed the ultimately more rewarding triumph of gaining more power for each when together *with* one another." Kern was concerned with the changing roles between men and women, but the same parallels have surfaced among same-sex lovers now that homosexual courtship and families have become ordinary parts of middle-class, contemporary life. More still do they inform the dream loves and the real loves between the races, where imbalances of power and expectation are often severe.

"I've had lots of lovers," Brandy went on, "and the moment I understand that their vision and their knowledge about themselves do not allow them to provide me the safety and security I need, living in a racist society, I drop those boys. I didn't hang around.

"We [gay black men] used to talk about having a black lover or a white lover. I used to tell people, 'I don't want a black lover for a certain reason, and the reason is, I don't need another oppressed person next to me and we're trying to pretend love. Because we're always dealing with the racism we get out there. When we go to work, for instance, when he goes to his job and I go to my job, in the course of the day, an African-American male goes through so much bull-shit—not just from white people, from black people, too—by the time you get home, you can't just talk about anything other than [that bullshit] because you're pissed. I didn't want to be in that kind of relationship. I wanted to have a relationship that offered me safety and security when I needed it. At the end of the day. During my off hours, I needed that. I thought I could get that through someone other than black. With most white males, and they were white males who had money, they could do that for me."

Even as he spoke, I felt myself flinching, unsure how to take this extraordinary confession. The pain and peril of interracial love in America remains so raw. The chances of its success remain so fragile. I had no doubt about the genuineness of the love Brandy felt for the two great companions in his life, the first, Robert, who still owned his house; the second, Eric, with whom he had traveled the world from 1987 to 1990. Brandy had believed he and Eric would go to their graves together; toward the end of his life, three years after the breakup, he said that a single call from Eric and he would sacrifice everything he had left. Like James Baldwin, who thirty years earlier had found the solace to write about America's racial torments only by living with a white European in France, Brandy seemed strength-ened in his political commitment to race matters through his love and reliance on white men. And he was stung by those other gay African-Americans who distrusted him because of his loves.

"For a long time," he told me, "I didn't participate in things like the conference where we met, simply because there was this whole thing about [only dealing] with black people in your life. You couldn't deal with white people. Well, darling, that limits me. I couldn't do that.

"There's always been that controversy, 'Well, you know, Bill, Bill doesn't really like black people.' That's their bullshit! How could I not love black people! I am the blackest of the black! How can I not love my own kind? People who always wanted to spend a lot of time with that discussion, they were out of my life very quickly . . . be-cause that gives [them] control over my life, and nobody tells me what to do. It comes down to that."

171

At our last interview Brandy lent me two of his personal journals, running from July 1990 to January 1993. Like most diaries, they are an assortment of ordinary, daily reflections, some insightful, some embarrassing, many painful as he began to see his time expiring faster than his accomplishments. The dilemma of how to express both love and solidarity is a constant. The first journal opened the night after he had seen the film *Longtime Companion,* shortly after his breakup with Eric. He was touched by the evocation of the lost lives of men like Eric and his other white lovers. At the same time he was angered and saddened.

7 July 1990

. . . The film . . . left us to wonder about single, not-so-rich, not-so-white men who have died alone and uncelebrated across America. Sad? Yes!! But not just because of the subject and plot.

I want to run from the narrow thinking of a world which knows not nor cares about the plight of men who look like me—in color, speech, and texture of hair. After all, aren't these the traits which deliver to me white specimens seeking one-night stands and sexual favors?

I want to make films, write books, create lasting memories of black men loving and knowing themselves; so that someday as somebody finds it interesting to look through the tapes—they'll find faces smiling, eyes aglow, and read of my passing through this world. So many thousands have moved between American shores in search of a place where for once they might breathe more smoothly and without the harsh white heat of racism and sexual primacy challenging their every move. It ain't been found yet.

A few pages later he remains doubly tormented, about the failure of his relationship and about the continuing failure of either gay or black leaders to mount a serious campaign to save the lives of African-Americans dying of AIDS.

27 July 1990

Opening up to live. Trying to get over all the hurt of childhood neglect and abuse; trying hard to erase the misgivings about past adult relations which soured and dried up, trying to relinquish anger from my recent separations and partings by realizing that my survival and joy are necessary and important to me.

If I am not afraid of death, then why would I be afraid to live? Answering those fears about living is possible; I can survive life's trials and I can achieve happiness. I love you, Brandy, I love you, William, I love you, Willie! . . .

■ ■ ■

Another friend has departed—filled with cocaine, *Pneumocystis,* and toxoplasmosis. Rumor has it that he died alone in a small room with only household spirits and insects to hear his fear and loneliness. His mate [in dark moments Brandy spoke of being "married to HIV"] had crossed the oceans to attend her offspring in America, leaving the silent killer AIDS to watch over her lover. Only moments passed after her jet blasted off into low space destined for sunny California when the deadly virus finally crawled to its mark on his brain and began eating away at 47 years of memories and pictures of survival as an African-descended man in the world.

No feeling was spared for his shy but boisterous nature or his bravado in the face of adversity. There was no friend there to hold his hand or press his temples when the pain became gigantic and loud in his head. He died alone—but we will remember Steve Simmons.

3 August 1990

Deadlines come and go. Sometimes they are just that—dead lines. No deals, no plans. Just dead lines. Days go by when there's only life wrinkles to worry about; memories of other men and other times. All gone by and dead. . . .

Deadline to forget pain (seize the time!). Deadline to clean up your personal life—wherever it seems dirty. Remember to always be real. Remember that AIDS is just a move toward man-to-man history.

> *Holding his fatness*
> *In my mouth, I hum*
> *Knowing that my vibration*
> *Will tickle him past*
> *Time, race and obsession*
> *Towards my desire; and*
> *The serenity of our*
> *Shared legacies.*

Reading these entries now, as I write this remembrance six months after Brandy's passing, I push myself to understand his eight-year-old's dream, lit up by a magazine photograph of a four-masted, white-sailed schooner, filled with black people, slicing into the ocean. In our last interview, when we were speaking about black people who would not forgive him his love of white men, and white people who cared little or nothing about the troubles of black people, he came back to his determination to navigate his life freely. "This is a globe," he reminded me. "We are all world citizens. That's what I always aspired to, being a world citizen. I wanted to see it all. It seems to me that the philosophy that you can only hang out with black people means that you're stuck. You're really stuck.

"I always wanted to be open and free, even though I still have to deal with oppression. I get oppressed by black people if I allow it, just as well as by white people. People of my complexion, people darker than blue, have never been allowed to live freely, and I have always sought living freely."

II. FRED HERSCH

Five people sit on chairs and a sofa in the SoHo loft where Fred Hersch has lived, composed, and occasionally produced jazz records since 1979. He calls it his Monday-night group therapy for jazz students. The five, one woman, four men, are his private students—all young, promising jazz pianists, who, rather like participants in a Gestalt-therapy circle, take their place at "the hot seat" and play a piece of improvisational jazz on his Steinway grand. Tonight they are working on ballads.

Michael, an intense man with bushy blond hair, finishes a piece. Fred asks the other students for their reactions, then offers his own comments: "Your last chords were really good. You really seemed to connect with the tune, but it took so long for you to get there. When you connected to the tune at the end, your sound cleared up. You're thinking too much about what you're going to play." Michael's fingering was precise, nimble, but somehow tight and overstudied.

"Ballad playing"—Fred pauses—"is like seduction. You've got to draw everybody in. You've got to not think about it too long. You've got to *do* it.

"The closest analogy to playing jazz like this is juggling. You have to think ahead and know where the balls are. You think too much and feel too little, you drop them. You think too little and feel too much, you drop them. Thinking and emotion. That's what makes it jazz, gives you that 'Wow!' when you just express yourself."

Moving beyond ballads, he speaks about the particular burdens of improvizational jazz, of how it demands all the technical expertise of classical performance while at the same time it requires the musician to dwell within a series of emotional moments—but more still, to inhabit those moments while hearing the music you are making, the music the other players are making, and to move through that riff in such a way that you can hand it off or pick it up from the other players. You must do all that, but never fear to plumb the emerging musical emotion as it happens, daring to play the phrase with a touch that you've never played, never heard before.

I listen as he probes the layered musical intentions of his students. His comments are occasionally technical, but as he tells me in advance, his method is to act as an analyst. He tries to assist his students in discovering their own musical intentions, then to realize those intentions in the language of jazz. Jazz, as some jazz writers have noted, is the most ruminatively interior of musical forms, the music most committed to examining the expressive self; Fred's technique aims at bringing his students toward more intensive self-reflection. The method recalls our initial encounter.

Fred and I ran into each other at the corner of Christopher and Hudson Streets on a spring evening sometime in the late 1970s. There was a light drizzle. It was just cool enough to need a jacket out. He was twenty-three, a brash kid down from the New England Conservatory of Music who had already worked on the road for Woody Herman. We meandered up Hudson for a block or two, arm in arm. He looked over at me—I wore a broad-brimmed leather hat in those days—and said only, "It's so incredible just to walk down the street here embracing another man." He leaned his face beneath my hat brim, and we kissed gently.

Something about the zest, the spontaneity, the joy of the moment, stayed with me for years. When I was in his loft later that weekend and heard him play for the first time, the same quixotic lyricism flowed out of him as his fingers touched the keys. A dozen years passed before I saw Fred again, at Kimball's West, a jazz club in San Francisco. He had his own trio, regularly toured all the major American jazz clubs plus occasional gigs in Europe and South America, and had played with several of the jazz greats from the fifties and sixties—trumpeter Art Farmer, saxophonists Stan Getz and Joe Henderson—as well as harmonica player Toots Thielemans, and bassists Charlie Haden and Sam Jones. He had become, critic Fred Bouchard wrote in *Down Beat,* "one of the small handful of brilliant musicians of his generation." He was a figure in American jazz, and I wondered, as I sat waiting for the first set, if he had retained the sassy, sweet lyricism I remembered from our meeting in the drizzle and the songs he had played in his loft.

I wasn't disappointed. All the humor, the quirkiness, the sweet musicality, had stayed with him. And he had grown. There was a poignance that I hadn't remembered. He seemed to descend into some deep heart of his pieces. He did Ellington, Monk, Coltrane, Miles Davis, but he also took old show music and sentimental stand-bys like "My Funny Valentine," "Bye Bye Blackbird," "If I Loved You," and "The Song Is You," and he turned them sideways, crawled inside them, searching out the spaces in his musical and emotional imagination that touched the mood and color of the tunes. A small, compact man with thick brown hair, he had begun wearing a beard since I'd last seen him. It was dark and close-trimmed. As always for his appearances, he dressed carefully—dark pants and a crisp, pressed long-sleeved shirt, stylish but not formal, cuffs rolled halfway up to his elbows. The further he moved into the most intense pieces, the further he seemed to drift from the room. His eyes would wrinkle shut as he lifted his head back toward the audience and his jaw would fall open; it was as though he had found that place within himself that was the music his body was producing.

We spoke after the last set, around one in the morning, had a drink, and began a conversation that has continued for several years about the relationship of art to sexual identity. Few topics provoke as much heat and passion in the queer zone as the question of queer art. Film, literature, graphic arts, are often infused with obvious homoeroticism, as any tourist who has studied the Vatican ceiling well knows. Rock groups, balladeers, and country-western singers more and more are capitalizing on queer themes. And there is a rich, if obscure, musicological debate on the question of homo-aesthetics in classical composition, highlighted by the recent book *Queering the Pitch,* which takes on the work of Schubert, Tchaikovsky, Handel, and others. But jazz presents a special problem. As Fred tells his students, jazz is a direct, active union of mind and emotion. All music expresses emotion, but in jazz, the musician must reach into his— and occasionally her—most intense and immediate personal emotions to make the music connect to the listener. However highly trained and polished the musicians are, their magic is that their performance is raw, fresh, and of the moment. Classical musicians may interpret a work, but the notes were there before the performance. In improvisational jazz, the notes may never have been played before and may never be played again as they are in a small, smokey club on a single night because, at its best, a jazz performance is a direct musical rendering of the self. If that self is a queer self, larded, strapped, and infused with all the power that queer desire provokes in our emotional lives, how could it not display itself in a music like jazz?

"The music is what sustains the player from beginning to end," the great horn player Art Farmer once told an interviewer, adding,

"That's where you get your life from. That's why you play jazz."
Slightly rephrased, Farmer was saying, "You get your life from your
music," not, "You get your music from your life." The latter is what
many advocates for a gay aesthetics would argue, that sexuality is so
fundamental that everything else flows from it. As far as Hersch is
concerned, the notion that there could even be such a thing as "gay
jazz" is "ridiculous." Jazz is far too abstract for such reductions, but
at the same time he acknowledges that his homosexuality is not un-
connected from the music he makes.

Take the Gershwin song "The Man I Love," a tune he has
recorded and plays frequently. "My interpretation is fairly straight-
ahead, but I reconstruct it in my own musical language. Is there anything gay about it? Not at all unless it's totally subconscious. It's not
as though I'm making a gay statement with the song. It's been
recorded by a lot of other male jazz artists who are straight. I just
happen to like the tune. I thought, well, people will construe from
my playing it that I'm gay, but what the hell? Why not? Instrumen-
tal music really doesn't have any concrete meaning. I don't think
there is such a thing as gay jazz. Each person gives it its meaning. I
may be a good ballad player, but that's not to do with the fact that
I'm gay. Lots of musicians play them well and they are straight."
What some people miss, he says, is that jazz is a language of its own
that speaks to the complexity of personal experience, but which also
informs that experience. The fact that jazz is the consummate music
of the individual as outsider is what attracted him to it in the first
place.

He grew up in Cincinnati, a rich if conservative cultural city, and
began playing classical piano when he was three. Later he added vi-
olin, sang, and acted. "I was kind of a music jock, and that already
made me feel different. I knew I was attracted to men by the time I
was thirteen. I'd look at these Renaissance art books that had a lot
of naked men. I'd come home after school and play the piano—that
was my escape.

"I constructed myself in a vacuum, like many gay men who feel
different and spend a lot of time alone. I did my own things." That
sense of difference—as a gay kid *and* as a piano prodigy—had a profound effect on his identity and on his art. "I wanted to be a 'nor-

mal' kid, so I had a lot of friends with whom I tried to erase myself. I'd talk about girls and play combat sports. I was sent to camp for eight weeks every summer. I was on the swim team."

His parents, affluent, Ivy League–educated children of Jewish immigrants, were concerned that their talented son would feel too much an outsider. "The message from home, from my family, was, 'Assimilate!' Like, 'You're different [because you're a prodigy], but we don't want you to feel too different for being a musician, so go be normal at camp for eight weeks.' But I didn't feel normal. I felt different. So I got a lot of mixed messages.

"I think I got involved in jazz, at least in part, because it was something my parents didn't know anything about. It's totally mine. Also it's considered 'lowbrow' music in the musical pecking order. James Levine grew up down the block from me—he's an opera conductor and a famous pianist; that's considered highbrow music.

"Jazz piano, playing in bars with older musicians, around alcohol and drugs, was something I felt I could be doing myself. I was appreciated for my talents. There was no social pressure on me. I could be myself just the way they were being themselves. Of course, as the years went by, I found I couldn't be myself because I'm gay and different from most of the other jazz musicians in the world."

That was during the 1970s, when downtown Cincinnati had four or five clubs playing live jazz regularly. He began to play the old, traditional way, hanging out at the clubs with musicians twenty or thirty years older than he was. At twenty, he got his first gig, playing piano at Robert's Neoteric Lounge, a funky club whose walls glowed with neon clocks and beer signs. "I'd carry in my electric piano and they'd let me play. There's a jazz tradition [that] you give kids a chance. I actually learned by sitting in and playing with people on the bandstand who were worlds better than I was. But I guess they saw I had talent. They allowed me to play and they also kicked my ass a lot. They would start tunes that I didn't even know, start playing them and make me take the first solo, and I would just have to figure out what the chords were as they went by. Or they would berate me for whatever I was doing wrong, rhythmically or if I got lost, then they would give me the freeze treatment. They would talk to me, say, 'Hey, you really should listen to this record, study this tune.' It was the right way to learn to play that particular music. I'm very grateful to those older musicians who helped me out, some black, some white. I loved it. I just loved it. Stayed up all night, had a blast, made a living."

He dropped out of college, where he was studying classical piano "to please my parents": then he transferred to the New England Conservatory. Moving out of Cincinnati released him to explore his music and his sexuality more deeply. In Boston, there were bars and a gay world whose codes and styles intrigued him. They existed in Cincinnati as well; he had glimpsed them at parties and on theater gigs, but there it seemed too camp, too strange, and he felt too anxious to do much.

■　■　■

In 1994, Fred Hersch released seven albums on compact disc. He was nominated for a Grammy for a trio disc entitled *Dancing in the Dark*. The biggest project of the year, however, was a record he produced and played on, *Last Night When We Were Young: The Ballad Album,* a benefit for Classical Action: Performing Arts Against AIDS. And he began to perform regularly at AIDS benefits, talking about his own health status—HIV-positive but asymptomatic. Other musicians who contributed to the record were Gary Burton, George Shearing, Bobby Watson, Janis Siegel, and Toots Thielemans, all of them people who, he says, "make music from the heart." Almost all of them had also lost someone to AIDS. It was with Toots Thielemans, the Belgian harmonica player, that he'd had one of his most important coming-out conversations.

Fred and Thielemans were working a gig in Italy during the 1980s. They were seated on a train between Bari and Pescara when the elder musician said he hoped Fred would meet a nice woman soon. "I told him I was pleased that he wanted me to meet someone, but he should 'just change the sex.' " After that, the two of them became closer, Fred became friends with Thielemans's wife, and Thielemans asked about his boyfriends. By contrast, his early years in New York, in the 1970s when I met him, were deeply divided. New York represented an enormous ambition to "play with the best." A few friends and family knew he was gay, but his family urged him to be discreet lest he damage his career.

"I was petrified that some of the jazz legends in those bands I was working with would find out. I knew no other jazz musicians who were openly gay, so I had no idea what the reaction might be—and my career concerns overrode everything. I was feeling disenfranchised from the community that I had so wanted to be part of, trapped in a psychological closet that I came to see was largely of my own design. He wrote about his situation in a 1994 piece for *Musician* magazine.

> One of the pivotal moments came for me in 1982; I was living semisecretly with a lover at the time. Stan Getz came over to our loft for a rehearsal, and I remember hiding my lover's toothbrush in a moment of panic. After the rehearsal, I realized that I was spending an inordinate amount of time and energy worrying about who "knew" and who didn't. Straight musicians talked about their wives and girlfriends, but I wasn't comfortable talking about who I was seeing. I was becoming a musical chameleon and erasing myself as an artist—being what I thought people wanted me to be.

That sense of being an artistic chameleon posed deep problems. The core of his aesthetic expression in jazz was about authenticity, jazz as freedom from external social expectation. To corrupt that expression, in a musical language that relied on intimate emotional exchange among musicians, was a violation of what made the music work. And yet, because the handoffs between musicians are so emotionally charged, from piano to bass to drums, it is fragile. There was more to worry about than what outsiders might think; he also had to be mindful of how his straight partners would hear his gestures, his choices of emphasis, even his choice of tunes, which were, after all, frequently about love and romance. All of those considerations impinge on a gay jazz musician's decision to be open sexually—and in Fred's view they help to explain why there are so few gay jazz players who are open.

"In the old days, people used to ask me why more jazz musicians weren't out. The usual answer is 'the macho lifestyle.' Okay, but I have another theory. I think that there's a certain intensity of emotion and passion when music is being created together with other people. A lot of gay people keep the passion in the music and don't deal with the other stuff. That emotion isn't just inside yourself. It's really about the synergy of all the different emotions on the bandstand at any given time. That's what's so interesting about jazz. You have to be confident about your own playing, and you have to be attentive and tuned in to what's going on around you—so you can feed on that or throw it out at the drop of a hat, because of what's going on and not going on at the moment. It's the group that prevails. Jazz is really about that combination of energies and points of view."

Finally the walls of denial and obfuscation felt like greater barriers to his musicianship than the risks of openness. His challenge was to integrate his life—not to subordinate art to sexuality any more than to subordinate sexuality to art. He put it succinctly in the *Musician* magazine essay:

> One can't be honest as a musician and dishonest as a person. I also learned to treat my sexual orientation as a matter-of-fact nonissue and, to my surprise, found that I (and other musicians) became more comfortable with who I was. As a result of my greater honesty, I began to come into my own as a creative musician: I found a group of my peers to play with [they were not gay], formed my first bands, began composing in earnest, and made my first records as a leader.

Did "being out" change his music? He believes it changed the quality of his performance, the ease and thoroughness with which he could enter "the moment." Since jazz is an art realized in such moments, it seems fair to say that his progression as a gay man has changed the progression of his music. That change, however, is subtle, and its implications are both technical and existential. In an interview with musicologist Paul Berliner, author of *Thinking in Jazz*, Fred explained how musical consciousness and technique converge.

"I was playing this week, and I played all this technical stuff that I couldn't sit down and play now—even if I could practice it for eight hours. At that moment, the music was happening. Everything just fell into place in my hands and in my head. I felt I was expressing something with everything I played. When I'm playing well, there's a certain freedom of just being able to do anything, really." Usually that freedom happens in the ensemble and the members' musical interaction takes them to unprecedented expressions. "I've played with bassist Buster Williams," he told Berliner, "and Buster's made me play chords like, like I couldn't even sit and figure out now. . . . It was just . . . the effect of the moment, the effect of playing with who I was playing with and really hearing everything, hearing all of his fingers, and you just start playing, you don't think of chords, you just play these structures, you know that just happens maybe only once. And they're gone."

I read that passage and asked Fred about it. The "music that was happening," he assured me, wasn't "gay music." It wasn't a "gay moment." The moment is both simpler and more profound. "The emotion of music when it's really happening," he said, "is transcendental, it's almost sacred."

■ ■ ■

In the loft, with Fred's five students, Sam is the last to play. He chooses a soft, sentimental jazz standard, "Blame It on My Youth." The piece is pretty, technically proficient, and a little flat.

"Your intro didn't do anything. It seemed generic," Fred says. He looks to the other students for comments.

"You took your fingers off the keys," the woman from Berlin notes.

"Okay," Fred says, "but musically, it was kind of . . . noodlie. Like cocktail-bar playing. Just keep it simple. When it got jazzy, it just lost me. When you had those emotional moments, it was just right."

Sam responds, "When I picked this tune, I liked it, once I learned the lyrics. But I don't hear any passing chords, for improvising. I can't *just* play the melody."

"Certain tunes I could play endlessly," Fred assures him. Sometimes he stays with the melody, sometimes he opens with an improvisation and then works his way back to the central melody. The class is not "the jazz patrol," as though there were a checklist of performance requirements. Be playful, he urges. "If what you feel in your ears isn't right, change the key. Wake up! Find the line between the convention and what you feel."

He pulls a small digital tape from a rack and puts it in a tape deck.

"This is the simplest tune I've ever recorded. You can hear everybody listening to each other. Sometimes it's not even the tune exactly, it's the feeling you can get out of it." The music is clear, fine, transcendent, but the point of playing it is to let the students know how hard it is to find that transcendent simplicity.

"We got about nothing on the first day and a half [of recording]—and about everything the last half of the second day. I'd been on tour with the trio in Houston the previous week, and I thought it would be a snap. But when we got back to the studio, I didn't like anything I was playing. I still had the sound of Houston in my ears. I wasn't playing in the moment. It took me a day and a half to get there, to get to the moment."

III. Bob Wingate

I am walking down Thirteenth Street toward the Hudson River and New York's meatpacking district on a Sunday morning in early June, one week after Pentecost. Pentecost is the blitzkrieg of Christian Sabbaths, the one when the searing tongues of flame shot down from the Lord and struck the apostles, granting them the power to speak in all the tongues of the world and thereby spread the gospel of Jesus. I'm on my way to watch a movie shoot at a leather bar called the Lure. Transvestite hustlers, scrounging for morning-after trade, shuffle by, and the bells of St. Bernard's roll through the hazy, humid air.

A twentyish man in a black leather vest holds his eye to a higheight video cam, mounted on a tripod atop a Toyota Camry, parked in front of the Lure. Another man, bronzed, buffed, wearing jeans and a white T-shirt, approaches the Lure from my direction. Just as he arrives at the door, he greets a great, bearded, bearlike fellow. Following behind the bear is a much younger, fair-haired man who keeps his sheepish, hangdog face focused on the ground. Both the older man and the younger one wear business suits.

"Hey, Chain, how're you doing! Haven't seen you in ages," the buff T-shirt exclaims. Looking the younger man over, he adds, "Like your boy!"

"You never met Gregg? He's been my slave since Christmas. I'm going away for the weekend and want to board him with the Manager."

"I heard they had a slave-boarding service. I guess it's true." The T-shirt's eyes salivate over the sheepish slave.

"The Manager's supposed to take good care of the boys," Chain continues. He pushes his "boy" forward to knock on the black steel door and turns to the T-shirt, who is playing the role of famed pornographer Bob Wingate. "What are *you* doing here? Why aren't you at the office turning out your smut?"

"I'm doing a star search here tonight for a film my mag wants to do. I came to drop off some rope, magazine, flyers."

The slave boy knocks, waits, then knocks again. At last the door opens and a middle-aged man, his porous face washed in aggravation, snarls, "Yeah?" He sees it's the bearish Chain and his boy, and the snarl twists into a leer.

"Bring him in!"

"Cut! Perfect!" yells a short, trim, graying man in a long-sleeved sport shirt. "Let's go. We're running an hour late." The man, his eyes shielded by round, wire-rimmed bifocals, might be your uncle Bernie, the bookkeeper, or perhaps that college professor you remember who taught Beowulf and Middle English. He is, in fact, the real Bob Wingate, director and producer of the film, an S&M bondage work to be called *A Night at the Lure* from Bound & Gagged Video Productions, of which Bob Wingate is the founder and sole owner.

"Bob Wingate" is a phony, WASP cover name for this middle-aged Jewish intellectual, a man whose nonagenarian Viennese parents fled Hitler in the early thirties, who himself fled Eisenhower conformity for the literary life of Paris in the late fifties, and who relaunched his life in the eighties as a successful pornographer. Besides making videos, Bob Wingate is the publisher of the smartly edited and grotesquely graphic journal *Bound & Gagged: Erotic Adventures in Male Bondage.*

I was first introduced to Bob one evening about twenty years ago when he was hosting a poker game in the apartment where he still lives on the Upper West Side of Manhattan. The other players I've long forgotten, though at that time they would have been journalists, writers, and political radicals who had cut their teeth on the antiwar and civil rights movements of the sixties. Of them all, Bob was the man of letters. After graduating from Antioch College he had lived in Paris for eleven years. He wrote literary and political plays in both English and French and scraped along with help from his family and as an assistant to avant-garde theater directors. Some of his plays were produced in Paris, some in London at a small theater where George Bernard Shaw's work first appeared. For much of that time Bob lived with or was married to a French physicist. After she ended the relationship, he returned to the States in 1971. He began seeking men for sex, moved in with a man also named Bob, and maintained a modest life managing a dance company, driving a limousine, at last settling in as reporter-editor for a trade magazine dedicated to the marketing of housewares.

None of us who knew Bob as a man devoted to literature and politics were up on his secret obsession. It was secret even to his gay friends, though now he tells anyone who asks that he can trace his earliest bondage fantasies to a prekindergarten classroom where the teacher was trying to read a Babar the Elephant book to the kids. As we talk, we are sitting in the offices of *Bound & Gagged* magazine, 89 Fifth Avenue. Bob has on a striped dress shirt and tie. Other employees are working in the outer office, designing the next issue and fulfilling orders from the *Bound & Gagged* "toy" catalog. He is waiting for a call from his printer, in Berkeley. The printer, who also handles the protofascist *Soldier of Fortune,* is balking at some of the images in *Bound & Gagged.* In the midst of his remembrance of kindergartens past, the call comes in. Bob, the leftist litterateur, tries out being the tough businessman. He seems to make some progress and hangs up.

We return to Babar.

"I remember there was a little hyperactive child who would not sit still listening to Babar, so the teacher tied him in his chair with a jump rope. Not very tightly. She just wrapped it around him. She didn't gag him. She just tied him into the chair and he kind of wobbled around and laughed. But I think she may have been stern enough to keep him quiet a little bit so we could hear Babar.

"Children remember early experiences of desire," he reassures me, even if at the time there is no sexual tinge to the event. He wasn't aware of the sexual overtones to being tied up until adolescence "when I thought of being tied up by my friend Stevie as I was jerking off. I shot to the ceiling. As soon as I saw a picture of somebody tied up, I got a hard-on."

Not until he was twenty-eight, married, and living in Paris did he bring himself to look at his obsession squarely. The Paris student rebellion was in full flower, and liberation was in the air: class liberation, student liberation, women's liberation, sexual liberation. And, as happens with measured regularity in France, there came along a scandalous book that *everyone* was talking about, *L'histoire d'O,* or *The Story of O,* which has sold more copies than any other French book ever translated.

"When I read *L'histoire d'O,* I was appalled. It is about a young woman who becomes this slave, and she is taken out to a château. I read the whole thing in this fever and sweat, trying to change every *elle* to *il* because I didn't want O to be a woman.

"I went into a frenzy reading that book because I couldn't believe that somebody could talk about what had been such a secret fantasy of mine for so long. But of course everybody around me was talking about it—not that I wanted to hear what all those French intellectuals were saying. Since my early teens I had buried it within my jerk-off fantasies, which those days tended to center on French firemen. Apart from being turned on by the occasional picture I came across, I was afraid to look closely [at bondage images] even in the privacy of my own room, lest anybody see that that page had one more wrinkle on it than the others."

Secretly, Bob began writing his own version of O, to be called *The Story of Y* ("If O was the cunt, then Y was clearly the cock and balls"). The more he wrote, the more excited he got ("I was forever interrupting the writing to jerk off in the toilet"). The book died, and so did his marriage. A year later he was frolicking with men in San Francisco ("mostly doing ordinary suck-fuck sex"), but sweet as that was, he quickly found out that many gay boys were at least as disturbed by bondage fantasies as straight folks were: "It was just my luck to do my sucking and fucking with guys who didn't need much probing to inform me that they looked on people with my kinds of interests as freaky and weird."

Another decade passed before he placed an ad in New York's gay weekly the *Native,* seeking others interested in forming a bondage club, like similar clubs in Boston and San Francisco. He was swamped with replies. Eighty the first week. Not knowing how to organize a club, he sent out a questionnaire to everyone who replied. The bondage club thrived. But what to do with the questionnaires? His original idea was to publish a book of true-bondage experiences, rather like the first-person narratives in Boyd McDonald's *Straight to Hell* series, *Flesh, Cum,* and *Meat.* "Those books were filled with the sound of real people talking. And the authentic voice is always hotter than fiction." The Boyd McDonald stories didn't always get him hard, but he found them "funny . . . and always good toilet reading."

"But then one day I said to [my late lover] Bobby, 'Jesus! These [bondage tales] have just piled up and I could probably make more money if I started a magazine than if I put out one book. So I started a mag." That was his night work. Daytimes he continued as a trade-mag editor covering the latest in hardware and housewares.

By the time Stonewall 25 had rolled out the lavender in the summer of 1994, all the *Bound & Gagged* enterprises were grossing around three-quarters of a million dollars and growing at a rate of 25 to 40 percent a year. The summer of '94 was also the year that *Bound & Gagged* found its way to a bookstore at the Ansley Mall in Atlanta, Georgia, and into the hands of a sunny-faced, blond Republican who had never once looked at a man and gotten aroused. That man's name was Lee, a recently divorced father with a nine-year-old son.

One of Lee's buddies, also divorced, had recently shown him a collection of female bondage magazines in which men tied up women. That idea repulsed Lee, but then, he thought, if they have magazines for tying up women, maybe there are magazines showing men tied up, too. That idea excited him. Lee is a very orderly man who runs his own consulting firm. One morning he gave himself a test. He had a client meeting that ended at 10 A.M. and another that started at 1 P.M.

"I decided to spend from ten until noon to see if I can find something. If I can, well, good news. If I can't find something, then it doesn't exist, and it's over. That's how I run my life." It took a little enterprise, but by eleven forty-five he had wandered to the back of the Ansley Mall bookshop where there was a whole rack of sex-oriented magazines. "Down on the bottom, I saw it: *Bound & Gagged*. And I went, 'Wow!' The next big challenge was, well, son, are you going to have the courage to pull it off the rack and go buy it. I said to myself, 'Shit! If you've come this far . . .' "

What had begun as a dust devil of curiosity following a buddy's question about kinky fantasies with women had swelled to a tornado of obsessive anxiety. Since childhood Lee, too, had loved the tying-up games that went with cowboys and Indians and the kidnapping tales from Disney films. He kind of knew that he was aroused by such tales, but never had these experiences produced fantasies of sex with the men who were doing the tying and kidnapping. Now, however, his erotic imagination was swirling fast.

"I was driving home on I-75, and I was lucky I didn't kill anybody. Leafing through this sucker, I was weaving down the highway. I got home by three o'clock, and . . . well . . . that suit had to go to the cleaners." As much as he loved the stories, he says, he skipped right past the sucking and fucking passages, like blipping the mute button during TV ads, to concentrate on the ropes and shackles material. He swooned when he got to the classified section, saying to himself, "Oh my god, this, too, can be yours. I found one ad that described everything I ever wanted to do. I sent off a letter. Nothing. Maybe it didn't get there, I wondered. So I sent off another letter when I saw the same ad in the next issue." Several weeks later, a return letter arrived—from no less than Bob "Wingate" himself, though Lee didn't know that at the time since Bob used his real name in the letter.

"I called him and we talked for thirty minutes. He was into this slavery bit. I played the game. He said he wanted me to come up. I told him I'd be up the day after tomorrow.

"It wasn't until I was on the final approach into La Guardia airport that I said to myself, 'What are you doing? This is insane!' " Nonetheless, Lee took a cab to an apartment Bob keeps in the Chelsea district, and he followed the orders he had been given. The door had been left open. He was to close it behind him and follow instructions left on a note. He stripped off all his clothes, put a gag in his mouth, a collar around his neck. He attached the collar to a chain hanging from a chinning bar, then blindfolded himself, and lastly, put handcuffs on behind his back. Then he waited . . . in silence.

Bob entered without speaking. He played with Lee's body, his tits, his cock, his balls, his butt, then unhooked the collar from its chain and led Lee into another room, where he removed the gag and pushed him to his knees.

"I hadn't seen him yet when I hear the zipper go down.

" 'Suck it, boy!' he says, and I'm thinking, 'Oh, I missed this somewhere in the fine print.' I'm trying to think, 'All right, all right, now how am I going to get out of this?' And it dawns on me, 'Son, you're not going to get out of this. It's too late. You bought the banquet. Now it's time to pay the bill. So, hold your nose and jump in. If it's terrible, you're going home in two days, and this never happened.'

"Quite frankly, I don't know if that period lasted ten minutes, twenty minutes, or an hour. But it was interminable. I thought it would never end. Then he took off the blindfold and I looked up and I saw him, and I thought, *'My God! He's a Nazi!'* He looked like a character out of one of those old movies, the little round wire glasses. Stern. Looking down at me. I thought, 'This is not good.' "

Lee and I have been talking in the poolroom at the Lure, while Bob is downstairs in the basement, directing one of the slave scenes for his bondage film. Ten months have passed since their first meeting, and Lee admits that he has taken to cocksucking like a debutante to champagne. He is helping out this weekend as Bob's general factotum, tracking down missing clamps and manacles, ordering lunch, serving as an extra in some of the bar scenes. He tells me—

and Bob agrees—that he is still not much attracted to men. Except for Bob.

"I keep trying to figure out what this deal is with me. I think it's purely a situation where I have met somebody who truly enjoys being with me. I have never had anybody treat me half as wonderful as he treats me. He makes me feel important. He does all those things anybody wants in a married relationship, in any relationship. We laugh, have a good time, share a similar sense of humor. We can be silly."

"And the sex is good?" I ask.

"Yeah. It's different. You stick it in your mouth. I don't stick it anywhere else. The touching is nice. The holding. It's what I wish I could have had in my marriage."

The chains, the collars, the leather, the cuffs, all the scenes in the film with naked boys and cum shots "doesn't do anything for me, but the actual playing, when Bob and I play, or when someone plays with Bob and me, that excites me. As far as this stuff [in the video] is concerned, the cum shots still kind of gross me out. I just figure, well, it's not for me, so don't worry about it, son." Our conversation circles back to early fantasies, the simmering images that led him into the mixed life he now leads, half in Atlanta as the father of a grade-school boy, the good Republican, the Episcopalian church-goer and businessman—and the bondage-boy lover of a New York radical, Jewish pornographer. He roams around his childhood fantasies, many of which were related to kidnapping.

"I've always been one of those people who absolutely takes control of everything. I run people's lives. I am Pollyanna and Mary Poppins rolled into one. People are so used to me taking charge, everybody dumps everything on me. It comes natural. On top of that I am the crown prince in the family. I was raised to be king someday.

"Sometimes I'd get so tired of always having to be the leader, having to be in charge, having to be right, always being on. There were so many times I've just wanted to disappear into thin air, go away. I'd think of running away, but you realize you can never run away. So, if you can't run away, why not have someone run away with you. As I got older, I used to fantasize about it. More times than not I was the victim. Because that's easier. If you're the attacker, you have to visualize who you're attacking. That way I didn't have to think."

■   ■   ■

Downstairs, the final dramatic scenes of *A Night at the Lure* are reaching a whip-cracking climax. The story line calls for the Manager of the club, who runs the slave-boy boarding service, to sell the boys for $100,000 each to an evil broker whose body is covered with steel piercing studs. Each slave is normally boarded inside one of six dungeon cells (actually former walk-in roasting ovens left over from the days when the Lure was a kosher turkey-roasting plant). But while the heroic Bob Wingate has been upstairs auditioning for tryouts, the Manager is busily taunting, tormenting, whipping, and ejaculating the several slaves, before zipping them up into sacks, leather suits, and mummy bags, after which they will be stuffed into pine boxes for shipment to their Beverly Hills buyers. Of course, Wingate gets a whiff of what's up and breaks the scheme wide open in the nick.

Only, a problem has come up for the "real" Bob. Two of his actors, who are about to be zipped and crated, admit to mild claustrophobia. They don't want to stay boxed up too long while the rest of the action is being shot. A short negotiation ensues resulting in a modest script alteration.

"All right," yells Peter, the assistant director and coscriptwriter. "Back to the mummification! Put Chuck in the sack! Then crate him. Put Ryan in the [straitjacket] suit. Crate him! Begin the mummification—and boom! Bob Wingate bursts in with the .45 and rescue!"

Nobody knows how many "pay-off shots" (trade talk for ejaculation scenes) they've taped. It's not easy reaching orgasm surrounded by cameras, lights, and cords on the filthy floor of an abandoned turkey oven. Consensus is they've gotten enough, and anyway, in a tie-me-up, tie-me-down flick, cum shots aren't the point. As the last action ends, the villains are being led away in handcuffs and leg irons by the cops. John, one of the arresting officers, stops to talk to the blond, buff, fictive Bob Wingate. Gesturing at one of the two bad guys, he says, "We've been on the trail of this scumbag for years. When you think of all the nice leather boys who've disappeared . . . Good work, Bob. Keep it up!" And the cop gives Bob a big, wet deep-throater kiss.

There were a few more ancillary background shots, but it was time for me to leave. I was walking toward the door when Lee sidled up. He wanted to add something about that first night he'd spent with Bob the previous summer, after they had had dinner and talked about ordinary things and begun to like each other. "It helped," he said, "that that night he chained me up to go to bed, he attached manacles to my wrists and ankles. I felt safe at that point."

six

Toward

a

Generosity

of

Place

I. A UNIVERSAL FREEMASONRY OF INVERTS

A thick, braided pigtail hangs down below the collar of the man I have been watching since before the Sayville ferry arrived. It swings like a silent pendulum as the wooden ferryboat bounces through the chop of Great South Bay. On the dock at Fire Island he sat alone in the flock of gay men headed back to Manhattan. Across the aisle a man in a gaudy shirt and an Australian safari hat tends his beagle. Behind the man with the pendulous pigtail a blond surfer-boy snuggles his head into the shoulder of a lover twenty years his senior, and on the back bench a russety, shaved-headed thirty-something entertains his mates with high-camp Island banter.

It doesn't get any queerer than the Fire Island Pines ferry in June. At Sayville, the pigtail and I exchange glances as eight of us pack ourselves into the two-dollar shuttle to the Long Island Rail Road. We wait a few minutes for the Cherry Grove ferry to arrive. Its load is equally queer, but a few women emerge from it—none of them headed our way. At the station, I figure it's my last chance to open a conversation with the dark-eyed, dark-haired man with the pigtail, to find out if he's a standoffish attitude queen, lost in solitude, or just shy.

Shy. He is delighted to talk. He's been alone in a house for three days. We trade standard pleasantries about the restorative mood Fire Island extends to its weekday visitors, especially on cloudy, blustery mornings. The train arrives. Its wheels squeal to a stop. I hold back to follow him up the metal steps. His calves are Baryshnikov's. He gestures toward a long three-person seat and I slide in against the scratched, translucent Lexan window. The LIRR is famous for its sightless windows and for floors that grasp your shoes tight as leeches.

He is Ken. He is an art director for a slick monthly magazine. He has been writing short stories. I note his calves and assume marathon bike-riding, but Baryshnikov was the better hunch. He'd been taking ballet lessons (though not this summer) since his early twenties. Writer-dancer-designer, he had grown up in Brooklyn, swimming distance from Coney Island, moved to the West Village, and made for himself the sort of queer life that millions of Midwestern faggot boys dream of.

We must change trains, he once for Manhattan, I twice for Brooklyn. On our first train the pheromones of Fire Island are still strong. Eight or ten of our ferrymates are in our car. On the next train, most of them switch with us, but a large infusion of other Manhattan-bound travelers cuts the Island fragrance to a whiff. Now a clutch of tattooed and head-shaved adolescents—gay, straight, bi, who knows?—gang into the two facing seats just in front of us. Eleven stops down the line, at Jamaica, I change for Flatbush Avenue, Brooklyn. By the time I make my last change, Ken and I have shared enough life details to locate each other again and meet for a coffee—though it's unlikely such an encounter will follow. Our passage seems complete in itself. We have converted what would have been an otherwise dreary trip home into an hour-and-a-half tickle of flirtation.

My train at last arrives at Flatbush terminal. Once a handsome city railroad station fronted with a beaux arts terra-cotta facade, it is now a warren of stark platforms connected to a stark set of escalators that feed the passengers upward to a final set of corrugated street stoops. Gene, my boyfriend-partner-lover, is waiting. The lateness of the train has dashed our evening movie plans. I tell him of the man with the pigtail. He smiles.

"What about Raffaelle?" I ask. Raffaelle is his buddy-boyfriend from the spanking club.

"Busy tonight," he answers. Raffaelle might have met us at the movie.

Instead of rushing to find a movie, Gene and I sit in his car at this dilapidated Flatbush Avenue intersection, and I recount the moves of my journey with the handsome pigtailed man. Only in telling the story do I realize the peculiarity that steadily overtook our innocuous flirting game. The farther our train pulled us from the homo-island, the more charged the flirtation grew. The more we exercised our peripheral vision to monitor our increasingly nonhomo fellow travelers, the sharper became the edge to our homo-chatter. At the Pines a blasé queer familiarity governed the whole troop of travelers, shaping our body movements, our glances, our readiness and reticence to speak. Confident, secure in our homo camaraderie on the Island, we were watchful not to appear too easy in our flirtations. There, everyone knows each other's games.

Removed from that homogeneity, relocated to a conventional zone of hetero-commuters, we reconfigure the sensory language of exchange, in eye, in touch, in ear. We shift our glances toward unmarked coquetry; we lightly brush thigh to knee; we cock the ear to meet the modulated voice: we transform the loaded language of overt camp into the sly double and triple entendres of invisible innuendo. I offer that I grew up on an apple orchard in Kentucky and that now we tend a wide variety of fruit. His dancer's calf flexes lightly as I recognize my unintended pun. He remarks that the strawberry plant in his apartment window box has failed to bear fruit; I note that in the sex life of plants it takes two, both male and female, to make a fruit. He turns away toward the smeary window and the evening silhouette of barren, brick working-class housing that is Queens, New York.

All pretty ordinary stuff. Only the aura of our difference, our homo knowledge that we are using words to speak to each other in a way—not only sexually, but homo-sexually—that our carmates should not understand, titillates us, changes and escalates the flirtatious potential of our words. What would have felt tired and banal on the departure dock at Fire Island carries just the slightest reverberation of risk: it is that readiness for risk that churns up our banal chatter, feeds our fantasies, drives our game forward.

Our coded exchanges, however, are not only about risk. Risk is only the shell that surrounds our exchange, the circumstance that drives us to code our language. The code is itself erotic because it is a moving metaphor. Constrained by the shortness of our trip and by the potential hostility of our surroundings, we cannot be literal. We present ourselves through metaphoric images that have multiple meanings, images that seem larger than the words themselves: sexy but respectful of solitude, domesticated but traveling far, professionally driven but playfully irreverent, queer but chary of ghettos. Metaphors work because they arouse. They lure us into the unspoken, imaginative territory between the words. They promise a conspiracy of adventures unimagined by our uncomprehending fellow travelers, transporting us from the tedium of broken-down railroad cars. We escape the surface of our lives.

As I tell Gene my little story, he joins it, just as I vicariously join his adventures with skinny guys and handmade wooden paddles at a club called Spank Me Hard. While we do not share each other's actual adventures, we relish the stories of our mutual adventures. Our stories complement and enrich our imaginative lives, drawing us to examine the ways in which we do or don't fulfill each other's needs. During three years of companionship and twenty years of knowing each other, we have become comrades, committed companions whose comradeship embraces other people and other passions. The newspaper term for it is *open relationship,* although like most newspaper jargon, the phrase poses more questions than it answers. Open to what, by and for whom? The answers, we are learning, come not in our declarations but in our actions: ongoing gestures of commitment, ongoing actions of exploration. Our camaraderie at its best becomes a zone of trust, a fraternal fellowship from which we both look outward to touch the lives of others among whom we also find and extend fulfillment.

It is a risky enterprise. Not because we are sexually promiscuous, though at times we are. It is risky because the further we extend our exploration, the more we risk learning about our frailties and the more we are challenged to find an ethics of interpersonal responsibility to regulate those frailties. As any child who has grown up in a large, extended family well knows, the calculus of an ethical emotional life is far simpler in the nuclear household than it is in the compound of multiple brothers, sisters, aunts, uncles, cousins, and grandparents.

Twenty years ago Edmund White wrote about what he called the banyan-tree nature of gay male life, the extended families of men who met each other in bed (or the baths or the park) and gradually became each other's extended-family members after the sexual liaisons had gone dormant. Age and AIDS have taught us respect for our microbial and emotional vulnerabilities: we are not invincible. But the utopian value of White's banyan-tree family remains a powerful force in the homosexual project. Not only does it pose a counter to the barren emotional life of the modern, coupled nuclear-family, but it also privileges emotional inquiry over emotional protectiveness. It values a dynamic ethics of human interaction over an inherited rule of domestic exclusivity. To be treated well ourselves, we must do more than follow the rules; we must ask of ourselves how we can help our companions fulfill their needs; we must acknowledge that only in the rarest of cases can two people alone meet the full range of each other's physical and emotional desires.

Increasingly I find that what I call homosexual desire is not altogether desire for another man but desire for an exploratory knowledge, for a relationship of exploration that becomes possible with diverse kindred spirits. The codes and metaphors of exploration become more erotic than the touch of the flesh itself: they serve as entryways, a zone of mutual recognition. Much of the stimulation I find in my homo-ness derives from the knowledge I infer of another's desires from looking into my own sensual experience. At the crudest level it is the tacit, physical knowledge shared by the band of orgiasts, who, as one of their members nears climax, lock arms and thighs together with him, pressing themselves into a straining web of muscle and sinew aimed not at their own release but at propelling *him* into greater, wilder ejaculatory pleasure.

For many men that is the essential homo-moment, a merger of self-identities released from the separateness of difference. Sublimated, socialized, reconfigured as language and artifice, that self-effacing merger of selves is a central fount from which modern homosexual identity flows, articulating a longing for the release from difference through a bonded union with one's own. Writing nearly a century ago, Marcel Proust, in *Remembrance of Things Past,* characterized the power of that identity as a "universal freemasonry of inverts," a sort of homosexual knowledge that transcends class, culture, post, and learning and lies at the base of the dream of community:

> More effective and less suspected than that of the Lodges, [it] rests upon an identity of tastes, needs, habits, dangers, apprenticeship, knowledge, traffic, vocabulary . . . in which even members who do not wish to know one another recognize one another immediately by natural or conventional, involuntary or deliberate signs which indicate one of his kind to the beggar in the person of the nobleman whose carriage door he is shutting, to the father in the person of his daughter's suitor, to the man who has sought healing, absolution, or legal defense in the doctor, the priest, or the barrister to whom he has had recourse; . . . in this anachronistic fiction the ambassador is a bosom friend of the felon, the prince, with a certain insolent aplomb born of his aristocratic breeding which the timorous bourgeois lacks, on leaving the duchess's party goes off to confer in private with the ruffian . . .

Proust's world lay at the intersection of a declining aristocracy and a rising bourgeoisie in fin de siècle France. Ours is a transnational fin de siècle consumer life at the end of the twentieth century. Proust's homosexual men verified the security of their place in the world by daring to jeopardize it through their commerce in the freemasonry of inversion. We queer comrades, understanding full well that no "place," social or geographical, is secure, grasp our "inversion" hoping to make of it a place of personal security.

Despite their differences, Proust's world and ours are united across time in that persistent "identity of tastes, needs, habits, dangers, apprenticeship, knowledge," by which we continue to know ourselves and each other. For Proust that identity was the subverter of politics. Not only did "inversion" place the beggar in the baron's boudoir, but more importantly it granted the "invert" a double status whereby he could participate in society even as he developed a radical, outsider's understanding of power and privilege. That radical "doubleness" is yet with us, but it has also produced the critical political conundrum in contemporary gay life.

Having remade our subterranean identity into a political movement, we are forced to ask what kind of politics to make of homo-identity. Is a "gay political movement" only concerned with issues of gay identity? As lesbian and gay lobbying organizations grow and become more powerful in state and national politics, should their only criterion of evaluation be the candidate's same-sex desire? If prejudice against homosexual people is a human rights abuse, does the movement for gay liberation advance in coalition with other human rights causes? If queers have generally been excluded from positions of public and corporate power, are the injustices of class central to the queer campaign? Or, if desire cuts across class and race lines, destabilizing the presumptions of power, does queer liberation call for another approach to human rights, another approach to pluralism, participation, and democracy? Are we struggling to legitimate the right to love our own gender, or is our target the liberation of desire from any constraining identity?

II. NATIONALISM AND IDENTITY

As I have argued throughout this book, the conundrum facing queer Americans is only a variation on broader, more fundamental American themes of community longing and personal destiny. To understand our dilemmas of difference, our troubled search for identity, it seems valuable to look beyond our experience. The most profound, most intransigent of American barriers remains race. While I would never argue that homosexual identity and African-American identity are equivalent, there is much for queer people to learn from the ongoing debate among African-Americans about the limits and utility of identity politics. Indeed the divisions over the utility of black identity come down hardest at the intersection of sex, gender, and race where women and queers (and especially queer women) have consistently been sacrificed at the hands of black nationalism.

No one has addressed these issues more powerfully than Cornel West. Writing in the introduction to *Race Matters,* West states succinctly the dilemma that black people (and all outsiders) face: "As long as black people are viewed as a 'them,' the burden falls on blacks to do all the 'cultural' and 'moral' work necessary for healthy race relations. The implication is that only certain Americans can define what it means to be American—and the rest must simply 'fit in.' " Black people who accept the bargain risk cultural erasure even though their pigmentation still leaves them subject to insult and abuse. Black people who refuse that cultural erasure are singled out by the majority as "separatists," producing a self-fulfilling prophecy as more black people take on "black-nationalist sentiments . . . in a revolt against this sense of having to 'fit in.' " West's position is clear: the barriers to inequality can only subside once the dominant white majority acknowledge the mutuality of America's racial history, that America's European cultural heritage is inseparable from its African cultural heritage, that a fruitful future cannot emerge from benevolent gestures by white people to include their black stepchildren.

Sharply critical as he is of white obligation, West is equally adamant about the pitfalls of self-defensive "black racial reasoning." He refers to the failure of most black political leaders to criticize the nomination of Clarence Thomas to the Supreme Court—despite Thomas's long opposition to almost all the objectives of the black civil rights movement—and to the fact that the ultranationalist Nation of Islam directly supported Thomas, despite its leader Louis Farrakhan's acknowledgment that Republican Party policies were racist. The predicament in which black political leaders found themselves at the Thomas confirmation hearings grew directly from their reliance on "racial authenticity" as a litmus for determining whether Thomas, a man of scant judicial or administrative credits, was truly "black enough to be defended." Could he *as a black man* fall in the footsteps of the revered Thurgood Marshall, the first African-American ever appointed to the Court, and represent blackness on the nation's highest court? For West that reliance on *racial authenticity,* on black identity, was the critically false step black leaders took in evaluating the Thomas nomination (and it is here that queer activists should listen most carefully):

What is black authenticity? Who is really black? First, blackness has no meaning outside of a system of race-conscious people and practices. After centuries of racist degradation, exploitation, and oppression in America, being black means being minimally subject to white supremacist abuse and being part of a rich culture and community that has struggled against such abuse. All people with black skin and African phenotype are subject to potential white supremacist abuse. Hence, all black Americans have some interest in resisting racism—even if their interest is confined solely to themselves rather than to larger black communities. Yet how this "interest" is defined and how individuals and communities are understood vary. Hence any claim to black authenticity—beyond that of being a potential object of racist abuse and an heir to a grand tradition of black struggle—is contingent on one's political definition of black interest and one's ethical understanding of how this interest relates to individuals and communities in and outside black America. In short, blackness is a political and ethical construct. Appeals to black authenticity ignore this fact; such appeals hide and conceal the political and ethical dimension of blackness. This is why claims to racial authenticity trump political and ethical argument—and why racial reasoning discourages moral reasoning.

Racial reasoning placed a phenotypic African-American on the Supreme Court, but it failed to address the standards of justice—the standards by which we live together ethically as human beings—he would bring to the Court. For the rightist Bush administration it was a double triumph. They had found a black man dedicated to thwarting the civil rights agenda of mainstream black leaders, and in doing so they struck a blow against liberal, democratic voices within black America. The success of the Thomas nomination, West points out, became both a political and a cultural triumph for conservatives:

For white America, this means primarily scapegoating black people, women, gay men, and lesbians. For black America, this

205

means principally attacking black women and black gay men and lesbians. In this way, black nationalist and black male-centered claims to black authenticity reinforce black cultural conservatism.

More than any other event in recent history the Thomas nomination exposed the vacuousness of an identity politics devoid of larger ethical and political commitments. By asking only *who you are*—black, white, gay, straight, Chinese, Latino—we learn little about *what you believe* or *who you care about*. To the contrary, reliance on identity alone specifically precludes an inquiry into the tougher questions of values, ethics, and justice. Least of all does it lead us to imagine new arrangements of loving and living with each other that could subvert existing barriers of race, power, gender, and class.

Homosexual people, including those who suffer racial stigma, face a particular dilemma when it comes to identity politics. If we do not embrace the idea of gay identity to some degree, how do we assert the fact of our existence? Much as I might agree that *blackness* only exists as a stigmatized political term when there are nonblack people who make it so, black people have known of each other's existence as long as they have had eyes to look at one another. Queer desire, which cuts across all races, is ineffable, ever-shifting in its aesthetic display (drag, leather, butch, faunlike), excited and celebrated in its secret encodings: if we would win its political legitimation, what alternative have we but to proclaim it as an identity? But then, whose queer identity would we mean and how would our gay terrain look?

Maria Maggenti, the filmmaker *(Two Girls in Love)*, writer, dyke activist, propelled herself dead center into identity trouble when she wrote a first-person essay for the *Village Voice*'s annual "queer issue" in 1995. Since adolescence Maggenti had been making love to women, but then after twelve years away from the male bed, she fell in love with a man. Hopelessly, deliriously in love.

"Because I have insisted on holding on to the word *lesbian* to describe myself, at the same time that I insist on claiming a man as my primary lover," she writes, "I find myself at the center of a never-ending argument about the nature of homosexual identity. Where does being gay reside? In our cunts, our cocks, in what we take for granted?"

A friend sympathizes, but only to a degree, telling her, "I don't care what you call yourself. . . . But why can't you say you're bisexual?"

"Ugh," Maggenti responds. "It just doesn't feel right. It's inaccurate considering my sexual life, and it doesn't reflect the cultural, political, and social meaning that go with the word *lesbian*. To me, calling myself a bisexual versus claiming a lesbian identity is the difference between Muzak and Mahler."

Finally she ends up at a restaurant with her roommate (male, gay), who has all along encouraged her gender infidelity.

"Is this what liberation means?" she asks him. Wisely, he listens and orders a second bottle of wine as she continues her self-inquiry. "The right to love whom you want, to fuck whom you want, to be free and safe no matter who that is? Is this what we fight for?"

A day after Maggenti's piece appeared I found myself in a troubled conversation with another longtime gay activist, a lesbian who is not a separatist, who applies the word *gay* to herself. "Have you read that piece by Maggenti, whining about wanting to call herself a lesbian even though she's been sleeping with a man for two years?" she asked me. "What is she talking about? *Fighting for the right to love who we want*. That's not what I've been fighting for all these years. I've been fighting for the right to love another woman—not for some abstract idea of liberated desire!"

Politically, it strikes me, she is correct. The intense determination that has marked this movement is every bit as visceral as the struggle of black African-Americans to free themselves from bigotry based on the pigmentation of their bodies. We fight most passionately for the freedom to be human *in our bodies*. Abstract values—fairness, economic justice, the freedom to express yourself, the respect for particular traditions—shape our sense of meaning and harmony in the world, but it is when those values directly impinge upon the use of our own flesh that we fight most fiercely for ourselves. After all, the trouble that Maggenti is likely to have in her life from boors and bigots will not be because she makes love and keeps house with a man even while she expresses her queer commitments.

207

Her trouble will come from demanding respect and recognition for her female lovers equal to what she gets for her male ones. Questions of parity and legitimacy will not even be posed about her heterosexual life. And still, I deeply mistrust a politics that organizes itself around such a singular approach to sexual identity. Does it not fall into the Clarence Thomas trap? Does it not place *authenticity*—being *authentically queer*—at a higher value than love, justice, and the imagination of the unknown?

The question, or at least the passion given over to the question, seems radically American. While the issue of sexual and gender authenticity has surfaced elsewhere (particularly among some French queer theorists), it rarely has much political meaning. In my conversations with queer Europeans, I have found shock and dismay over American activists' preoccupation with who is genuinely "gay." During an intercontinental telecom exchange between Amsterdam and New York at the opening of the Stonewall 25 celebrations, a Dutch activist was dumbfounded at the exclusion of several groups from the main march past the United Nations. "Of course we have some divisions here, even different parades on different days," he said, "but how can you as gay people suppress different groups in your own movement? Aren't you doing the same thing the government does?"

The American groups in question, which organized their own march, included leather brigades, Radical Faeries, and the much despised (by the mainstream gay leadership) North American Man-Boy Love Association (NAMBLA).

What distinguishes the Dutch activists' approach from our own is our two cultures' widely divergent approach to political legitimacy. Gay politics in the Netherlands reflects divisions and commitments in Dutch politics generally: local versus national, ideological identification with political parties, concerns over housing, class, and income—all of which affect the interests of different gay people in different ways. The key divisions in American gay politics concern who is truly gay: Are "bisexuals" part of the "gay" movement? Can "transgender people" vote with lesbians once they have breasts (and what about the pre-ops who identify as female)? Are the men of NAMBLA gay? (My friend Eric Marcus, who wrote the first oral history of the lesbian and gay movement, regularly answers, "No, NAMBLA is not a gay organization. It's a group of child molesters.") Each of these questions reflects not only gay concerns but more importantly the quintessentially American propensity for relentless excavation of the self, or as Harold Bloom might put it, our gnostic search for an essential spirit, which is the root of meaning. Coming out, we come into our essential identities, revealing our place in the multispectered American dream.

There, alas, is where the dream all too often blinds us. If a gay democrat like Eric can share no identity with his homo-cousin who gets aroused by high school soccer players, if a spirited dyke who has spent her lifelong passion in the rubyfruit jungle shares no identity with the dyke who nightly sighs at the caresses of her male lover, how does an American queer identity save itself from its own gnostic Balkanization—much less align itself with any broader conception of social and political justice? Perversely, the gnostic essentialism we have derived from our Emersonian-Whitmanesque past leads us into a politics of individualism that fails to celebrate the fluid mystery of individual desire.

(I do not mean to suggest that the debate among sex/gender theorists, now two decades old, that sees homosexuality as either "socially constructed" or "essential" is a purely American affair. The nurture-nature inquiry has preoccupied European writers as diverse as André Gide, Oscar Wilde, Edward Carpenter, Magnus Hirschfeld, a number of contemporary gender theorists, and not least the genetic and biological scientists who are searching for brain-structure, hormonal, and chromosomal differences between homosexual and heterosexual people. Those who see homosexual or heterosexual desire as innate, or essential, to the individual's makeup come from many lands and cultures. What has distinguished the American gay rights movement is the political form it has taken even among people who see sexual identity as shaped by our social and psychological circumstances: that some identities are legitimate to the movement and some are not, and that their legitimacy results not from some broader ethical-ideological commitments but from whether their desires are *authentically* homosexual, and therefore constitute an identity worthy of inclusion in the gay movement.)

As the English gay activist and writer Jeffrey Weeks has pointed out, the central characteristic of modern Western life is fragmented identity. As individuals we live at the intersection of multiple identities, by heritage, by gender, by economic class, by geography, by family status, and by choice of therapist. The relative social stability of even the pre–Vietnam War era, when most of our intimates, friends, and coworkers looked like us and shared stories like ours, is gone. No amount of antediluvian hate-mongering from Pat Buchanan or anachronistic fundamentalist pulpiting from Pat Robertson or Tory lecturing from Bill Bennett can unscramble the omelette of postmodern life and stuff its yolks back in their fractured shells. Identity, whichever one we embrace, is, Weeks argues in *Against Nature,* "striven for, contested, negotiated, and achieved, often in struggles of the subordinated against the dominant, [and moreover] it is not achieved just by an individual act of will, or discovered hidden in the recesses of the soul. It is put together in circumstances bequeathed by history, in collective experiences as much as by individual destiny."

Weeks, the preeminent historian of English homosexual history, is by his own confession a "social constructionist." That said, he would be the last to define homosexual identity as an incidental accident of history or to deny the central *political* importance of lesbian and gay identities. "On the contrary," he writes, "it is because I have a strong sense of their contingency, of the conditions of their existence in concrete historical circumstances, and of their critical importance in challenging the imposition of arbitrary norms, that I am deeply committed to their value, emotionally, socially, and politically. Lesbian and gay identities, and the communities that made them possible, and which in turn they sustain, are the precondition for a realistic sexual politics in the age of AIDS."

The key word here is *contingency.* Whatever the nature of our desire (to be tied up in ropes and whipped by a master or to be sweetly caressed by a faun), whatever the sources of our desire (from aberrance on the Xq28 gene to the dissolution of patriarchal families), the only source of our ability to act, our only possibility of making political change, comes from our current circumstances. If we fail to acknowledge the contingent nature of our current sexual identities (or remember, as Jonathan Ned Katz has shown, that neither "homosexuality" nor "heterosexuality" were understood as "normal" sexual categories even 150 years ago), we risk falling into retrograde, neoreligionist identity camps that obstruct growth and imagination. Yet by failing to embrace any identity we suffer in silence.

Weeks proposes that only by understanding the present as a product of the past can we proceed toward a humane "politics and ethics of sexuality . . . a set of values that can help to shape the way we live."

III. SEX, GENEROSITY, AND FORBEARANCE

Usually when I hear talk about an "ethics of sexuality," the hair on the back of my neck tends to get itchy. So much of what has been offered as sexual ethics has only been a lightly veiled version of conservative Christian morality, of so-called family values that rank chastity, monogamy, and procreative (baby-making) sex above sex as a method of communication and pleasure.

Ongoing debates persist among gay men about sex clubs, video stores, and porn shops where men search out strictly anonymous sex. Many gay activists and public figures regard them as community embarrassments, holdovers from the unliberated pre-Stonewall days of furtive "dirty" sex. "I don't want to live next door to a porn shop," declared Terrence McNally, the author of Love! Valour! Compassion!—the banal celebration of gay angst, musical beds, and dazzling dicks that won the 1995 Tony Award for best new play on Broadway. The timorous, neoconservative Bruce Bawer grows pale when confronted with the surfeit of erotic imagery on display in most gay neighborhoods, convinced that it further jeopardizes his seat at the table of American respectability. A not insignificant number of lesbian and gay writers argue that the consumption of pornography and the pursuit of anonymous sexmates confuses pleasure with "addictive obsession," a therapeutic construct hardly likely to figure high in their code of ethical progress. And then there is the further moral weight brought on by AIDS, now sweeping up a third generation of young queer men who have embraced the bacchanal as a form of contemporary psychic liberation.

211

Against such a minefield of ethical-moral passions, each of them reflective of how different people experience their own queer identity, how should we even begin to approach an ethics of sexuality *among* homosexual people, much less encourage it on the whole of a nation world-famous for its long-standing sexual prudery?

At the risk of sounding ridiculous, let me suggest that the determination to arrive at a pluralistic (not relativistic) ethics of sex among queer people can illuminate a renewed vision of political ethics in the culture at large. Sex is vital to any discussion of contemporary democratic life, not only because it addresses the question of who controls our bodies, but even more because so much of the hope, rancor, and anxiety associated with contemporary identity politics come out of contested sexual space. To talk about the claims of women at home and in the workplace, of racial minorities to a fair access to social and professional privilege, of parents to educate and shepherd their children (and of children to develop their own voices in a world of incoherent, conflicting parental messages), of the elderly and infirm on the young and healthy to pay for their health care, is to touch upon the radically changing rules of sexual freedom and sexual obligation.

Just as sex has become inescapably implicated in the most painful issues of making life and dealing death, so, too, the shadow of sex lurks behind most of the divisive debates in contemporary political life. The challenge for an ethics of sexuality is not to decide in advance which acts are good and which are evil, which identities noble and which despicable, but to imagine a theater of political life in which all the actors can find a voice without shouting each other down into self-defensive silence. That claim of being a pluralistic theater of divergent voices is how America has presented herself to the world since her founding.

Alas, not even our most revered democratic heroes fully believed in a truly pluralizing society. As de Tocqueville noted approvingly, the first "Americans," the Indians, never counted at all for anyone. Women never entered the political consciousness of the framers. As for black people, Thomas Jefferson and Abraham Lincoln believed "the race problem" could only be solved by deporting black folk to some place beyond the horizon. Ben Franklin had no use for black people and not much for Germans. The famed nineteenth-century minister Horace Bushnell, like most WASPs, had little use for the Irish Catholics or in fact for anybody but "the British family, the noblest of the stock [that] was chosen to people our country." *The homosexuals,* as identifiable persons possessed of their own voice, had not yet been born. All these, as the political theorist William Connolly puts it, existed *outside* political pluralism. They were people who were "under justice," beneath the interest or concern of the justice system wherein political ethics were to be evaluated. The business of finding your own voice, of establishing your own identity as an outsider, Connolly calls the "politics of enactment," the politics of becoming an actor on the political stage.

Connolly's *Ethos of Pluralization* is one of the most refreshing meditations available on the ethics of modern identity politics and particularly queer identity. Connolly draws us to reconsider one of the first concepts we ever encountered in civics class, the Latin phrase inscribed on every penny, nickel, dime, quarter, and silver dollar that passes our palms: *e pluribus unum.* From the many, one. The hallmark of a single pluralist society. The question beneath the bromide is how to determine the boundaries of the *pluribus* that forms the *unum.*

For just as blacks fighting for the franchise gave small attention to the grievances of the suffragettes, so the grievances of feminists a century later paid scant attention to the petitions of lesbians and gays (any who doubt the discomfort expressed by early feminists for their queer sisters need only pass half an hour perusing Betty Friedan's *The Feminine Mystique*). Pluralism includes only the disparate voices already onstage. By pluralization Connolly asks us to embrace a dynamic ethic of welcoming and encouraging voices not yet recognized as actors on the stage even though they may be climbing forward from the audience into the wings demanding to make their entrance. All of which may sound reasonable until we realize, first, no actor currently on the boards cares to be upstaged by new arrivals; and second, the clear implication is that today's justice will always be tomorrow's injustice.

However radical the framers legitimately understood themselves to be in 1787, we now also see them as racists and misogynists. The imposition of abuse, the articulation of grievance, the formation of identities by those who are aggrieved, is eternal. It does not end. Denied omniscience, we cannot even know all the insults we are extending or the potential grievers we are creating by our ignorance. Thus a universal justice, Connolly argues, is no more possible than is a universal alphabet of sexual expressions and identities:

> Future (possible) gays are constituted as homosexuals; future (possible) carriers of nontheistic reverence as atheists; future (possible) participants in cross-national movements as irresponsible citizens; future bearers of the right to die with respect as doctors of death. The contemporary constitution of each places it—to varying degrees—under the regime of justice/injustice in a way inadequately captured by the retrospective discourses of dialectics and hypocrisy. Justice now trembles in its constitutive uncertainty, dependence, and ambiguity. And it is just that it so tremble.

Neither God nor nature nor any abstract logic defines the shape of justice. And at the same time, neither God, nature, nor logic privileges the outsider's and the newcomer's claims with moral value. Instead, we are all called upon to engage in a *critical responsiveness* that relies upon a spirit of *generosity* from those whom society already acknowledges and a spirit of determined *forbearance* on the part of those whose identity is just emerging. Thus, while we would not be called upon to accept a cult of child sacrifice, we might well be (and have been) called upon to honor others' sacrificial rituals of Santeria.

Connolly, who is straight, considers one of the most divisive issues in the gay movement—pedophilia. Sex between Catholic priests and choirboys in the United States, he notes, differs significantly from relations between the aristocratic citizens and adolescent boys in classical Greece even though the pederastic acts may be the same. Why? Because the general cultural norm in the United States takes the sodomizing of boys by men as an abuse of power, a violation of the body, whereas in classical Greece older men's sexual relations were "surrounded by an ethic of restraint and taken to reflect natural human desires." Still more importantly, these cultural values shape how we (and the Greeks then) use our bodies, which in turn shapes how we experience "exploitation or reciprocity, injury or gratification, degradation or respect, naturalness or disorder."

To elaborate with a personal experience, I once pointed out to an editor colleague at National Public Radio how a report on child abuse had grossly distorted the nature of child-adult sexual conduct in different historical eras. In an introduction to a series of reports on the subject, the host, with more than a little shock in his voice, remarked that the ancient Greeks had even approved of having their children "sodomized." Our use of the word *sodomized* clearly suggested violation; yet there is no indication that the Greeks ever regarded such man-boy couplings as a violation. Setting out a parallel example, I described how even today the Sambia tribesmen of New Guinea require all male boys above age seven to fellate older males because *within the Sambia cosmology* that is the only way a boy can gather enough semen in his body to reach manhood and warrior status. Thus, not only were these man-boy sex rites never regarded as abusive; they were understood as essential to healthy maturation, celebrated, and remembered among all the males with fondness well after they had become procreating, "heterosexual" adults. My then editor-friend, who had always thought himself highly liberal and progressive, ground his jaw and smirked, "You can always find a way to justify abuse."

The point here is not to honor some more "natural" moral code on the part of the Sambia or a more "enlightened" moral code in our world. In each case the meaning of the act depends entirely upon how sexual use of the body relates to existing relations of autonomy and abuse. What is to be honored is not any single code of singular rightness, but a respect for an ever-changing dialogue of different actors in different places. Progress occurs, Connolly argues, not when any single group has won respect for its own identity but

> when a larger number of constituencies come to terms with the relational character and element of contingency in what they are. The cultivation of critical responsiveness grows above all out of the appreciation that [emphasis added] *no culturally*

constituted constellation of identities ever deserves to define itself sim-
ply as natural, complete, or inclusive.

When we realize that our current privileges are all contingent upon prior recognitions—gay, female, black, Catholic, etc.—and when further we realize that the modern world has given us multiple intersecting and sometimes contradictory identities (e.g., gay Puerto Ricans, who must negotiate through racial, sexual, and ethnic familial allegiances), we open ourselves to empathy with others at odds with ourselves, not out of naive altruism but "from prudence today toward the adversary [we] may need to align with tomorrow."

Once again, Connolly's claims regarding the necessity of generosity and forbearance speak to the central act of gay experience and gay politics: coming out. If we conceive coming out principally as a personal declaration of individual identity, it relieves the closeted man or woman of the shameful burden of hiding. It probably encourages other similarly closeted people to follow suit. But it may do little to advance—or even reverse—the readiness of nonhomosexual people to recognize homosexual identity. In almost every successful gay coming-out story I have ever heard, there has been a concomitant "coming out" by the "straight" family and friends of that queer person. Hearing the gay declaration, they have had to enter into an act of imagination. They have had to reimagine the life of their friend and in doing so reimagine how they will see, hear, touch, love, and respect that friend. Along the way they realize that they have "reprogrammed" the limits and possibilities of their own imaginations about the erotic. They have "come out" into a new way of being.

Only when we realize that our collective petition for recognition requires a parallel "coming out" from the majority nongays, only when we act with forbearance toward those who have had no call to examine the presumed naturalness of their own sexual identities, can we expect them to engage with us in Connolly's critical responsiveness. What we have won, moreover, is far more than grudging respect for our own identity: we have brought them to acknowledge the contingency of their own identities. We have brought them to recognize that if Maria Maggenti could understand herself as a lesbian and still enter into a relationship with a man, then they may not be as confident in the "naturalness" of their own sexuality. There are of course no such guarantees, nor does the prospect of such "pluralization" of recognition relieve us of the necessity to hang tough or engage in forceful political confrontation. What seems clear, however, is that a genuine democratic ideal is a replication of what we hope for in the coming-out dance that we undertake with our intimate friends and family—namely that both we and they will be changed by the process, transformed into new identities born of our new relations.

IV. The Kids from Canarsie

Taking the Long Island Rail Road home to this polyglot place called Brooklyn only intensifies my sense of how rich and perplexing the contemporary gay movement has grown. I look at the world Gene and I share as we move through the interstices of gay identity. We could not lead the lives we do without the world of organized "gayery," its cafés, clubs (including sex clubs), community centers, newspapers, legal defense and lobbying groups, bookstores, and vacation retreats. These are the institutions and social forces that we and other urban gay people rely upon. And yet we are not exactly of it. Yes, he is a founding member of one of those gay institutions, the Knickerbocker Sailing Association, and he sends small contributions to several gay service groups. And I, through my writing and reporting, am a producer of "gay culture." I contribute to the store of images through which other queer people recognize and distinguish themselves as unique. Higgledy-piggledy, this is how a public identity is born.

Like a growing number of lesbian and gay people we have located ourselves well outside the most obvious gay terrains. Gay people are not absent from our neighborhood, but they are by no means dominant. Koreans, Caribbean islanders, second-generation Italians and Jews, and longtime Irish-Americans are our neighbors. In adjacent Prospect Park, there are two gay-male cruising zones. Park Slope, the next neighborhood toward Manhattan, has a national reputation as a lesbian hometown. And out near Bay Ridge, toward the Ver-

217

razano Narrows, is a huge gay disco where John Travolta danced his way to fame in *Saturday Night Fever.*

A man named Paul Del Duca, who grew up in working-class Brooklyn, spoke to me one spring afternoon about the perplexities of queer life in New York's biggest borough. Paul was vice president of the citywide Stonewall Democratic Club. He had been an activist on his campus, spoke at gay rallies, and because of his position, often attended high-level receptions involving city council members and the city's gay political leaders. He was, in short, thoroughly integrated into New York's public gay world. Still, it was the sexually idiosyncratic world of middle- and working-class Brooklyn that felt most comfortable to him.

"I am perfectly comfortable here in Brooklyn," he tells me. We are sitting at the kitchen table of his mom's house in Canarsie, a working-class Italian and Caribbean neighborhood. Paul's sixteen-year-old sister dodges in and out of the bathroom as he jokes about all the sexual episodes he used to have with his high school buddies after they dropped off their girlfriends. Nodding toward his bedroom, he confides that it was right in that doorway that his dad caught him making out with one of his high school boyfriends, and right at this table where we are sitting his dad asked him if he was gay and he answered yes and his father answered back, "You're my son and I love you whatever you are, but don't tell your mother." Around five-thirty Paul's mother—she and his friends call him Pauley—drops in. He introduces me and I explain that I'm interested in hearing about straight and gay life in Brooklyn.

"You wanta listen, that Pauley knows how to talk," she advises with a practiced smile.

"I have gay friends here in Brooklyn who don't really go to Manhattan that often," he continues. "I have two friends over in Brighton Beach [near Coney Island], Peter and Glen. They tend to be the center of our social life in Brooklyn. A lot of my gay friends are more comfortable in Brooklyn. They don't like the Manhattan scene. They just, like, hang out in the house and chill."

In his Manhattan-based gay political life Paul finds most of the gay people he meets are transients, "people who have come here because they feel this is the place where they can fulfill their identity.

218

I find myself [there in Manhattan] surrounded by people who have come from outside the city, and their idea of gay identity is different from mine. Gay identity for them has to do with being part of a community that identifies as gay, and it doesn't for me. . . . The way it worked here for me, I would just wind up having sexual encounters with my friends—and I had a lot of friends.

"I remember the first time I walked into a gay bar, being looked at by everyone and how much that bothered me. I have learned to deal with it, but to this day it bothers me. I don't like this objectifying feeling I get. It is a community predicated on sexuality."

Paul is a wiry, intense young man who gets more and more wound up in his story. He laughs a lot as he talks, but his laugh seems as much a release of tension as it is a reflection of his sardonic humor.

"Why are we all here?" he asks rhetorically about the gay world of bars and clubs in Manhattan. "We are all here because we all sleep with men, and I guess I wanted something more than that. Because I was used to something more than that. Because the guys I was sleeping with were not only sleeping with men. There was more going on. There was a different type of interaction."

He begins to tell me about his teenage years when he was fourteen, fifteen, sixteen, running with a group of guys who called themselves the Twenty-second Street Crew. "We would hang out on a corner on Avenue U and East Twenty-first Street. The guy who owned the video store was a young guy. Friends of mine would work in that store, and there would be a band of ten or twenty of us some nights listening to music, hanging out. Some of the guys [were ones] I would fool around with in secret, and they were all very macho. Some boys would call themselves the Avenue Boys. Then there were the Kings Highway Boys. They were like gangs, and occasionally they would fight one another. Some of them would spray-paint. There was a time when I was spray-painting."

Paul had a girlfriend then, but there were also three guys he was sleeping with.

"One guy, Joe, lived on my block. We used to hang out on weekend nights in my friend Mark's basement, and Joe at one point would always make these advances. At some point we would dim the lights so it was dark and everyone would go off drinking. Joe would always end up taking me into Mark's parents' bedroom and say things like, 'Let me feel your dick,' and things like that and I would let him, and he would wind up jerking me off or giving me a blowjob."

Another of his buddies, a Puerto Rican man, always wanted to play top with Paul, until a year or so ago, after he'd been living with a girlfriend. Then he came to Paul and asked Paul to fuck him. Twice. Most of Paul's teenage buddies are still friends, though most of them now are also married. Many are cops. They know Paul considers himself gay and speaks out at gay events. A few may also know that he still sleeps with women sometimes.

Like Francine, a friend for four years who knows he sleeps mostly with men.

"Francine has gotten more and more . . . *temptuous* toward me and been very clear about the fact that she would like to sleep with me. It was last December and we were alone. One thing just sort of led to the next, and we wound up sleeping together." It had been more than a year since Paul had slept with a woman, and it was a puzzling experience for him, emotionally and physically.

"When I was in bed with Francine, I found myself looking for her penis. I said to her several times, 'I wish you had a dick.'

"She answered, 'Well, I don't,' but I was looking for that. Her body felt different. I mean a man's body feels more rigid and pronounced. A woman's body feels very Jell-O-y, and I didn't like that as much. Yet it was much more intimate, much more emotional. It was about here are these two people who have known one another, and now we're connecting in a deeper sense. I could see myself having a child with someone like her because there is such a deep emotional and sexual feeling."

Paul tells me that he is "somewhat uncomfortable" with his attraction to women. It is a zone of eroticism that remains unresolved, that, as Maria Maggenti says, isn't quite covered by the word *bisexual*. What I find most interesting is how completely he has turned the sexual world of twenty-five years ago on its head. In his Brooklyn world of cops and carpenters and garbagemen, of family, friends, cousins, and grandparents, Paul's homosexual desires are just a part of Paul.

"There was this sense," he says, "that we were friends. Like we grew up on the same block. We grew up together, and even today when they all know I am gay, none of them has a negative attitude toward me. It is sort of like, 'Oh, Pauley. We know Pauley. We *know* him!' I'm another person. I just happen to be gay to them."

Partially that is true because the lesbian and gay movement has made it possible to talk openly about homosexual desire. Partially it is true because the comfort Paul feels in his own sexuality disarms those of his friends who don't share his desires and enables them to love him as one of their own. And maybe mostly it is true because more and more men and women like Paul, in America and in the world, have rejected a twisted, contorted morality of sex for an exploratory ethics of human sexual relations. More and more they ask of themselves and of their mates not "Who am I?" but "How should I act?"

source notes

The books and articles cited below are gathered under the particular chapters to which they are most relevant, although in a series of personal essays of this sort, sources for one chapter frequently apply to earlier or later chapters as well. Additionally, many of the books and essays are included for those who would like to further explore the territory discussed.

CHAPTER ONE

Altman, Dennis. *The Americanization of Homosexuality, the Homosexualization of America.* New York: St. Martin's Press, 1982.

Baldwin, James. *The Price of the Ticket.* New York: St. Martin's Press, 1985.

Bawer, Bruce. *A Place at the Table: The Gay Individual in American Society.* New York: Poseidon, 1993.

Bergman, David. "The Agony of Black Gay Experience," in *Gaiety Transfigured.* Madison, Wis.: University of Wisconsin Press, 1991.

Burnside, John. *Who Are the Gay People.* San Francisco: Vortex Media, 1989.

Butler, Judith. *Bodies That Matter: On the Discursive Limits of "Sex."* New York: Routledge, 1993.

————. *Gender Trouble: Feminism and the Subversion of Identity.* New York: Routledge, 1990.

D'Emilio, John. *Sexual Politics, Sexual Communities: The Making of a Homosexual Minority in the United States, 1940–1970.* Chicago: University of Chicago Press, 1983.

D'Emilio, John, and Estelle Freedman. *Intimate Matters: A History of Sexuality in America.* New York: Harper & Row, 1988.

Foucault, Michel. "Friendship as a Lifestyle: An Interview with Michel Foucault." *Gay Information* 7 (spring 1981): 4. As quoted by Ed Cohen in "Who are 'We'? in Diana Fuss, ed., *inside/out: Lesbian Theories, Gay Theories.* New York: Routledge, 1991.

————. *The History of Sexuality.* 2 vols. New York: Vintage, 1990.

Herdt, Gilbert H. *Guardians of the Flutes: Idioms of Masculinity.* New York: Columbia University Press, 1987.

————. *Third Sex, Third Gender.* New York: Zone Books, 1994.

————, ed. *Gay and Lesbian Youth.* Binghamton, N.Y.: Harrington Park Press, 1989.

————, ed. *Gay Culture in America: Essays from the Field.* Boston: Beacon, 1992.

Katz, Jonathan Ned. *The Invention of Heterosexuality.* New York: Dutton, 1995.

Leeming, David. *James Baldwin, a Biography.* New York: Knopf, 1994.

Lorde, Audre. *A Burst of Light.* Ithaca, N.Y.: Firebrand Books, 1988.

Perchuk, Andrew, and Helaine Posner, eds. *The Masculine Masquerade: Masculinity and Representation.* Cambridge, Mass.: MIT Press, 1995.

Sedgwick, Eve Kosofsky. *Epistemology of the Closet.* Berkeley, Cal.: University of California Press, 1990.

Singer, Bennett, ed. *Growing Up Gay/Growing Up Lesbian.* New York: New Press, 1994.

CHAPTER TWO

Aalan, Joshua Canon. "Italy for Foreigners." In *Guida Gay: Anno X, 1993–94*. Milan: Edizionis Babilonia, 1993.

Aldrich, Robert. *The Seduction of the Mediterranean: Writing, Art and Homosexual Fantasy*. New York: Routledge, 1993.

Belmonte, Thomas. *The Broken Fountain*. New York: Columbia University Press, 1989.

Bleys, Rudy. "Homosexual Exile: The Textuality of the Imaginary Paradise, 1800–1980." In Rommel Mendes-Leite and Pierre-Olivier de Busscher, eds., *Gay Studies from the French Cultures*. Binghamton, N.Y.: Harrington Park Press, 1993. On travel and homo exile, movement as Dionysian counterpart to bourgeois domesticity.

Boswell, John. *Same-Sex Unions in Premodern Europe*. New York: Villard, 1994.

Caldwell, Joseph. *The Uncle from Rome*. New York: Penguin, 1992.

Cornelisen, Ann. *Torregreca: Life, Death, Miracles*. Boston: Little, Brown, 1969.

Douglas, Norman. *Sirens Land and Fountains in the Sand*. London: Secker and Warburg, 1957.

———. *South Wind*. New York: Dover, 1981.

Evans, Arthur. *The God of Ecstasy: Sex Roles and the Madness of Dionysos*. New York: St. Martin's Press, 1988.

Fernandez, Dominique. *Le rapt de Ganymede*. Paris: Grasset, 1989.

Griffi, Giuseppe Patroni. *Scende giù per Toledo*. Milano: Garzanti Editori, 1990.

Halperin et al. *Before Sexuality: The Construction of Erotic Experience in the Ancient Greek World*. Princeton, N.J.: Princeton University Press, 1990. Especially chapter 4, "From Sex to Politics: The Rites of Artemis Triklaria and Dionysos Aisymnetes at Patras."

Knight, Richard Payne. *A Discourse on the Worship of Priapus and its connection with the mystic theology of the ancients*. London: Dilletanti Society, n.d.

Malaparte, Curzio. *The Skin*. Trans. David Moore. London: Picador, 1988.

Onians, Richard Broxton. *The Origins of European Thought.* New York: Cambridge University Press, 1951, 1991. On genius, Part II, "The Immortal Soul and the Body," chap. 2, "The Genius, Numen," etc.

Putnam, Robert D. *Making Democracy Work.* Princeton, N.J.: Princeton University Press, 1993.

Schwartz, Barth David. *Pasolini Requiem.* New York: Pantheon, 1992.

Chapter Three

Bornstein, Kate. *Gender Outlaw: On Men, Women, and the Rest of Us.* New York: Vintage, 1995.

Califia, Pat. *Public Sex: The Culture of Radical Sex.* Pittsburgh, Pa.: Cleis, 1994.

Colomina, Beatriz, ed. *Sexuality & Space.* New York: Princeton Architectural Press, 1992.

Simmel, Georg. *The Sociology of Georg Simmel.* Ed. and trans. Kurt Wolff. Glencoe, Ill.: Free Press, 1951.

Chapter Four

Bercovitch, Sacvan. *The Puritan Origins of the American Self.* New Haven: Yale University Press, 1975.

Bloom, Harold. *The American Religion: The Emergence of the Post-Christian Nation.* New York: Simon and Schuster, 1992.

Butler, Samuel. *The Way of All Flesh.* New York: Macmillan, 1925.

Hillman, James. *A Blue Fire.* New York: Harper Perennial, 1991.

Kant, Immanuel. *The Critique of Judgment.* Oxford: Clarendon, 1978.

Klein, Richard. *Cigarettes Are Sublime.* Durham: Duke University Press, 1993.

Paglia, Camille. *Sexual Personae: Art and Decadence from Nefertiti to Emily Dickinson.* New Haven, Conn.: Yale University Press, 1990.

Signorelli, Michelangelo. *Outing Yourself.* New York: Random House, 1995.

———. *Queer in America.* New York: Random House, 1993.

Thompson, Mark. *Gay Soul: Finding the Heart of Gay Spirit and Nature.* San Francisco: HarperSan Francisco, 1994.

Zeeland, Steven. *The Masculine Marine.* Binghamton, N.Y.: Haworth Press, 1996. See also Zeeland, *Barrack Buddies and Soldier Lovers: Dialogues with Gay Young Men in the U.S. Military* (Binghamton, N.Y.: Harrington Park Press, 1993), and *Sailors and Sexual Identity: Cross the Line Between "Straight" and "Gay" in the U.S. Navy* (Binghamton, N.Y.: Haworth Press, 1995).

CHAPTER FIVE

Berliner, Paul F. *Thinking in Jazz: The Infinite Art of Improvisation.* Chicago: University of Chicago Press, 1994.

Gallagher, Bob, and Alexander Wilson. "Michel Focault: An Interview—Sex, Power and the Politics of Identity," *The Advocate*, No. 400, 1984.

Kern, Stephen. *The Culture of Love: Victorians to Moderns.* Cambridge, Mass.: Harvard University Press, 1992.

Rorem, Ned. *The Nantucket Diary of Ned Rorem.* Berkeley, Cal.: North Point Press, 1987.

Thompson, Mark, ed. *Leatherfolk: Radical Sex, People, Politics, and Practice.* Boston: Alyson, 1991.

CHAPTER SIX

Adam, Barry D. *The Rise of a Gay and Lesbian Movement.* Boston: Twayne Publishers, 1987.

Altman, Dennis, et al. *Homosexuality, Which Homosexuality?: International Conference on Gay and Lesbian Studies.* London: GMP, 1989.

Awkward, Michael. *Negotiating Difference: Race, Gender, and the Politics of Positionality.* Chicago: University of Chicago Press, 1995.

Bersani, Leo. *Homos.* Cambridge, Mass.: Harvard University Press, 1995.

Chauncey, George. *Gay New York: Gender, Urban Culture, and the Making of the Gay Male World, 1890–1940.* New York: Basic Books, 1994.

Dollimore, Jonathan. *Sexual Dissidence: Augustine to Wilde, Freud to Foucault.* Oxford: Clarendon Press, 1991.

Found Object 4 (fall 1994). Especially before and after Stonewall section.

Garber, Marjorie. *Vice Versa.* New York: Simon and Schuster, 1995.

Goldberg, Jonathan, ed. *Reclaiming Sodom.* New York: Routledge, 1994.

Greenberg, David F. *The Construction of Homosexuality.* Chicago: University of Chicago Press, 1988.

Hamer, Dean, and Peter Copeland. *The Science of Desire: The Search for the Gay Gene and the Biology of Behavior.* New York: Simon and Schuster, 1995.

Hinsch, Bret. *Passions of the Cut Sleeve: The Male Homosexual Tradition in China.* Berkeley, Cal.: University of California Press, 1990.

Hutchins, Loraine, and Lani Kaahumanu. *Bi Any Other Name: Bisexual People Speak Out.* Boston: Alyson, 1991.

Lacqueur, Thomas. *Making Sex: Body and Gender from the Greeks to Freud.* Cambridge, Mass.: Harvard University Press, 1990.

LeVay, Simon. *The Sexual Brain.* Boston: MIT Press, 1994.

Lind, Michael. *The Next American Nation: The New Nationalism and the Fourth American Revolution.* New York: The Free Press, 1995.

Mercer, Kobena. *Welcome to the Jungle.* New York: Routledge, 1994.

Miller, Neil. *Out in the World: Gay and Lesbian Life from Buenos Aires to Bangkok.* New York: Random House, 1992.

———. *Out of the Past: Gay and Lesbian History from 1869 to the Present.* New York: Vintage, 1995.

Parker, Richard. *Bodies, Pleasures and Passions: Sexual Culture in Contemporary Brazil.* Boston: Beacon, 1991.

Rorty, Richard. *Contingency, Irony, and Solidarity.* New York: Cambridge University Press, 1989.

Scott, Dariek. "Jungle Fever? Black Gay Identity Politics, White Dick, and the Utopian Bedroom." *GLQ* 1 (1994): iii.

Stavans, Ilan. "The Latin Phallus." *Transition* 65 (spring 1995).

Tiefer, Leonore. *Sex Is Not a Natural Act & Other Essays.* Boulder, Colo.: Westview Press, 1995.

Trevisan, Joao S. *Perverts in Paradise.* London: GMP, 1986.

Warner, Michael, ed. *Fear of a Queer Planet.* Minneapolis: University of Minnesota Press, 1994.

Weeks, Jeffrey. *Against Nature: Essays on History, Sexuality and Identity.* London: Rivers Oram, 1991.

————. *Sexuality.* New York: Tavistock, 1986.

————. *Sexuality and Its Discontents.* London: Routledge and Kegan Paul, 1985.

White, Edmund. *The Burning Library.* Ed. David Bergman. New York: Knopf, 1995. Especially the essay "Paradise Found" from *Mother Jones,* June 1983, on the banyan-tree model of gay life.

index